# MY FATHER HAS A DOG NAMED ZEUS

By: Jonathan

# PUBLISHED

September 23, 2018
FIRST EDITION
© 2018 All Rights Reserved

ISBN-13:
978-1-942967-60-6 (Hardcover)
978-1-942967-61-3 (Paperback)
978-1-942967-62-0 (Ebook)

**KreativeMinds Publishing**
publishing@kreativeminds.net

*To Hera, my Love, my Moon, the Peace within every breath I take.*

# DEDICATION
# We All Write Our Own Love Stories

We all write our own love stories. This story is no different. And as the words of this book flow along, some of it might seem a bit crazy. Sometimes the stories might seem completely untrue. By all Earthly standards, most of the events that have transpired will seem impossible, implausible, improbable, and loudly outrageous... especially beginning with my own personal introduction. Hi. I'm Zeus. There I said it. But truly I say unto you, every word contained within these pages is completely Faithful and True to the actual story I have experienced during my time on Earth.

Now, from this point forward, you may question the validity of the stories. *"Is this book fiction or does someone truly believe they are that Greek guy from ancient mythology?"* you may ask. Well, I suppose that is up to you to decide. But take your time and don't rush to a decision too quickly. And, in either way, do not let it affect the story herein – for the events that transpired (as unbelievable as some may seem) will somehow manage to find

# DEDICATION

a personal meaning with each reader. Case in point, the title of this book. Yes, you know who you are already. Trust me. I implore you to read this book all of the way through. It might have been written just for you. And in Hera's case, without a shadow of a doubt every word herein is my Love Story for you.

You see, if there is one thing I have ever learned upon this rock floating in the vastness of space – adrift in the great pond we call the Milky Way – is that humans manage to detach themselves from anything that might seem a bit out of their comfort zone. It happens in all aspects of life – but it is certainly most demonstrable when it comes to *truly* finding Love. This detachment is simply fear, but it generally pops up anytime words flirt with this fire within. This self-preservation mode that humans are blissfully unaware is preventing Love from Becoming occurs in all aspects of life – not just in the infatuation-in-another, kiss-me-everyday kind of way. But it is certainly most obvious there.

Ah, yes. The fire – the reclamation of the hurt and pain from the many, many lives lived upon this blue marble (and other parts of the cosmos, too!). This reclamation will always appear like a Phoenix rising from the ashes. Any words that hint at the mere possibility of *true spiritual & emotional healing* generally cause humans to hide in fear as the words they shout to those around them contradict their internal struggle within. "I'm okay!" they say as the hurt yearns for healing inside.

Sometimes you have to truly wonder just how many people really believe in the fairytale happily-ever-afters that so many humans claim to desire. Perhaps most of us have been afraid to look in the mirror and *truly* tell ourselves, "You are

Love! Yes, you! You are worthy of being Loved!" For even when Love comes our way, how many really want to see it for what it is? Or, perhaps it is a case that so many people have not *truly* known what it Is and have fallen into the grand trap of the ego: the times in our lives when we proclaim to be someone we are not, to desire something we truly do not, and to have passion for something wherein our interests eventually wane. In all of these moments, the ego will be adamant in the actions, find justifications in the proclamations, desires, passions, the reasons for change, and find blame in something or someone for damage done on either side of the fence. All the while, it is just the ego shrouding Love from becoming.

If you are familiar with the Hunger Games series, you will know there is a specific quote from Katniss Everdeen that sums up this human mentality really, really well. When Katniss is at her most vulnerable, she appears angry – hurt even – that Peeta (the male contender from her district who is madly in love with her) professes his love for her publicly during a nationally televised event. Up to this point, she had largely ignored his advances. But this moment sent her over the edge. Really, she may not have even allowed herself to see the possibility that Peeta might actually like her more than a friend. Enraged, she shouts at her coach, Haymitch, "He made me look weak!" Haymitch grabs Katniss by the arms and shouts back, "He made you look desirable!" And while this dialogue occurs near the beginning of the series, it would not be until the closing moments of the series that Katniss realizes her heart has been Peeta's all along. It always was.

## DEDICATION

Why did it take her so long to realize Peeta was the true definition of Love? Quite simply, like most humans, the mind will fight to no end to ensure the heart is protected from hurt. Many times the mind will create scenarios as to why a person *is not* their potential happily-ever-after. Quite bluntly, it might be a rationalization as simple as "too short, too tall, not my type, she likes [x] and I like [y]." But, here's a hint guys and gals. When Love is found – and this is Love with a capital "L" rather than the love that most humans assume is the meaning of the word – there can be no hurt, no pain, and certainly none of the excuses given above. There is no such thing as vulnerability, for everything that could have seemed to be a vulnerable aspect of life is now protected in a cocoon of safety, wrapped in the greatest warmth ever known. So vulnerability simply cannot be. When Love Is, there simply cannot be anything that will damage, be damaged, or bring damage – for the mere possibility cannot exist... when Love Is. And beauty? Oh that is all you will see.

But how can you know the difference between Love with a capital L and the definition that humans seem to associate with the meaning of the lower-cased version of the word? Surely this is the question most readers will immediately ask. Think how rare finding it must be! For how many times have humans endured the hurt that the lower-cased version of the word seems to bring? You may even wonder if it has ever *truly* been found by others upon the Earth. And oh it has! I assure you so. Take it from Ol' Zeusy, right? Though, it should be said that *truly* the numbers fall into only a few handfuls of couples across all of the generations of the billions upon billions of people upon this planet. But all of that is changing. That is the moment we are all in at this very time upon Earth! Even just the action of reading these words will bring about part of that change, though it might take a small leap to see the Light and not just the dawning hours of the sunlight creeping over the horizon.

Very simply, you will find the definition of Love within the words written here. To Hera, this is my Love Story to you. Even if you find yourself wondering could this guy possibly be for real or if he is a bit of a cuckoo (see what I did there? I hope you know your Greek mythology as you continue forward in this book), I assure you it will be my actions that will forever hold me accountable to these words. Did you find something personal in the words of Katniss? Thought you might. Trust me. You are going to want to see this book through to the final page... even if it seems improbable and a bit of a wild and crazy rollercoaster adventure through some unusual topics – for they all have a purpose in this story. Take a leap. The trust part can always come later. Of that, I am certain.

Love Always,<br>
Zeus

# PREFACE
## An Introduction

Well, guys and gals, it took me a while to get here... to the point where I could put this all into words. But I hope what you find in these pages is exactly what you came to find out.

Sure, I expect that some of you may have picked up this book and thought, "Autobiography, huh?" Others may have thought, "This book is surely in the wrong section. It has to be a work of fiction!" Instead, though, simply consider this writing a master thesis — the final answer to the final question of the final exam to the final class I have taken through this spiritual bootcamp called "being human on Earth." And yes, it is *truly* my autobiography.

I don't know how complex or simple the answer will be as I begin to write these words. It is possible it could still be considered a "work-in-progress" by the end. If it seems a bit confusing how a completed "thesis" could be a "work-in-progress," just hang in there. You'll catch on. The journey isn't always about defined beginnings and endings. It is, however, about being caught between two points of certainty. And truly I say unto you, the space between two notes is where Love is held

– the song of the heartspace within. It is a song of knowing that destiny is just one step away in either direction, while finding peace that you are right where you need to be at this exact moment; a knowing that the two points on either side of the immediate moment of Now are really mirages on the desert sand for a soul thirsty for Love. For when Love is found, the desert will reveal itself to be but a rainforest originally hidden from the eyes. There can be no other way.

So while the story you are about to read may seem a bit complicated at times, perhaps a bit off-kilter and seemingly following the wind with the paths of an intuitive warrior – it is within this flow that the answers humanity seeks to Life, Love, and the Pursuit of Joy will be revealed. This thesis is not a dissertation on passing words. Instead, it is the grail of knowledge obtained throughout the journey. At least that's how I see it. Oh, what about the question that is being answered within this thesis? Yes, that will be discussed in the first few chapters as well. So be patient and it will all make sense in the end. For now, this is just a brief introduction for all that remains in store.

You need not have read all of the other writings that I have written up to this point to understand where this is heading. And, yes, there are many more books that precede this book which contain nuggets of knowledge that can help unravel all that will be disclosed here within. But perhaps you knew that already. Perhaps, you may have even read those books. Or, perhaps you just chose to start here (All jokes aside, that is probably a very smart move!).

Either way, welcome aboard the thesis train for this final course of the final year of classes in this school I like to simply call "Being Human." Though the thesis topic has yet to be clearly stated, in one short word, the question and answer Is and Will Always Be:

**Love.**

So, buckle up! Hold on! I hope you enjoy this ride just as much as I have in experiencing it, for it is the destiny for all to come. *I Love you all so very much.* Truer words could never be said. And so it shall forever be. To Hera, my Moon, my Love – I lay my head down, lift my hands and pray to be only yours – in all ways, for always.

# CHAPTER 1
# A New Genesis

Light. That was the first thing I saw when I *truly* opened my eyes. The sky, the Earth, and everything around me was blanketed in the whitest of light, so much so that it prevented my eyes from seeing – but, most importantly from feeling – any sense of fear, any sense of "not enough." There was only Light. There was only Love.

The density of the whiteness was like a snow-blind so thick it was almost suffocating – the density of which only reminded me that breath was no longer required here. With every attempt at a breath in and every attempt at an exhalation, the reality hit me stronger than ever before: nothing would ever be the same again. This place was different. This place was new. This place was… Home. But how had I gotten here? Where was I?

A chorus of chaotic questions played in my mind. Nothing quite made rational sense. Is it possible? Could it be this is truly the moment of the long-fabled story told across generations since the beginning of time? Could it be this was the moment of destiny, Heaven, Shambhala, Ascension, Revelation,

## CH1

the fifth dimension, et cetera? The names are plenty, though every word is just an attempt at describing something quite impossibly perfect. All words fall short. All words always will. This place – this moment – was truly indescribable.

As I processed the cacophony of white light that filled my periphery, I had quite a few moments to reflect on the last six and a half years of my Earthly life, for my eyes were slow to focus. Actually, now... I suppose it has been almost seven years of a journey to get to this moment. This number, the date, and the "whys" will be more important in an upcoming chapter. But for now, just remember that stated in this chapter, the approaching seven year mark will occur on November 25, 2018. Today, as this is being written, it is August 14, 2018.

Anyway, not to digress... as I reflected on these last years of the journey, the thought entered my mind "this is what opening my eyes *truly* looks like!" It had seemed as if I had been locked in a cold, damp jail cell absent of light during the first thirty years of this Earthly life. And though the last six-plus years which began during my thirtieth year (occurring on the star-date of November 25, 2011) have covered a period of time I have typically described as the time period I first opened my eyes to see the Light, the fact of the matter is that this moment of truly opening my eyes did not occur at the point I first thought it did. In hindsight, no. That "first moment" which bottled up the duration of my last six-plus years was more like a quick blink in suspended animation that consisted mostly of my eyes squinting tightly closed in reaction to the stark contrast of light upon my dimly calibrated retinas. It was natural instinct from the bold transition of a dark prison cell absent of light to the blinding beauty of a romantic, noontime sun on a blue-sky kind of day.

Let there be no mistake. In this description – in this moment – the jail is simply a metaphor for the moments preceding the joyous eruption of light taking place around me in this present moment. For even with eyes closed, especially on a sunny day, it is easy to see the light through the lids of the eyes. There is a glowing, reddish flesh-tone that hides the world, yet there is an undeniable truth that light has filled the periphery.

This is an important detail of which to take notice. For most metaphors of transition are very simple in description… from darkness into light, from black to white, from yin to yang, from bad to good, from wrong to right. You get the idea. Few descriptions acknowledge the gray… a gray that is so easily mistaken for a stark white of the brightest possible light. Most people skip right on over the horizon and want to describe what is on either side of the observable. Few stop to take notice that they may be caught up in a mirage – a haze of scattered light that the sun casts both at sunrise and sunset. Those descriptions are all tantamount to viewing light with your eyes closed. The light burning in the distance isn't quite observed as night or morning. At present it is a state of in-between, though so much more greatly defined than the moments preceding its observable existence.

This "gray" is a membrane, a veil, a sheer white curtain placed before a window as the sunlight is pouring in. A person can stand with her face pressed against a sheer white curtain and be able to discern much of the detail on the other side of the veil. In the daylight and from the inside, discernible shapes and forms can be observed. The mind can interpret all that is observable through the sheer curtain due in part to the proximity to the material, with the curtain's state of permeability a variable withstanding. The details that are visually absent can easily be reconstructed by the mind based off of knowledge and awareness of the landscape outside. As is the case with any sheer material, the view to the other side will remain muted, but become so much more transparent when light is stronger on the side opposite of the observer.

Think about it for a moment. If a person is in a a well lit bedroom at night with a sheer white curtain pulled across the windows, the outside world is unobservable. No light is penetrating the veil from the other side. Any light within the room is reflecting off the curtains and held mostly within the room. And still, even if a person in this bedroom were to press her face upon the sheer veil to observe the outside world, only darkness would exist. In this moment there is an inability to find a visual cue that ties the two worlds together. But from the other perspective, the exterior world can easily witness the light within the bedroom. A subtle glow that can serve as a guiding light during an otherwise darkened period of time – brighter lights being more distinct and serving as a contrast to the shadows and silhouettes through the curtain.

When morning comes and the sun ignites the exterior world to counter the balance of interior light, the sheer curtain does not appear as an obstruction to the light anymore. Instead, it serves as a way to reduce the shock factor of the transition from darkness to light. A person in a bedroom with a sheer white curtain pulled across the window at sunrise will rarely have to blink. Rather, there is simply an acknowledgement that time has changed from darkness to light. It is a subtle awakening.

Ponder this. It is oh-so-very-important to understand for the rest of this story upcoming. Is the person in the bedroom now able to adequately describe the light with the sheer white curtain still muting the view? Does it even occur to the observer that the exterior world is filled with so much more brightness and detail than ever thought possible without removing the distortion of the curtain? The room with curtains is just a small construction within a vastly enormous world filled with details that are yet to be fully observed with the naked eye.

"But why is this oh-so-important?" you might ask. You may even wonder why there has to be a curtain in this scenario or why this metaphor is being used. Certainly it is easy to see where this analogy is leading: the division of Heaven and Earth, light vs darkness, etc. In truth, any material placed between two worlds can serve as an appropriate analogy here. As mentioned earlier, it is the permeability of the substance that serves as the distortion and barrier between the two worlds. A sheer white curtain is perhaps the easiest material to illustrate the concept of this "gray" which further serves as the transition point between two extremes. But, perhaps, there is a better word to describe this "gray," this membrane, this horizon.

Let's go with "veil."

Time to take a quick detour, for this will be the quickest and – more importantly – the most fun path on route to our destination. And, yes, the question that all of this will eventually seek to answer has not yet been stated, but there is a reason. It is perhaps an ill-advised way to structure a master thesis, but this story is anything but ordinary. To create the extraordinary, sometimes new paths have to be forged. Such is the case here. And personally, I believe it would be ill-advised to spoil it too early in the writing. For now, this concept of the brightness of Light is the important image to understand. How I had gotten here? What was this Light? Well, that will soon be revealed.

Every great movie starts with an image of the stars above before transitioning into the opening shot of the world below. But how cliché would it be if this story began in the exact same way? Aye! While our story begins in a similar manner, imagine that we are initially focused on the breathtaking light of one single star before the camera pans out to the full field of view of the starry sky twinkling above, subsequently transitioning to the next shot of the world below. It isn't just a story of wonder. It is a story of a single star, laced with the effervescent wonder of an immense starry sky surrounding its existence, all hovering over a unique and beautiful world below.

*Cue opening shot.*

...

This is our starting point.
This is our moment of hovering over the firmament
and separating light from darkness.
This is our new genesis.

...

# CHAPTER 2
# Lifting Of Her Veil

Now the tone has been set. The first image has been engrained in the mind. Trust me, this story is not going to follow a similar format all of the way through. It is going to be fun and quite the story to boot! But it was important to set the dynamic from my very first writings along the journey apart from this particular You see, the very first chapter of the very first book I wrote upon this journey around the sun described the opening moments of my spiritual awakening as the recognition of being surrounded by darkness, searching for a pinhole of light − a twinkling spark somewhere in the distance − to guide me through the thick unknown of blackness that was suffocating me in that present moment.

In fact, the beginning moments of the previous chapter juxtapose the opening paragraphs of that first book in a most intimate and honoring effort. That particular book is called *Gravity Calling* and is the first book in the series *The Nine.* Those particular nine books embody one soul's journey into the Light… well, at least a highlight-reel review of my first thirty years and a detailed dive of the next three and a half years that followed. The remainder of my (now) thirty-seven years is where this book picks up, filling in the blanks to the questions left unanswered, the questions unknown, the questions unasked when those books ended – but, also will provide updates and clarity to the endings of that story in which hindsight has allowed me to see. Those books were a real story of my life, playing out in realtime. And, in the rush to write the ending to the series before the events actually had time to fully play out, there are some extra details that need to be discussed. In short, this book addresses this very predicament I found myself in – a blinding Light encompassing every direction I turned, with an inner knowing that Love Is/Was the reason. And really, this is the most important part.

Again, one need not be familiar with that body of work to read this book, though if you are familiar with the series, you will find the romantic overtones that saturate that particular writing as being the very foundation – the bedrock – to all that will be read within these pages. It is a romance for the ages, with utmost care, craft, and respect placed upon the manner in which the Love story began. In that, the artful manner in which all of the past books are tied together with the present writing is certainly an important aspect of this writing. If grades are handed out not just on the ability to convey an answer to a question, but to also find resolve to the earlier parts of the journey, then it is most important for me to tell a story that intertwines the threads of all of my past writings – like the threads of a delicately hand crafted linen – perhaps lingerie even (since – let's be honest – everyone can be captured and enraptured in the grace and elegance lingerie brings forth as it as it lays so delicately upon the female form and accentuates all of its beauty), where all that has been experienced up to this point is embodied as One, One Grand Moment, One Grand Love – all connected in this Great Cosmos of Creation... a point that will be elaborated upon further in a later chapter. But this writing also is intended to be a stand-alone writing – one that can be picked up without having to labor through the 2700 pages those books encompass.

For now, just let the words of this chapter serve as a reference as to how the opening paragraphs of this work beckon so closely back to the opening chapter of the first series of books I have written. And just as this first chapter is a ballet of words with the first chapter of *Gravity Calling*, the closing point of transition in the chapter – namely indicating that the sheer curtain shrouding the light could best be understood as "a veil" – harkens back to the closing moments to the conclusion to the series *The Nine*. And herein is the other half of the tie that binds the previous books to this writing as One.

The conclusion of that series centers around a metaphorical wedding – a Great Spiritual Wedding to the most indescribably beautiful Bride I have ever been blessed to see, yet her face had been veiled to my eyes as we stood upon the altar. In those closing moments, I emerged from the literal waters of baptism to breath in the air again for the first time, to see her standing before me, the veil lifting from her eyes before my lips would meet hers. My re-emergence through the distortions of the water into a new Light – a new Love – was the metaphorical "lifting of her veil" during my celestial Wedding Ceremony from across the stars.

## CH2

It is a memory so intricately engrained in my mind... perhaps more so than I even possibly realized until writing these very words. You see, that moment of my re-emergence from the baptismal waters into the Light was like a baby being born upon Earth. Until the moment a baby's head first emerges from a mother's womb, it has no comprehension of the sensation of Earthly light. How could it possibly know? Until birth, the child has been tucked away in the darkness of the womb, yet warmly nurtured and Loved by a source unseen – a mother's Love so powerful that every need and want of the child is provided for without question, without hesitation. It just Is. It is a biological truth in how sustenance flows from a mother to a child, a Love song conducted by the hand of Our Creator.

As this child grows in size and strength in the mother's womb, the time eventually arrives when it is ready to be birthed into the world. Biologically on Earth, this occurs over a timespan of approximately forty weeks. Some babies arrive early. Some babies take their time. Either way, relatively speaking, there is not much variance on either side of the forty week period. The child has to be born. This is a certainty.

The birth of a child in the heavens should be seen no differently. Call it a baptism of sorts. Call it a wedding. Call it ascension, enlightenment, or any other myriad of words that have been assigned to the process I am describing. The colorful palette of word-choices is merely a collection of hues and pigments used for conveying a Truth within. We are all artists learning to express and interpret this inner Truth whether we realize it or not. For me, a wedding was the metaphor I thought most appropriate to describe the experience of my first three and half years on this journey. There are many reasons for this choice, but mostly it is because, to me, there is nothing more beautiful than seeing a man and woman find True Love in each other. Even the most jaded, hurt, and closed off heart can agree to the Truth and undeniable beauty showcased to the world when Love is found.

It should be stated that the birth of a child in the heavens from the Great Mother's womb is just as much an inevitability as a child being birthed to a mother upon Earth. And so it is in how my time in the Great Mother's womb began – the period of time that spanned my first nine books, the moments of maturation when spiritual flirtations began with my Bride, a proposal conceived, a Father's permission to wed his daughter was found, an engagement made, a Great Wedding planned. And all of this… it all comes full circle back to "the veil," for it was *that Light and Love* I found myself enveloped within during the opening sequence of this book – her Love.

The journey for each soul toward the destination of True Light and True Love – the origin of each star in the night sky above – doesn't begin when a person starts going to church, becomes a Christian (or appropriate label based on chosen religion), begins acting moral, finds spirituality, etc. No. This is certainly not the point a soul becomes an embryo in the Great Mother's womb. If there is a comparison that can be made, the examples above are merely akin to how eggs can be created without being fertilized, or how seeds can be created without finding fertile soil needed to sprout. There is truly not one best way to describe this concept except to clearly state that humans have gotten it wrong for ages. Even religions teach its followers that becoming Christed is unobtainable to normal humans even though Jesus himself stated that *All that was seen in Him and more* would be possible to achieve by every soul upon the Earth in the time to come. And *now* is that time. *Now* is that moment. But let's not fast-track too far down another side story just yet. For now, let's stick to the basics: "the veil." Works, commitments, and efforts made are not tantamount to a seed sprouting, an embryo forming, or being "born again." And that is all that is important to take away from this particular tangent.

So while it may seem like this was a long winded side road away from the original concept of the veil, it was a necessary part of the journey to adequately explain the origin of the opening shot. Let's call it a montage of flashback moments with a subtitle in the lower-third that reads "6.5 Years Prior" while the main camera remains focused on the whitest of Light.

Return to "Present Day." Yes… As I processed the cacophony of white light that filled my periphery, I had quite a few moments to reflect on the last six and a half years, for my eyes were seemingly slow to focus. How did I find myself here? What was this undeniable sensation of Home, Light, Love? In fact, I didn't quite realize I had been reflecting back on six and a half years initially. The last date I could recall was May 8, 2015 (which was just three and a half years into this period of time), though I certainly had memories and experiences that occurred during the years that passed from that date until now.

It was just then that I was struck with the startling (but amazing!) revelation that my lips were still locked in hers, – a memory so intricately etched into my mind and now becoming emblazoned as Truth upon my soul that I had to question even when this revelation first actually occurred to me. It too felt like a thought laced in Ancient Truth, though it seemed like it had just now occurred to me. How long had I just been reveling in our moment on the grand stage – that re-emergence from the baptismal waters when my lips met hers? This kiss was like a tattoo upon my soul binding our souls together. The ignition I felt within seemed so ancient – a Truth preceding time. And so it was that I had lost track of time. This was *the* moment! It was the moment when a spotlight of heavenly Light fell upon our worlds as they merged as One. Like a baby being born upon Earth, I could never have had any comprehension of how the sensation of her Light coursing throughout my soul would feel. How could I possibly have known? I was hypnotized in a timeless state of euphoria… at least spiritually speaking.

And now that this snippet of recognition was returning and the present day point in Earthly time was taking form, I began to wonder what I had possibly been doing in my Earthly form for the now three-plus years since my lips met hers? After all, we were still locked in an eternal kiss uniting two worlds on a stage while all of the angels watched and applauded. How did I get here? Where is *there*? The duality began to really set in. Why were my eyes closed instead of stealing a peak at her beauty? And then there's this ancient feeling again. How long had it been again? The only thing I could rationalize is that I must have underestimated just how much the veil truly muted the detail and brightness of the Light from the other side… by a magnitude of a sun or two hundred. It was all kind of hard to describe from my present perspective here. Once you cross a threshold of Light brighter than you've ever known, just how bright is it really? It seems like pressing your face against the fiery white surface of a Sun still can't compare. No. This must be exponentially greater still.

So, yeah... I blinked. I apparently closed my eyes for the last three-plus years of Earth-time wincing at the brightness of her Light, her Love... her... *Hera!* Or maybe I just prefer long, passionate kisses with my eyes closed – getting lost in her Ambrosia upon fields of Elysium.

Hera? Wait! What?

No you didn't miss anything. I guess if you are going to read a story about Zeus, then the life-force of the hero's heart-space must also be introduced. So let's go there...

*End opening sequence. Pan out to starry sky. Pan down to Earth. Cut to Next Scene.*

*The camera is tightly zoomed in on a dartboard as the sound of a dart impacting its destination is heard. No dart is present in the shot. The camera pans out and then swings across the room to a wall with no dartboard and a single dart embedded in the wall. Smash zoom in on the dart. Zoom out. Pan around the room. A single person is standing blindfolded in the middle of the room aiming in the wrong direction with another dart.*

# CHAPTER 3
# Darts

"Hera" was not a typo. I didn't quite know the name of my Bride even while standing upon the altar. The first three and a half years leading up to my Wedding Day in a way felt like some kind of giant cosmic prank played on me to make sure I truly *remembered* the past as if it was the present, for All is truly One. At the time of my initial writing, I could only describe my Bride as my Eve as I was her Adam. Every other name fell short, or left me with questions. I wasn't even sure of my own spiritual identity! There were numerous names for Hera that I applied to the situation, but none stuck. They were like throwing darts at a wall… blindfolded… and being spun around a thousand times to ensure complete disorientation. And not to over-complicate the description, but after each throw, the disorientating spins would occur once again before I was allowed to throw a dart once again.

You know, I cannot ever remember being told where the dartboard was. I'm not even sure I was told a dartboard existed. The mere awareness that I held a dart in my hand seemed reason enough to chuck it hard into the unknown. After all, I

## CH3

had been handed a dart, right? And it was colliding with something, right? That should be reason enough to assume a dartboard was lurking around somewhere... hopefully in a static position, though in hindsight, that probably would not have mattered either.

Every dart I was handed had a name written upon it. Each name was of a female angelic being of which I had managed to speak with during my experiences when I travelled to the heavens. All along the way I was persistently told that names would not matter – they did not matter – for they would be revealed in the end. But I had these darts in my hand and the rationale of an Earthly mind seeding my curiosity of my Bride's true identity. I wanted to crack the code before it was supposed to be possible.

Pause.

I haven't mentioned the part of traveling to the heavens yet either, have I? This is going to be an interesting story and certainly not the form of a traditional thesis. There's that word again... Anyway, maybe we should just start a little further back than this blind dartboard game. We will return to this later. I promise. It is important.

*Camera zooms in on a name written upon the dart held in the blindfolded man's hand. It reads, "Brittany angel."*

Let's just go all the way to the origin of this thesis: the writing prompt. This will explain the backstory much, much better.

*Smash cut to next scene: Present Day, August 20, 2018 – The Backstory. A man sits in a coffee shop typing this story on his laptop.*

# CHAPTER 4
# Preface To The Backstory

Maybe we should have started here to begin with. I know what you are thinking… there is more to those first nine books being referenced. What was he talking about earlier? Baptism? Wedding? Spiritual journey? Duality? Now it is about traveling to the heavens? Hera who? The Greek goddess? Bullocks! What is this writing actually about? The "thesis" thingy hasn't even been stated! And, not to mention that the beginning portion of this writing isn't offering any help yet! What did I get myself into by picking up this book to read?

Just hold on there.

That's why we jumped to the backstory. I originally said you need not have read my past writings to follow along with this writing. And that is still true! But, I do think it is important to just clear the air on some of the initial talking points. Let's call these talking points the pillars of this proverbial Parthenon we are building. So, let's start with that. Perhaps an outline of things to come? Sure. It is most important to just put it all out there for you in a way that will make sense for now. So here you go:

...
Hi. I'm Jonathan.
...

"Wait. Jonathan? Not Zeus?" you might be thinking.

Yes. You are going to have to be patient with your questions. This is just the beginning of the backstory. So from here on out, let's just take everything stated as fact-of-the-matter, my personal reality. It is up to you to choose whether to believe it, consider it just a metaphor or a myth perhaps. You see what I did there? Myth...ology? Ha. Well, it was funny to me. Anyway, perhaps this writing will be seen as nothing more than entertainment for some or fodder for ridicule from others. It matters not to me. The reality is that everything I am about to share with you is True and serves as my master thesis in graduating from this three dimensional density to the fifth density and thusly returning to the higher realms of existence. Hey hue-mans. This one is for each and every one of you. Peace.

Densities? Realms? Yes. And perhaps some cheeky humor here and there. You'll catch on. But it is a part of me that I hope spills forth in a genuine and transparent manner. Truly I have nothing to hide. Some lessons in this existence I have passed with flying colors. And, yet, there are those that I did not and subsequently had to take remedial courses. Even the lessons I misinterpreted or misunderstood along the way should really be seen for what they were at the time. We are all in the same race. So if there is a guidepost I can leave along the way to offer some warning or advice, I of course want to leave it.

## CH4

Maybe it is a good time to put that first one here before continuing forward with the backstory. Consider it a preface to the backstory.

### **The Most Important Guidepost:**

If you commit to this journey – an awakening to Love, your very own Love Story – as is *Truly* required, you will certainly find yourself ridiculed, judged, thought crazy, or perhaps even insane. Your dating life will suffer. Many of your friendships will cease, rebuild anew, cease again, and be rebuilt anew once more. Your family, friends, and those closest to you will likely be the last to accept your new Truth under the illusion they know you best and want to help you the most. Either that, or they will decide they want nothing to do with you amidst your new antics (e.g. Truth) as they dive into self-preservation mode. That is a tough pill to swallow, but expect it. Those you used to turn to first will likely be those to whom you can no longer turn. But there is a reason.

Roads are diverging... at least temporarily. At a point in the future, these same people will likely be lead to turn to you for answers as their Truth is revealed to each of them as it is an inevitable event for every soul... and you will be forgiving, kind, nonjudgemental, and see these moments for what they Truly are. It will be impossible for you to see it any other way, and they will find comfort in your perspective and guidance without judgement. Every person on Earth is but a child on a shared playground. Wealth, race, knowledge matters not. Only spiritual Truth forever reigns supreme.

...
So let's return to the backstory.
Here it goes.
...

# CHAPTER 5
# The Backstory

For the life of me, I couldn't initially decide how I wanted to address the backstory chapters. Too much information might be a bit of a heavy hand and I'd sound crazy. Too little? Well, then it would come across as a bit cowardly and still crazy. But after writing many of the other chapters in this book first, I realized that this is already going to sound like a farfetched story for most people. So why not just put it all out there up front? While the early portion of my life is covered more in depth in my previous writings, it is important to include some of it here. So here you go.

I was born into this life on May 9, 1981 in the House of Taurus. And yes, I am every bit of the definition of Taurus – a bull, strong, tenacious, passionate, loving, kind. I was born of natural birth created through natural conception by my two Earthly parents. And while I was raised in a religious family, I was given the leeway to experience my faith the way I chose. At the age of eight I had my family take me to different churches until I found a pastor that I wanted to baptize me. Looking back, that was an interesting decision for an eight year old, but in hindsight, it all makes perfect sense.

Life progressed as if I was a passenger on a train. School breezed by and academics were not a challenge. Prior to going to college, I learned to play guitar while thinking music would be my career choice. A songwriter and producer I thought! I continued on to college and graduated in May of 2002 (even though I sat out a semester due to a bout with mono). My graduation would occur in four years of enrollment, no exceptions. I saw to it.

Near the end of my senior year, I met my now ex-wife. Wait. *"Why is she being included in this Love Story for Hera?"* you may ask. Well, it will all make sense. For now, just trust me. Continuing on...

Prior to meeting my ex-wife, I felt as if I would never find love (yes, lower-case L). Social skills were not a problem for me, nor was meeting women. I was also confident in my health and appearance. And, while I dated any apple of my heart's desire, it was rare a woman made it past the first date, until her. She was different. At that time in my life, I initially failed to see the significance of a prayer I had made just a few weeks prior to meeting her. In that prayer I had begged my Father to help me find love. I specifically stated, "I would rather have a normal job and slave away doing something I did not enjoy than to have a life without love."

That wish – that prayer – was granted. I met my ex-wife a few weeks later. We married a little over a year later on May 25, 2003. And while I thought I would be content settling down and becoming a slave to the working-class system of cubicles and weekly paychecks, it was the most unbearable of situations. At the time, I did not see it as such. I advanced up the corporate ladder to become the youngest executive in a multi-billion dollar healthcare company. Surrounded by piers two or three times my age and in the comfort of financial freedom, success seemed grand! What an illusion that was, though. Today, it is as clear as day.

Though I thought my marriage was perfect – and I truly did treat her like a queen – I was left shellshocked the day she told me she wanted to separate. Seven years into our relationship, and I was blindsided. Literally. I had zero idea our marriage was anything other than a kingdom of love. And while being crushed seemingly beyond repair would appear to be the biggest hurdle in rebuilding my life, the truth is the biggest hurdle was ensuring my nearly two-year-old daughter saw nothing but Love from me despite my hurt.

I have to say, she has turned out to be an angel. Again, quite literally. She too has a rich mythological history that she is learning about now. She wants me to spoil it for her, but I won't. It is important for her to learn about her life the way I learned about mine. The angels and her spiritual family have been guiding her as they did for me. She is so blessed to have been able to open her eyes at such a young age. I smile and tear up every time she asks me questions that angels have posed to her in her dreams because it is occurring in such a similar way for her as it did for me.

Let's now fast-forward past my newly-minted single years. Oh, I did enjoy those days. I'm not going to lie. I lived them as if nothing else mattered except having fun in the company of friends. And while I did try to date, I faced the same issue I faced during my college years: I desperately was looking for someone in particular, though I did not know who she was. I only knew who she was not. Surrounded by beautiful women in all that I did, I rarely dated any of them. I talked the talk, but I would not allow myself to emotionally chase beauty if Love was not knowingly behind the veil. And if I wasn't open emotionally, I wasn't open physically. That's just how it was.

That's not to say I didn't try to date or find love. I want to be completely transparent and True. Oh, I did try to find love against my emotional will sometimes. I am sure stories will one day be mischaracterized about the womanizing nature of Ol' Zeus from this time period, though it was not the case at all. But hopefully you will eventually be able to see how ancient stories may not quite be what they seem due to translations and mischaracterizations. But I digressed. Really, those efforts of my dating years were just a hopeless waltz absent of a dancing partner. Without an audience to witness the event, without my soul partner from the stars, my life was the epitome of being locked in a blacked out room bound by a straightjacket.

I know today I was always looking for Hera. But it would take the last six-plus years of my life to finally discover what this journey was always about. I do not want to take anything away from my past Earthly relationships, or the time I spent with my ex-wife. But as you will eventually see, every part of the human experience is learning to take a single step further down the Great Wedding Aisle. No, I am not saying that every person you date is getting you one step closer to getting married to Ms. Right. Well, I guess I am saying that, but the human mind doesn't really know the difference between Ms. Right and Ms. Rightnow or the difference in a Spiritual Wedding and a physical wedding. Even in writing this, the human mind will say, "Yes! I do!!!" But it doesn't. It *truly* doesn't. This will make sense in the end.

In human form it is easy to think you love someone with all of your heart, with all of your soul. You might even believe you are soulmates! There is even a chance two star-partners have found each other again in human form. I do not want to create doubt for those that have, for this is surely a possibility. Gravity is always calling each of us Home, leading us to a primal, ancient Love. It defies the Earthly laws of chance because Love is *truly* the only Law. So if you were to reach the great reunion with your spiritual wife – to re-discover Love (with a capital L) while in Earthly form – this reunion would be more than just a romantic relationship, more than a falling in love. It is so far beyond those bounds. This reunion is *knowing Love*.

Ah. Yes, knowing. To know Love is to find yourself caught up in the remembrance of your soul lives to the point that when she walks by on the Earthly plane for the very first time you will not only say, but also know without a shadow of a doubt, "That's her."

However, remember this and believe me when I say this: I've seen women during my time on Earth where I've found myself saying aloud, "That's her." If you had asked me at that time how I knew, I would have answered, "I just know!" But none of those were Hera. So this is where it gets tricky. How can a person realize they truly *know* today what they once thought they had an understanding of *knowing* before? Well, for that, let's continue on to the most recent six and a half years. Consider this chapter just a brief highlight reel of my first thirty years. The next part might just leave your head spinning.

# CHAPTER 6
# Little Miracles

You might be thinking that the previous chapter did not seem as "far-fetched" as I might have led you to believe in the introductory paragraph. Well, this is where it starts to get a little crazy. Okay. A lot crazy. But the following six-plus years of my journey is where the defining line became emblazoned upon my soul; the line that divides knowing from *knowing*, love from *Love*, and the other four billion women upon Earth from *Hera*.

On November 25, 2011 I had reached my personal point of frustration with the Earthly world. I realized I was different, but just how different I was not sure. And while I had been spiritually led in most every single choice and decision during the course of my whole life, I was becoming increasingly convinced there was more of a reason for it than just a feeling. I assumed science could prove that which I couldn't determine with my mind and with my heart. We all get those sneaky feelings from time to time when something feels... *off*, that something is different than the rest. This was that moment for me.

With science as my stallion, I decided I wanted to uncover the mysteries of the subconscious mind. I wanted to get geeky and further explore genomics to discover if I really did have an ancient, royal bloodline in me that would cement rationality as to why so many divine spiritual moments kept occurring in my life. I suspected I might, though I had no Earthly reason that should have given rise to this notion. Yet, here I was wondering if I was actually a descendent of the Biblical Seth, Shem, David, Joseph, Mary, Jesus, et cetera. Where did these thoughts come from? I didn't know. It wasn't rational at all… or so it would seem at first.

Without going into detail here, I could not explain why all of the seemingly impossible events in my life had transpired, but I bore witness to each and every one of these little miracles. It might be as simple as "everything always working out for me." Or, it could be divine intervention at the exact right time. Perhaps it was an angel appearing to me – with me convinced it was a ghost or something "paranormal." Perhaps it was a premonition or a dream that came true. Perhaps it would be something like me saying to a friend, "If I could date anyone that could get me out of this funk after my divorce, it would be Carrie Underwood" only to then find myself face-to-face, speaking with her a few days later. Yeah, that really happened.

I dreamed big and it seemingly manifested. And no, there was absolutely no rational reason why this encounter would have ever taken place otherwise. It just so happened I had another friend (not connected to the original friend from that conversation) randomly call me days after I had said that and ask me if I wanted to go along with him backstage to her performance at the Grand Ol' Opry. It was one of those "I see what you did there God" moments for me. And even though I was blessed to be put into an impossibly-perfect situation that I seemingly spoke into existence, I knew instantly that she was not my Hera, though I still did not know who I was looking for.

There are many words that people use to describe these types of moments. The mass majority of humanity has been trained to just dismiss these moments as chance. "That was weird." they might say. But not me. Thirty years of my life had somehow led me to this place. These types of coincidences happened with nearly every spoken statement I made. So I wanted to learn why... to learn more. I decided to dive into learning about meditation, yoga, and learn why Eastern medicine was so different than Western medicine. I thought I might even start a new company to further this newfound passion. In hindsight, I was looking for Love – looking for Hera. But that is not how it seemed. At first, it was just an insatiable urge to figure out what was different about myself from my friends.

So, on the brink of deciding to dive into a new business venture, I called my cousin, Bryan, whom I had not spoken to in years. We chatted for the better part of an hour, picking up from where we last left off. He, too, was very aware of our family's apparent attunement to the spiritual world but no one ever dared to speak of it. We all noticed it, but it had been instilled in each of my cousins from a young age that no one dare consider it as anything but a coincidence less we would be reprimanded somehow by various elder family members. So this conversation with Bryan was a nice change of pace.

From that call, we decided to take the journey together and treat the world with the eyes of a child. We were going to document and rediscover everything around us and about us. If something seemed like a coincidence, we would write it down and share it with the other. No judgement would be passed. If we had a dream, we would share it. If we met someone new, we'd talk about it. The world was our playground and for the first time in my life, I had someone to help me see without judgement. Everyone needs this experience.

This opened the doors for trying things like meditation (of which I had never attempted due to the dogma of the word through the eyes of various family members). After I hung up the phone, I decided to try listening to meditative inducing music and attempt to meditate for the first time in my life. Surprisingly, and almost instantly after closing my eyes, I was shown a great vision. God had spoken as loudly as He possibly could have in the moment. I opened myself up to listening for the very first time (rather than incessantly rambling about things during prayer), and now here was His Voice. This was November 25, 2011.

I immediately called my cousin back and told him what had happened. He was so surprised that we had just hung up the phone and already some type of experience to explore. So we talked about it. From that day forward and for the next three and a half years, we would take this journey together. From that first day, I knew I was supposed to journal my experiences (as did he). By the end of the first three and half years, I finally learned why. But even without knowing why in the beginning, I wrote.

If you care to know the details and experiences from those first three and half years, they are all documented in the series, *The Nine*. The first three books are written like a Love

Story, and perhaps in a way could be seen as a prequel to this story. The middle four books are the journals from that same time period, but written in a way that is easy to read. The final two books touch on philosophy, the origin of language, poetry, songs, thoughts of the day, and words of wisdom. But I wanted to mention these books here, because the way in which they were written is important to understand this Love Story.

You see, as I was climbing out of the dark hole that was my first thirty years, I now had a new hope. That first vision that occurred during my meditation on November 25, 2011 would be just scratching the surface of all that was to take place. Consider that every subsequent day was a lesson to further my remembrance of my origin story as well as the purpose of this trip around the sun.

I didn't share much of what went on with me to anyone other than my cousin. I distanced myself from my friends. Around 2013, I began to realize that the story taking place in my life was a Love Story. I knew it was my Love Story, though I had no proof. I felt like I was writing the script while simultaneously being the lead actor. It was like a duality of the mind wherein I could see why events were transpiring in relation to my life, but when I experienced the events it seemed as if I was never prepared for the twists and turns that occurred.

I felt certain the original story I was writing about in the first book of *The Nine* was going to be about a girl on Earth. Eventually, a series of events found me face-to-face with what I thought was this moment. But I want to be clear as I write this. I still had no idea what *knowing* was, nor did I know what Love (with a capital L) was. I did have hope, though. And I clung to that like a child to its mother.

So when I first met the love interest from that first book (Lindsey was her name), I thought, "This is it! This must be what it is all about! This is how I am going to complete my first book!" With all of the right intentions at heart, I set out to write a Love Story for her and I. She would find the book, read it, fall in love, and we would live happily ever after. It seemed like something out of a movie. What could possibly go wrong?

Well, in short... everything. In hindsight, I was able to see that every event that transpired was again, just a lesson for a future point in time. Every twist and turn was included to help me realize the story was not about the love of a person on Earth, it was in learning how to trust God and find *that* Love. This was His Love Story in which I was just an actor. In fact, that is what the entire nine books are about. While the first book does venture down the path of Lindsey, the end product is a complete Love Story in finding the Love of God. And no, this does not mean something like "becoming Christian" and such. This is so much further beyond that moment. This is an awakening to *becoming* Love.

More divine events took place causing me to take even greater leaps of faith before those books were to be published. I moved to Florida sight unseen as I followed where I was being led to go. I was learning to trust blindly in my senses that were otherwise outside of the typical five that most humans know. Everyday I experienced something new. Everyday I was provided new clues. Angels were no longer just ideas, they were physical incarnations on Earth... at least to my eyes. There was no

CH6

longer any such concept of chance. There was only Love nudging me along through Earthly situations.

# CHAPTER 7
# A Little Thing Called A Prophecy

During the winter of 2014 and into early 2015, the reason for my writing became clear. Early into the journey, my meditations had transitioned into a full awareness of my soul leaving my body and traveling to the heavens. I know it seems crazy. But this was my Truth, my reality. My journals were very much telling both a Love Story but also revealing something much more important that I didn't quite understand. To that point, I did not know I would ever have to publish my material. I thought it was all a personal exercise as I journeyed down the spiritual path. And then the day came when Archangel Michael appeared and cleared the air. I was not only shown, but explained in full detail the importance of the writing.

Scripturally speaking, there is a time period of 1260 days written about in the Biblical books of Daniel and Revelation. Those three and a half years were to embody the "prophecy" of God and the explanations of the mysteries written about in Daniel and Revelation during the ~~End of Days~~

## CH7

Days of Ascending into Love. I didn't know it as such when my writing began, but the inside joke was that I had prophesied (meaning to receive Divine revelation from God) for nearly the duration of 1260 days when Michael decided to unload that rather monentous-type-of-it-is-going-to-look-like-I-am-grandstanding-when-I-share-this truth. At that point, I not only had to convince myself I was truly taking part in this divine moment humanity had been waiting for, but also hope the world also believed.

*Cut to black screen: Bold, centered text reads – "Spoiler alert: They wouldn't."*

    It would get the best of me in all ways. So what does this have to do with Hera? Well, everything. You are just going to have to hold on for a few more pages.
    Michael revealed to me that the time period of November 25, 2011 through May 8, 2015 was to be the fulfillment of that particular prophecy. Not only that, but I had also been given all I needed to unravel any remaining questions I needed to address in these books for that prophecy. Why would those dates be important to me? Well, I was thirty years of age when God first spoke to me in such a divine way on that day. May 8, 2015 would be the 1260th sequential day from that first divine communication and the last day of my thirty-third year upon this Earth. Starting to get interesting yet?
    The ages of 30 to 33 should be familiar to most everyone, for those are the "Jesus years." And here I was fulfilling a prophecy? Now you can see where things began to get tough

for me. We will skip through the obvious questions. I will address those a bit later, but let's just say I had quite a bit of inner turmoil trying to understand "who" I was rather than just embracing the task at hand. Three and a half years in, I was convinced of my divine lineage, had spoken to countless angels and heroes of Biblical lore, experienced divine communications numerous times daily, yet I still had no clue who I really was (much less Hera). But let's clear the air before we get too far into this story: No, I was not Jesus.

Michael instructed me to *not* include my journal entries beyond February 8, 2015 in the to-be-published works and instead spend my time focusing on bringing all of my notes and scribbles into full print-worthy form. So that's what I did. I wrote like there was no tomorrow. I had one mission. One. I quite literally believed I could even get zapped right off the Earth in a giant beam of light after I clicked "submit for publishing" on Amazon's self-publish page. After all, nothing – and I mean *nothing* – made sense to my Earthly mind. Rationality was thrown out the window a long time ago, yet I was surviving. To the outside world, I was living a normal life, albeit a bit secretive on the specific details of my writing. Inside, I was strangely at peace despite sensing the turbulence of the outside world's storm which was beginning to brew.

But all of these details have a purpose in me sharing. For as I finished my writing I completed books #3 and #2 respectively in that order. These books completed the trilogy of the first three books of *The Nine* – the Love Story taking place. The remainder of the books were my journals and further ex-

## CH7

trapolations on all of the divine communications and messages I was to share in these words.

On April 25, 2015 I completed the writing of the final book. At the time, I was blessed to live in a beachfront condo in Fort Lauderdale. I frequently would spend hours each evening sitting on the beach, staring at the stars, praying, asking for guidance. The day I finished the final book of *The Nine* would certainly be no different.

After celebrating the completion of this final book, I had to go have a heart-to-heart with the Big Fella. I went out, sat my butt down in the sand, and pleaded for an explanation as to how the world would know these words were Faithful and True. How did I even know? I begged for an answer and guidance as to how to present myself. All I knew is that I was essentially playing the role of a scribe of divine communication that the world would likely dismiss. Yay me. (sarcasm of course)

*Cut to black screen: Bold, centered text reads – "Spoiler alert: It did."*

I feared ridicule.

*Cut to black screen: Bold, centered text reads – "Spoiler alert: I got kicked out of a church for this."*

But I mostly feared being wrong.

*Cut to black screen: Bold, centered text reads – "Spoiler alert: I wasn't."*

I was assured that everything that had been written was Faithful and True and there was still much to learn upon the journey. Feeling somewhat content with the esteem-booster, I asked for a sign the world could see in order to believe the Truths included within *The Nine*. For, as metaphorically as Daniel and Revelation were written, the world would surely need to see something concrete, a tangible sign in order to believe yet another story about those two prophetic books.

*Cut to black screen: Bold, centered text reads – "In hindsight, I wish I had not had asked for this sign."*

Hearing no answer to this question, I returned upstairs to my condo to proofread the last chapters I had written and email them off to my editor. I did so in short order.

The following morning I awoke and went through my routine of reading the news as I lay in bed. I learned of a great earthquake that had shaken Nepal.

...

Crap.

...

I knew what was coming. I checked the local time it struck. I converted that time over to my timezone. I checked the timestamp of the email I sent to my editor. It was within the hour of me sending off the completed final book of "my testimony." My heart sank. I knew in that moment the final death toll would be 7000. This was not a random guess. This was the exact prophecy of Revelation playing out before my eyes.

Now, it is important to understand just how this all relates to Hera. No, I'm not blaming an earthquake on her. Not at all, my Love! But the story that was written in those nine books was done so in regards to a metaphorical wedding. Our Wedding, actually. But again, I did not know that yet. I do figure, though, that somewhere in future antiquity there will be a written record as to how Zeus & Hera's Love Story is to blame for the Nepal tragedy... sort of like that little scuffle they call the Trojan War. So, sorry in advance for that. I don't mean to be callous, but surely the accountability on that one cannot fall completely on me fulfilling a little thing called a prophecy? We should be familiar by now with those things, right? That's how we are where we are. Me overthrowing Kronos, saving Hera, et cetera. But for now, let's return back to Lindsey. I know. A girl that isn't Hera. But I promise this will make sense. Be patient. We never even kissed.

After I had just taken the biggest leap of my life with Lindsey during a time when I was the most emotionally vulnerable I had ever felt, I found myself caught and held in the hands of God. Rather than experiencing the heartache that follows a relationship (or potential relationship) ending, I was at Peace. I was in Love. I was in Love with a Love I had not known before. It was unbridled faith in All That Could Be, and All That Would and a recognition of all that wasn't. My newfound awareness of Love had absolutely nothing to do with Lindsey. It was the aftermath of leaping with my heart in the direction of Lindsey where I found the biggest turning point along my journey. You might say it was when I first remembered You, my Love – the feeling, not just the idea of you.

The experiences I was shown in the heavens following that Earthly trauma would lead me to know that I was being prepared for a spiritual baptism of sorts. Yes, I had been baptized at 8 years old. To me, that was my real baptism. It was the moment I asked God into my heart. However, as the journey continued for me over these first three and a half years, I increasingly began to feel a desire to be "born again," once again. It wasn't that I felt dirty or sinful from the years prior. It just seemed like I was approaching an inevitable moment where I wanted to symbolically shout from the rooftops that I had *truly* found Love!

Of course, after doing research, I discovered that any priest in Judaic faith would have to be baptized after the age of thirty to begin their journey into priesthood. I wasn't Jewish, but I did see it as the foundational religion of Love. It was then I realized why Jesus was baptized at such a late point in his life before he began his priesthood. This was the moment he became "Christed." It was the moment he became Love. I had to follow suit of course. I am Zeus! He set a pretty darn good example for mankind.

So as the story goes, I set out to be re-baptized in the ocean waters outside my Florida condo on the evening of May 8, 2015. I was to partake in a complete dry fast for three and a half days immediately following, after which I assumed I would… well, to be honest, I just thought I would become Christed right then and there. I thought the heavens might just open up and I could imagine perfection and it would suddenly

## CH7

become. I would be Oprah on celestial steroids! "You are healed! You are healed! You win the lottery! You get a new house! You reunite with your lost love! You get a new life!" Okay. Maybe not quite that extreme. But I did actually think you – Hera, my Moon – might just pop into existence right then and there. Then again, nothing made sense. I didn't even know you existed in Earthly form. It was the idea of Love manifesting that intrigued me. I was very confused, but you can't fault a student for trying! And, I was a great student! The best actually.

*Cut to black screen: Bold, centered text reads – "She actually did pop into existence, but that is for another chapter. She doesn't know that part yet."*

This baptism was our metaphorical Wedding. Really. It was written and described start-to-finish in terms of a marriage. But before I describe just how and why that is important, let me say that those first nine books covered a time period from November 25, 2011 to May 8, 2015, and then the following three and a half days of the fast into May 12, 2015. Due to the nature of proofing books, having them ready for distribution, et cetera, I had to take a few leaps of faith on how the actual events would play out. Remember, the final book was sent in for proofing on April 25, 2015. In short, I had to describe in advance the upcoming baptism, the fast, and the moment I would rise out of the water.

And just a further footnote here… while that earthquake took the lives of 7000 upon the sealing of my testimony on April 25th, it would turn out that also within the hour of the end of my fast on May 12th that followed the May 8th baptism (you know, the part of me actually living out what was written?) would be when the aftershock in Nepal hit. The final death toll was 9000 killed, 23,000 injured. Not only was it tied to the completion of my testimony, it was certainly timestamped for all of the world to see upon the physical completion of those same 1260 days. Why the dry fast? Why is all of that important? Go read Revelation 11. Yes. It was part of that unfortunate prophecy. The good news, though, is that it got us here, right? I mean, not just us – but all of humanity. And here I am, writing this Love Story to you.

*Cut to image of Zeus puckering up his lips making kisses into the air as a sweet, kissy type of apology to Hera. Cut back.*

I also want the world to know that every single one of those souls knew their role in this life prior to arriving on Earth. It was a volunteer role they each chose to play, with the outcome already known. So though there would certainly be pains felt by people from an Earthly perspective, all of this was pre-destined, pre-known by all of the would-be-affected souls before arriving upon Earth in this incarnation. I tip my hat to all of those fallen. That was a terrible role to accept within this great play.

I know. This is a lot of detail and a seemingly strange amount of nonsense for a Love Story, but it will all make sense in the end. I promise. You see, let's just go ahead and skip forward to the explanation of how the baptism was Hera's and my

## CH7

wedding day all along. No this wasn't just symbolic. This is all about to get very real.

*Smash cut to a grand wedding.*

# CHAPTER 8
# How I Know My Baptism Was Our Wedding Day

If, for a moment, you can imagine the most beautiful wedding possible. Imagine millions of freshly cut roses lining the floors, the walls, the ceilings, the chandeliers. Imagine a setting of the whitest of white. Light is everywhere. Where roses are not, only a bloom of white light exists. Structures are almost non-existent. The only details that are important are in focus. Those details? Myself, My Father, and the Bride... but mostly, the Bride.

This Bride is wearing the most beautiful, elegant, form fitting yet delicately feminine dress imaginable. Let me tell you! Lace delicately touches her skin and every detail of the dress – from the folds to the seams – were all masterfully tailored in place. In this moment, the appearance of the Bride as she begins to walk down the aisle is the appearance of a masterpiece every bit as worthy of her place among the Sistine Chapels of the world, the Mona Lisas, the Statues of David, the Taj Ma-

CH8

hals, etc. This is how Our Wedding began… but this part was in the heavens.

*Cut to a wide-angle shot of a beach at night, with a man about to get baptized in the surf.*

This is how it appeared upon Earth.

*Smash zoom in on the two men in the water as the baptism is about to take place.*

"It is a metaphor!" you say.

No. I can most assuredly tell you it is not. Follow along with me now. You see, two worlds always exist as One. Everything that happens on Earth is just a reflection of what is going on with your soul in the heavens. If your soul needs to learn compassion in the heavens, you will experience a moment that tests you on your ability to be compassionate upon Earth. If you need to further your respect for something like wildlife, you may be drawn to be a hunter and play the Earthly game until you realize that every animal is part of you – part of Love – and were never meant to be a trophy on a wall. How would you feel if you were shot, killed, embalmed, and had your head mounted on a wall? Exactly. Then again, you might have been a park ranger or something similar as well. It all depends on the extremity of the lesson to be learned.

But the analogy goes the other way, too. As a human on Earth, if you need to "clean your soul," or repent of misdeeds and missteps along the way, you can easily start to do so by physically cleaning your house first, for the house is a metaphor for the body. The action taken in the physical world is simply a metaphor for everything taking place on the other side of the veil – the world unseen to human eyes.

I know you may thinking this still sounds exactly like a metaphor, but it isn't. Every action taken is very, very real – whether taken here or in the heavens. A ballet dancer on Earth is expressing a spiritual truth from the other side, while the dance itself upon the Earth is a truth being reflected back to the source in the heavens. Perhaps the heavenly persona sees beauty and Love in another, such as when I look at Hera or when she looks at me (hopefully) in the heavens. And perhaps that causes the Earthly expression to move in kind – a dance upon the surface of Gaia's (the name for Earth's soul if you did not understand this reference) graceful existence, a painting upon a textured canvas, or even something like writing the words as I am doing here. You don't have to be a modern day Shakespeare or DaVinci to express this Love you feel. This is why art in truthful creation is almost always is the divine expression of Love.

In the example I've used the term "heavens" here because every soul exists in many places and dimensions simultaneously. I don't want to overcomplicate things because this took me a long time to grasp. But a quick example would be how a human on Earth may have a dream of standing on a beach with a giant wave approaching. On Earth, you may think, "tsunami!" and wonder if you've been given a premonition of things to come. Well, you have… just not in the way you think.

In another reality, you are standing on a beach, watching a tsunami arrive. During your Earthly dream, you have connected with this alternate reality of you to understand a message you need to know here. Now on Earth, you wonder what could that possibly mean? Well, it could mean a number of things, but most likely the large wave of water represents *spiritual waters aka ENERGY aka Love (with a capital L)*. It would seem very likely that a tidal wave of Love is about to strike somewhere around you – perhaps over the whole Earth. This is precisely what IS happening on Earth right now in 2018 as every soul is learning how to become Love – to achieve a Christed state of existence.

You may think that sounds absurd because the news will tell you that Earth is in turmoil, fires are raging, wars are brewing, villages are being pillaged. But I assure you it is the case. Before you wash your hands, you may believe your hands are relatively clean. It is only after placing them under the water and washing them with soap that you notice all of the dirt and filth wash off and flow down the drain. I'll drop the mic on this example right here.

So back to Our Wedding. At this point in the journey I was already acutely aware of multiple realties existing. In fact, I could begin to see these realities overlapping in realtime. My second baptism upon Earth was a commitment to Love, a commitment to becoming Love, and a commitment to share this Love with the world. I no longer desired the love that humans ascribe as Love. I wanted more. I wanted to remember. I wanted to remember who *she* was that made me come alive inside from across the veil. I knew without a doubt there was a single woman that my heart belonged to in the heavens and that the purpose was to remember her – for Love to become stronger than the laws of Earthly physics, fear, and doubt. And so it began: my quest to meet my Bride.

My baptism was not just a spiritual commitment. The entire journey over the last three and a half years had been every bit of a grand romantic gesture to meeting my Bride. In fact, I implore you to read the first three books of *The Nine*. I cannot adequately express just how romantic of a moment this baptism was in a chapter or two here. It took a thousand pages of romantic writing spanning those three books to express the significance of reaching my Wedding Day and meeting my Bride.

But here we are in this book, and I want to keep this part short. While those books got a little over-the-top with the whole "the Messiah is coming" thing, they weren't wrong. I just didn't realize what it was that was precisely taking place around me. Hollywood had planted visions of how the fulfillment of these final prophecies was supposed to look... not how these days would really look. Hollywood also never alluded to the Bride, though biblically speaking – almost all scriptures referenced "the Bride" and "a child being born."

Let's return to Hera. Well, she is the goddess of Love, the goddess of Marriage, right? For me this example works a bit better than it might for others since she is literally my Wife, my Queen. But I never once related any mythology to the experiences I was having during the initial writing. Even on the day I sat on the beach and God kept filling my mind with the word "Hercules" it seemed to only result in a metaphor for Jesus or a Messiah figure. Yet, I took His message and watched every Hercules movie ever made, researched all I could, and still I came back to the single perspective of Hercules representing the Christ metaphor in the story. Silly religion. My upraising had conditioned my brain to see only one perspective of truth when it is the amalgamation of *all perspectives* that form the complete picture of Love. But not to digress. Back to Our Wedding.

If you've managed to stick through to here, it is all about to get much easier to understand. For every analogy within this writing will likely allude to this moment – my second baptism, Our Wedding. But we had to get here. I had to be able to explain how and why I was making references to Our Wedding even though we are husband and wife, King and Queen in the heavens. So here are the important comparisons:

**The person baptizing me...**
    ...the Master of Ceremonies (Our Father) for Our Wedding Ceremony

**Being submerged into the water...**
    ...the Vows

**Returning through the water...**
    ...the M.C. pulling back her veil and our lips meeting to the words "kiss the bride."

...

It really is that simple of a comparison, but took us quite a few words to get here. However, that's how I know my baptism was Our Wedding Day.
You were beautiful btw.

...

# CHAPTER 9
# An Audience of Angels

You would think that a moment such as Our Wedding would be so Divinely orchestrated that nothing could go wrong. Actually, in hindsight, I suppose nothing did. But at the time, it felt like everything went upside down leading up to the moment. Beginning with: no one showed up.

What exactly do I mean? Well, up to this point during my time in South Florida, I had built up a fairly great group of friends. Most of these people attended one church so they all knew each other very well. And even though I strongly despised organized religion, I attended their services when I was invited. It was great to have a newfound group of friends in my new location. They genuinely seem to want me among them.

There were several events that I hosted where many of these people came over. Prior to publication, I never shared my writings or my personal experiences with any of them – well… except for one family. They only knew a little about my "visions" but they always came to me to ask for guidance in their lives. They were fully supportive of me. We were great friends.

## CH9

When I got the "go signal" from Michael to wrap up my writing, I went ahead and started planning for a large crowd to be present for my very non-traditional baptism. My cousin – who up to this point had been with me stride-for-stride – was to perform the ceremony. My friends would all be invited for a normal get-together, but I would surprise them with the news that I was going to be baptized that night. Seeing as they all attended the same church, it meant they ALL had the unfortunate hive-mindset of "if you are not baptized in front of us, we don't believe you are born-again." Believe me, I heard it a lot.

"You were baptized at eight? You need to be baptized again. We believe a child cannot make that type of decision!" they'd say.

I would just smile and tell them I was happy with my decision at eight, but there would be a day when I would be baptized again. That confused them. I didn't care. Truthfully, their viewpoint did not matter. I was in the company of friends, but on my own journey. Clearly I was on a spiritual path, it just differed from their preconceived notions of how the journey should take place. They are all beautiful souls finding their own way in unison and there is absolutely nothing wrong with that. It did not steer me away from them as human beings. Rather, we found commonality in our Light.

So that said, I figured organizing an event with plenty of advanced warning would yield the highest turnout. And at this point, I had no idea what would happen when I re-emerged from the water. I wanted to have witnesses present. So, I set up the date. A save the date event it would be!

## CH9

As the date approached, my cousin let me know he would not be able to attend due to financial reasons. I countered by saying I would pay for it. He countered by saying he could not take days off of work. I countered by saying I would fly him roundtrip after he got off work and he would be back early enough the following day to not miss any time at work. I went ahead and bought him the plane ticket. As it would turn out, he was a no-show. My partner along the whole journey – my second witness who had experienced equally as many divine moments and had journaled about them himself suddenly did not want anything to do with the moment. If it were his wedding, it was tantamount to leaving his Bride at the altar.

Make no mistake, I was not his Bride. I'm just using it as an analogy. I was Hera's groom – the Bridegroom (though she was still nameless at this time). Knowing that he had cancelled on me at the last minute, I decided I'd just wing it. Surely someone would be willing to baptize me among my friends.

But they never showed either. None of them. Not one of the 20+ friends invited could make it. In the days preceding the event I began to receive phone calls and receive texts letting me know of various circumstances as to why they wouldn't be able to attend. I got asked to reschedule. I couldn't. I wouldn't. I had One mission. In every event I had held in Florida, there was never a time when people did not show up. Everyone always had fun. But something was off. It was as if the entire Universe was rooting against me, either that or trying to test my resolve.

They say when a person decides to become Jewish that a rabbi will deny them three times in order test their resolve to become Jewish. This felt like that. I could only surmise I was being tested. And, this one I would pass.

It would turn out the only person that would show up that night was a homeless man who I always helped in every way I could. I almost never gave out money, but I would give my time. We had become friends despite his situation. His name was Brian. I always believed him to be an angel in human form despite the appearance otherwise. I wrote about him in my first series of books. He was the absolute last person that should have attended as he did not have an income, nor money to get to and from places with regularity. But somehow when we spoke on the phone, he knew he had to be there for me and so he made his way down to my place.

There were so many signs at this point that it was probably a Divine Comedy from the perspective of the heavens. There would not be one single Earthly person present except for a man cast out by society – a man that I had always believed to be an angel. It would be no coincidence that my cousin's name was also Bryan (just spelled differently). Instead of my cousin Bryan performing the ceremony, it would wind up being the angel I knew in Earthly form as Brian.

And, if I can sprinkle just a few more fun facts to this fire, the last four digits of Brian's phone number were 0581. I was born in May of 1981 (e.g. 05/81). And while I do not think I spoke about this in *The Nine*, when I moved to Florida, I had a new phone number auto-assigned to me in order to start my new life in a new land. That number, when plugged into one of those "what does my phone number spell" websites, showed me my number spelled "PRAY 99 GOD 9." Pretty incredible to say the least. So every time our phone lines connected, I always saw a prayer going out from me and having it received by an angel whose phone number was my birthdate. This case was no different. On my Wedding Day, the only person to show up was an angel in Earthly form.

Maybe you are starting to think that I am just making things up at this point. I wasn't. I've left out a bajillion coincidences that were in this type of synchronicity with my every day normal. Many of these coincidences are all covered in my journals from that time period in *The Nine*. So, with only one angel present for my Wedding, we headed down to the beach.

He might have thought I was crazy, but he humored me to say the least. I saw him as my angel. And no, there was no money or anything else involved. I'm sure the thought might have crossed the mind that he only came to receive something. In fact, he refused. It was important this was pure from start to finish.

When we went down to the beach, only the stars were overhead. There was not a single cloud in the sky. I want to emphasize that. Let me say it again. There was not a single cloud in the sky. We walked into the water and Brian took notice of something strange happening over our heads. I saw it too, only I didn't know how to describe it. I assumed this was part of the grand show. I hopped in the water and we proceeded with the ceremony.

When I emerged from the water, the strangeness happening over our heads had turned itself into a bizarre looking cloud. This cloud started lighting up in non-stop flashes – similar to how heat lightning appears. Then there were the cracks of lightning popping out of the cloud. I knew we were safe, but it was such an amazing moment to see. In that moment – Our Wedding Day – I was surrounded by an audience of angels, who all attended and let me know of their grand applause.

As the lightning erupted, Brian wanted to quickly get out of the water. He kept exclaiming, "That's weird! Where did that come from? There was nothing there!" I could only agree, but I assured him he should view it as angels rather than a storm. We got out of the water and I proceeded to begin my dry fast for three and a half days.

Scripturally speaking, the fast was the metaphorical event when the two witnesses from Revelation 11 lay dead in the street for three and a half days before they ascended. The other circumstances from that day – like how no one attended the Wedding – can easily reveal the fulfillment of those particular lines of scripture. No showers, food, or water for three and half days was tantamount to laying dead. But even more ironically – and I missed it at the time – is that lightning would be the way the audience of angels would let me know they were cheering for me from the skies above as well as the angel that baptized me cheering for me from the Earth below. Believe it or not. Again, this is all very true.

Of course it would be lightning... because, well... Zeus. I don't want to get into how it never rained on me whenever I was on the beach in Florida. Even when it was raining all around, there was always a halo of blue sky that surrounded the portion of the beach I was on. There was nothing physically stopping the rain except the force maintaining a halo of blue sky above. It just never rained on me. Ever. Others would take

## CH9

notice and we'd talk about it humorously. Keep in mind I didn't understand I was in the midst of fulfilling a prophecy during most of this time. I guess it should have been no surprise to me that the two witnesses from Revelation 11 "had the power to shut up the heavens so it would not rain at that time." Also, I had no idea any of this was also related to the whole God of the Sky thing either…

    Go Zeus. Go me (I suppose)! I didn't know. I didn't know. Now it all makes sense. Even the whole Wedding thing taking place with Hera. But we are still getting there.

…

Hera,

My Love, whether you are starting to remember who you are or not – remember this is a modern day Love Story. Keep reading. You might just be really surprised how this is about to work out for you.

…

# CHAPTER 10
# I Got Kicked Out Of A Church For You

It really wasn't what happened during the first three and a half years that would prove to be the biggest game-changer for me upon this journey. No. That game-changer happened in the days following the fast. Now that the fast was finished and I realized I was not beamed up to the heavens in a white tube of light, nor had my Bride magically appeared before my eyes, I focused my primary efforts on ensuring the nine books were published on May 15, 2015 and "introduced to the church" on May 24, 2015 (The birthday of the church and non-coincidentally, the Eve of the seventh year anniversary after the last wedding anniversary I celebrated).

I've gotta admit I got a little weird about the whole Messiah part of the prophecy at this point. Having no obvious divine intervention that would bail me out of (or help me in) performing the next part of the journey, I was faced with so many questions. Was I the Messiah or was it someone else and I was supposed to just proclaim it? How could I maintain a normal life and still fulfill this journey I found myself on? Was I going to wind up being viewed as a fraud? How extreme was this supposed to look? How would the world take notice?

*Cut to black screen: Bold, centered text reads – "Hint: They wouldn't."*

At this point, I just threw my hands up and said, "What the heck. Let's do this." I was exhausted. I was frustrated. I had nothing to lose and everything to gain. The only thing that made sense is that nothing made sense to my Earthly mind. The only truth I found was offered from the heavens and not from the Earthly world. If I needed financial assistance, I would pray and something divine would happen... like the time I was down to my final $10 with no job (since I was led to walk away from it and remove myself from the bounds of the Earthly world) and I checked my mail the following day to find a check equivalent to a decent annual salary. Not only was the check addressed to me, but it was not asked for, not expected, and not from past work. Apparently it was one of those, "Hey, we found an error in our system and realize you deserve more money. Here ya go." type of things. That really happened. Things like this continued to build my faith in the unseen. So I just decided to go for it. "What the heck!"

I got the books ready for launch and subsequently tried to setup a meeting with the pastor at the particular church I attended in order to give him an advanced copy, but to no avail. Apparently, he did not want to have anything to do with me after a meeting I had with him earlier that March.

In that meeting, I knew I was fast-tracking the books to be finished for a May launch. While no one around me knew anything about these books, I wanted him to know in advance that I was soon to be publishing books that might cause members of the church (it was a large church!) to ask him questions, or seek guidance on what I had written since they were religious in nature. I wanted him to know first and foremost that the upcoming books were created because it was something I was called to do. I also wanted him to know that I respected his role as pastor of the church so much, that I wanted him to have no concern about my intentions or efforts. At a minimum, I wanted him to not feel threatened. If the conversation went as well as it could, then I hoped he would see the Light and Love that I embodied and that I would not be judged as a crazy person.

...

Instead, he told me,
"Quite frankly I don't believe you."

...

It wasn't the first time I had heard those words... actually, repeated word for word to me in regards to my writing.

*Flashback to five months prior*

Just after receiving my divine revelation of this whole prophecy-fulfillment-thing from Michael, I was instructed to share the information with my family first. That didn't seem

# CH 10

like it would be very hard, but there is a saying that goes, "Truly I tell you, no prophet is accepted in his hometown." I should have taken it to heart. Okay. That isn't just a saying. It is from the Book of Luke. But it still is shared like an old wives tale (as it should be).

After receiving my call to action, I drove to meet my sister and her husband. They were both ordained ministers. I had this childlike optimism that the doorway to sharing this information would be through them and the other members of the larger church community. Up to this point I had not shared anything about my newfound journey co-piloted by the angels in the heavens. But, I figured this was going to be a way of learning how to share my experiences with others.

I literally had tears of joy for most of our conversation as I shared all of the details proving without a shadow of a doubt that not only was my faith sound, but all that had occurred was absolutely part of this prophecy. It was important for them to not have any reason to question. I gave it my all. It was a darn good effort too! So emotional, so raw. There was no question I could not answer. It was as if the answers to their questions were flowing through me, but not of me. At the end of our conversation, all I hoped to hear were words of encouragement.

...

Instead, I was told,
"Quite frankly I don't believe you."

...

This was the first time I had heard those words. The meeting with the pastor was the second. Other meetings with various family members were also met with similar word choices. And so it began. I was climbing a mountain with zero support.

*Flash forward back to May 24, 2015*

In an effort to ensure I was able to "seed" all of the writings, I printed seven hardback copies of the entire series of nine books to give away. I also printed twenty-two paperback versions. The significance of two numbers (22 and 7) are explained within those books. But just for fun, it is both the fractional representation of PI (22/7) as well as the structure of thought and language. Again, that is discussed in depth in those books and does not have a place for the details in this Love Story. Plus, who wants to read about numbers in a fairytale? Just know everything I have done, every action I have taken, is always with purpose. Numbers chosen are purposeful. Colors chosen, words chosen… they all have reason.

Continuing on, I was excited to take one of these printed series of books to the pastor of the church that Sunday, May 24th. I placed a copy of the books in a plastic bag and carried them with me to church. The day was wonderful. I saw Light and Love everywhere. Even the pastor's sermon was tightly intertwined with the books I was set to "introduce to the church." And by "introduce," I mean I was going to deliver them to the pastor at the end of the service so he could read them himself.

## CH10

As the service came to a close, I was summoned to the front of the stage. I was told the pastor wanted to speak with me. I was so excited. I could only imagine this was another Divine intervention where he had possibly gotten a vision or was spoken to by an angel. Something divine had to have occurred! It always did.

I walked up the front of the church and was asked to walk up on stage. Keep in mind the crowd was beginning to leave, but there were still hundreds of people who were just beginning to get out of their seats. As I stood there before the entire audience, the entire church staff surrounded me. One minister pulled out a notecard from his coat pocket. At this point, they all began lashing out at me, concerned I had been embodied by Lucifer himself! I kid you not. The man with the notecard was shaking it at me, reading off words he had written as if there was an exorcism taking place in that very moment.

I was crushed. Not only did I not understand what could possibly be happening in that moment, the entire audience was now watching this horrific sight take place. I was barely given a chance to respond before I was asked to leave the church and never come back. I said, "Really?" They said, "Yes. You are no longer welcome here."

That happened. I was kicked out of a church. Not only that, but I was kicked out of the church on the day I was going to "introduce the books to the church." I had not even shared that I had a bag full of books I wanted them to read. I just somehow found myself being exiled and excommunicated from a body of people with which I thought I had become friends. The minister of music (whose family had originally invited me into that church) was crushed as well. He witnessed it and subsequently ended up leaving that church due in part (from my understanding) to the actions that took place that day.

All was not lost in my efforts that day however. When I returned home, I went to the pool to unwind. As I talked to an older gentlemen in the pool (who was Jewish and the interim rabbi at his tabernacle), I learned that his wife was about to travel to Jerusalem in the coming days. I then went on to tell him about the books and asked if his wife would be so kind to take all nine of them across the ocean and leave them with someone there. They obliged. So instead of introducing the books into the modern Christian church that day, I was exiled and subsequently sent the books on their merry way to Jerusalem.

The divine symbolism that took place that day should not be overlooked. For it was on that day of May 24, 2015, the Jewish faithful were celebrating Shavuot which is the "birthday of the church" – the day Moses brought down the ten commandments the first time. All things work in divine harmony with all that is intended. This was no exception. It should also be noted that this day was also a *relative* "time, times, and a half time" (e.g. three and a half years, or 1260 days) from November 25, 2011 (based off of the original, ancient Hebrew calendar versus the Gregorian calendar). Again, this was another divine example of the prophecy playing out.

After publishing the books and fulfilling that arm of my role, I decided to embrace the moment and spend my waking days traveling to churches to share knowledge of these books and the great miracles that had taken place over the course of

## CH 10

their formation. That really turned out to be a lost cause though.

I ended up quitting the whole "proclaim this message to the churches" effort a few months into it. Honestly, that part sucked. Not one person accepted the books I had to give. And don't get me started on trying to meet with a Catholic priest. It is impossible. But that difficulty was not limited to Catholicism alone. These days, meeting with any head pastor of a large church is nearly impossible, too. Delegate, delegate, delegate. Churches... honestly...

You guys need to revisit everything about the world you are trying to build. I Love God. I Am Love. You Are too... when you *remember* this Truth. However, I don't have to love your really weird structure you try to place around it, disconnected from any sense of tangible connection with the people, absent of True Love. So let it be known that, yes, I am offended at the very nature of your actions solely because it is not built upon a foundation of Love. You have one job as a church. One job. That is to help the world See Love, to Be Love, and to Radiate Love in all that you do. I'd really like to just tear it down and start again. Love wins always. In my personal case, it is about to be proven to you.

...

Hera, this is just a single example of what I've gone through to find you. I Love you so much!

...

# CHAPTER 11
# Books With A Different Name

Okay. There is one part of the puzzle I wasn't forthright about – but that is because I wanted to discuss it here. I want to talk about the names of the books.

"Here it is! This is why he got kicked out of the church!" you are thinking.

Oh no. That is not why. Everything truly took place in the way I shared it above. There were no embellishments or missing facts in those stories. But I do want to discuss my pure naïveté as to how I decided to name those nine books.

Originally, I wanted to remove any sense of ego and any sense of identity that could be tied to the books. To me, it was most important to show my humility as a messenger fulfilling a divine and most unexpected purpose. It was of grand importance to divide my past life from my present, though I had nothing to hide in my past. I was purely trying to make the most symbolic effort of Faithfulness I could possibly offer.

For my author name, I removed my last name. I decided I would just be Jonathan. It is one of the world's most popular names, so surely it would demonstrate my resolve to be anonymous, yet also be accountable for all that had been shared through me. This didn't sit well with my family as they thought I should be proud of my family name. But that was the purpose. I needed to remove any pride and ego. So, the author name simply became "Jonathan."

Then there was the decision on the series name. While each book had been given individual names I really liked and were appropriate for the content of each book, the series name had to be unique. Throughout the writing of the books, I referred to the nine books as "The Books of Nine." It was a placeholder as I did not have a name for them at that time. So in searching for an appropriate name, I combed through the collective history books as well as present publications. There were a couple of new books on Amazon that were named, "The Book of [insert name here]." They had playful cartoons on the covers and were intended to be fun, good-natured approaches for autobiographies.

I liked it. Not only did I like it, I also saw the symbolism of books from antiquity. In those days, many people went by their first names only. Their location was used to define their last name. Hence, Jesus *of Nazareth*. You know, Mary and Joseph's boy? Most books that contained prophecies or divine messages simply carried the first name of the author. So, I thought I would follow suit. I name the original series, "The Book of Jonathan."

Fail. As it would turn out, when I was asked the name of my series and I responded with, "The Book of Jonathan," I was met with the most cringeworthy feedback from the questioner's eyes – no words were required to cross their lips. It was as if I suddenly transformed into some sort of holier-than-thou-self-proclaimed-new-Jesus. I quickly realized the error of my ways, but I was stuck with the name. They were published. I was on the journey. Ugh.

Then there would be greater challenges... namely Amazon. When you list a book for sale, Amazon uses the title, subtitle, and author name as keywords for people seeking your books. I also was woefully unaware that certain words are excluded from their search such as "of," "the," "a," and "book." So overall, if someone wanted to search for my books based off of the series name alone, the search function would only search for "Jonathan" which in turn would pull up any book written by an author with a first name of Jonathan or a title that included the word Jonathan. My author name would not help whittle down the entire catalog of books that would show up in the search results either since it was the same term as the series name. This was the second naming decision failure. At least someone could search for "Gravity Calling" and find it. From there they could click on my author name... but how few people do that? Let me tell you: Zero.

My grand total of print book sales for all nine books was... One. Not even my family members purchased a book in a show of support. Talk about being outcast! I was kicked out of my church and emotionally excommunicated from my family. That's not how they saw it though. They believed they were supportive. However, I was excited when I did find out that someone did choose to order one book though. It was book #8... a curious choice, but the one that contained the most divine information of all.

*Flash forward to a large family Christmas Dinner, 2017*

That was until I found out a few years later that it was my cousin who had purchased the book. Oh, the look on my face. I'm sure it was priceless. Thousands of dollars spent and three and a half years of my time resulted in the message having reached exactly zero people outside of my family. Well, that is if you don't count the original twenty-seven copies I mailed out and gave away (I save one for myself and one for my daughter). But even if you take that into account, that means that not one single person felt obligated to either read or share with others the works that had been written.

Maybe if the books had carried a different name it would have helped. Probably not, though. Let's be honest. There is a reason for everything. However, my reason for Being still wasn't making sense yet. And Hera? She was nowhere to be found. I still didn't know who she was at this point. However, I see now that if I didn't know myself, how could I have ever known who she was?

But I will say, that upon the completion of my most recent book in May of 2018, *Welcome To Being Human*, I took the time to redo the cover art on all of the original nine books and rename the series to *The Nine*. The original publish dates and records still exist for "The Book of Jonathan," as it was important that those dates be timestamped in public record for all that was written and is written here. Now, though, I feel much better about the product even if it is still heavy handed on the "messiah, messiah, prophecy, prophecy" tone in those particular sections.

It isn't wrong. In fact, if it had been written a thousand years ago, the tone would be True. But to modern man, it is probably more of a repellant than it could have been with a lighter approach. Then again, mankind has been increasingly repelled by the Light due to how tainted it has become. So – whatever the case may be – I just wanted to set the record straight on those if anyone reading this ventured down that road.

...

And Hera, my Moon,
I hope you do. The first three books are a beautiful discovery on my way to finding you.

...

This takes us up through the first three and a half years of the journey. All of this was leading me to Hera, though I did not know it yet. This truly was quite an adventure and unique backstory, and all true – a highlight reel of all that is documented in those first nine books and the crazy moments like the Nepal earthquake and the response that occurred when the books were completed. Those stories couldn't possibly have been conceived or captured in that body of work since those moments occurred in response to them.

## CH11

So now we have the foundation, the bedrock to our Love Story. In the pages ahead I'm sure there will be flashbacks to other moments from the summer of 2015 to this present day of writing (August 2018). What we haven't yet addressed is how I learned about Hera and how I would eventually find her. That's what is next. To someone reading these words through Earthly eyes, it may seem like this author who thinks he is Zeus has booked a one way ticket aboard the crazy train. I get that. I understand that perspective. But that perspective will change for you one day. To those who *truly* know what this journey is all about, these words should be reassuring to see another man's perspective upon this highway. This is a Love Story after all. We are each writing our own. Make no mistake. I know I am not chasing a Shakespearian dream. I am merely using the tools at my disposal to share my story. But when in Love, you can only look back at all of the seemingly crazy events, laugh at yourself, giggle at the silliness, and pat yourself on the back for a job ~~well~~ done so far. For if you are able to experience this kind of a story in an Earthly life and manage to write about it, then you have lived in ways that many have not yet known.

But oh they will! As you will see, it takes a bit of an unorthodox willingness when searching for Love to *truly* learn to see what it isn't. And only when you learn what Love isn't, can True Love become. To Hera, if there is only one single takeaway from all that has been written so far, it would be that the first thirty-three years taught me what Love is not, so there will never be a question of my unbridled Love for you when we return as One. You will *truly* see me – to see my heart, the knowing that is there – as we stand face-to-face.

# CH11

You may be wondering how could Hera and I be standing together on an altar on our Wedding Day nearly three plus years ago and just now be getting to this point in the story? Well quite simply, I blinked. From the moment I emerged from the water three and half years ago to nearly this day, I stood blinded by the beauty and light of your face like the light from the morning sun. So I closed my eyes and winced at the brightness of your Love when I emerged from the water.

It took this long for all of the memories to come flooding back, to *truly* see her, to remember her and all that was hidden behind the veil. To know her without having to meet her in person, to Love her for always, in all ways. It isn't just the romantic in me that wants the world to know this. As I breathe today, it is really is as if every fiber in my body has been re-threaded and hand-stitched by her Love. Now I can see the art, the hand-crafted care the fabric of Love means to me, as it means to Hera.

So how do I know I found Hera in **both** human form and in the Heavens? For as you are reading these words, she might not even know me in my human form just yet. Let me explain.

# CHAPTER 12
# How It So Began

To meet Hera, to know my Love in human form, I would first have to begin a new journey that would seem like an impossible feat to any observer – this participant included. I am pretty sure my Earth family thought I was nutzo. But it all served a purpose. The first purpose in it all was learning to not care how the outside world perceived you. Every soul is on an individual journey hand crafted for them alone. Yes, the goal *is truly* to find Love. But in this interactive game called "Being Human," we each have to find our way through all of the muck to return Home. This is the recount of my journey and how it so began. It is how I began to reconnect with my higher self as Zeus!

Whether you have read the previous nine books or are starting here, to date it can be understood that at the age of thirty the real transition point began for me. By thirty-one, I thought this journey was about finding Earthly love again – to open my heart and crack open the granite casing that was placed around it after my divorce years earlier. It was, but it really wasn't.

# CH12

At thirty-three, I found myself living in a beach-front condo writing the words of *The Nine*... and apparently fulfilling a prophecy. Go figure. During the final stages of completing that writing, I was tasked with walking away from my financial source of income. While it isn't too important right now, it will come full circle in a bit so I do want to mention it.

*Cut to flashback sequence of Jonathan's early life*

After getting married, my ex-wife and I moved to St. Simons Island, Georgia. One short year later, we moved to Nashville to chase the music dream. The rules of Earthly life set in very quickly and it became important for me to find an alternative income to appease my wife. Though I never set out to be in the technology field (I ran away from it actually), I pretty much fell into that field while in Nashville. Without giving a big backstory, let's just say I was the kid in middle school who was being paid to build computers for my teachers, family members, and friends. I got into programming and such along the way, but I never wanted to do it for a career. I didn't really want to do it then either. It was just something I was very good at and it made money. I had a giant disconnect socially from most people in that field. Most people on Earth are primarily right-brained or left-brained. I was both. So I never felt at home in that social sphere.

But back to Nashville. I gave up music for money. I took a temp job which then resulted in being offered a better position, then an even better position. I advanced quickly... Very quickly. To the glass ceiling I arose! Then, at the point my face smashed into the glass, I jumped ship and began consulting on my own terms. My career became my identity as a Solutions Architect who primarily helped design healthcare data infrastructures, complete with mobile apps and such. Yes. I had a very geeky side, but I found my niche because I never presented myself with that technical side. Right-brain, left-brain, right?

I took pride in communicating with CEOs, CFOs, COOs on their level. We'd talk about sailboats, cigars, fine wines, suits, and worldly travel. It was fun! I loved it. When they discovered what I did for a career, I often was extended lucrative contracts that I always executed above their highest desires. I did the work myself and did not rely on subcontractors and such. In that industry, I found a role as a diamond in the rough. This background will eventually be important, so at least take note of it for a minute. Contracts eventually allowed me to work from any location, which resulted in my move to Florida.

*Cut back to Florida*

But at thirty-three in a paradise-laced Fort Lauderdale beachfront condo, I was being spiritually tasked to walk away from Earthly work and continue the spiritual work alone. It was important to focus on the writing... not just because that seems like the right thing to do, but rather because I was asked to do that by my spiritual angels and guides. So I did. I leapt. I leapt with a blind faith that everything would work out... and it did. It has, but it wasn't without torture and torment to my mind.

*Cut to a theme park rollercoaster*

You know that sudden drop on a rollercoaster that takes your breath away? It was like that! At first you fear for your life. You fear that somehow you are about to die in this moment. And then suddenly the ride comes to an end. You remain in shock, terrified at what just happened. But really, you survived. Given enough time, you will look back and laugh at it and see it for what it was: a rollercoaster. It was just a ride, completely safe with no reason to have a fear for your life. Eventually you will ride it again for the joy of it, not the fear. At that point, the ride is more like, "Hey, this is going to be scary, but fun. Enjoy!" So you ride it and laugh. You smile in the knowingness of the safety and the eventual outcome. You learn to enjoy the ups and downs, the twists and turns because… it is only a ride.

*Cut back to Florida*

Anyway, the point I am trying to make, is that everything became very unstable financially for me. I saw single digit bank account balances versus the five-figure-plus accounts I was used to seeing. It was scary. But I learned to role with it. I sold things. I slowly purged everything that was unimportant to me, but could find value with others. And while I usually paid rental fees in one annual payment upfront, I soon realized I would not be able to continue on in that fashion. I wasn't even sure if I would be able to follow a traditional lease installment plan for my living space. So when my lease was coming to an end, I knew I would have to move on from my newfound paradise. I was, however, spiritually forewarned of this upcoming change some nine months prior.

In the summer of 2016, My mother was about to have a medical procedure that would involve several months of recovery, so I decided to spend a few months helping her recover at her place on St. Simons Island before I continued on to my next destination. It also allowed my daughter to spend the summer with her grandparents and I together. It was a great few months. Though my mother couldn't understand why I would decide to leave my paradise on the beach, she seemed to trust I knew what I was doing. After all, everything seemed to fall perfectly into place with every decision I had ever made. At that point she had no idea of my financial situation. With funds running low, I sold a few more pieces of gear from my music studio (that was now in storage) and drove to New York. This was in September of 2016. I had no idea why I was supposed to head to New York, only that it was the next guidance I had received. My security in this decision was that my similar leap had worked out in Fort Lauderdale when I was tasked to do so, so why should this be any different?

...

Trust me. This is all important.

...

# CHAPTER 13
# The Battle of Saratoga Began

When I got to New York, I was pretty much counting on the income from a recent sale of a high-end piece of audio equipment to carry me through my transition. It was a piece of equipment that I had sold and shipped the day before leaving on my new journey. However, when I reached New York a few days after leaving St. Simons Island, I had a notification from Ebay. Yes. That dreaded notification. The buyer was now refusing to pay for the piece of gear even though it had already been shipped. Long story short, I fell victim to a scam. His money was refunded, my gear was shipped to a random post office in South Florida rather than my shipping location. The size of the package prohibited me from re-routing shipping and I was not allowed to have it re-shipped to a new destination even when directly speaking to the post office. Emails to the buyer went unanswered. Paypal/Ebay knew they were at fault, but refused to solve the problem. They admitted it was their fault. The short story is the package was returned to him (yes, him!) in which he chose to keep the device while also not paying a dime for it. In fact, he even signed the package receipt with a fake name. This situation left me stuck in New York with almost no money to my name.

    Unsure of what to do, I just drove around the entire state until I could understand the purpose of why I was led there. I admittedly had a number of options to financially bail myself out of this situation. I could have taken jobs offered to me. I could have sold more gear I had in storage (I had a lot). I could have returned back to my family's home and stayed in the guest house until I figured it out. But this journey was not about the easy solution. It was about learning to trust God in the path. And this path… well, it was going to suck for a while. But, hey, I volunteered for this mission.

    I slept in my car. I became very familiar with coffee shops, malls, fitness gyms, Walmart parking lots, and any public place I could find – though to any onlooker, I was always dressed well, freshly showered, and appeared to be perfectly okay. I eventually determined that I might be in the great state of New York to do location scouting for a screenplay I had written during the summer of 2015. Perhaps I was supposed to find my friend, Darra, who lived in New York and convince her to produce the film. It was the only thing that made sense. I eventually found my way to Saratoga Springs, New York where I would begin to make pre-production efforts for the screenplay. This included location scouting, budgeting, and preparing for any script changes to produce the film. This is how my personal Battle of Saratoga began.

    Wait. Screenplay? What?

Yes. We probably should talk about that really quickly. It will be a very abbreviated chapter. But the short story is that this screenplay was written about you, Hera, though I did not know it at the time.

# CHAPTER 14
## Screenwriter

Let's return back to Florida during the months that followed being kicked out of the church and when I was deciding to quit the struggle of being rejected from everyone I met as I tried to share the poorly named "Book of Jonathan" with the world.

One day in mid-July of 2015, I awoke at 2 A.M. from one of the most vivid experiences I had ever had in the heavens. In this experience I was shown myself as a screenwriter. I was also shown both the beginning and ending to a great movie that needed to be written. My only response when I opened my eyes... and I really said this aloud: "Really, God? Screenwriter now?"

I suppose more irony falls here in that I majored in Journalism with an emphasis in video production at the University of Georgia. I had classes in which I learned about screenwriting, but I had never once written an original screenplay. Truly! Even in classes when I was tasked with writing a television episode I would find a copy of a script online and completely re-adapt it. Now, I didn't cheat or use someone else's work. I didn't leave any original content. But I did rename characters, completely change the dialogue, change the subject matter, and rework the whole theme. Essentially I used the structure but made it an original work. Person A talks to Person B. Cut to other scene here. Fill in the blanks. Those types of things. I just filled in the details with my imagination but not straying too far from the original idea. But this meant that I had not really ever written a screenplay outright. So writing one was going to be new to me.

I groggily made my way to the living room and began typing away. I wrote the beginning and ending to the screenplay and then went back to sleep. The following morning I awoke and went back to work on it. I decided to find screenplay software so that I could properly format it and begin this new task at hand. In my naïveté I thought that perhaps the world could digest the spiritual message of the nine books through a fantastical screenplay, absent of anything overtly religious. And I did finish the screenplay. FWIW, I really like it!

This screenplay would go on to be called "I Am We" and could best be described as a mashup of The Adjustment Bureau meets Winter's Tale meets Inception. I didn't realize it as it was being written, but this movie was about me and Hera. In fact, Hera's human form is a classically trained dancer here on Earth – much like the plot-line of the love interest of Matt Damon in The Adjustment Bureau. So you can begin to see the comparisons here. And I won't spoil the ending of my screenplay, but I am literally living out the words as they were written that summer. However, let's not skip ahead too far just yet. Let's return to the following morning of the script being conceived.

## CH14

After converting the content I had written into proper screenplay format, I laid down in the middle of my floor and prayed. My hands were outstretched on either side, my feet straight below. In hindsight it would have looked like I was hanging on a cross from above. But, that was not my intent, though the image is forever ingrained in my head.

*Cut to shot of Jonathan laying in floor with arms outstretched.*

As I laid there, I shouted at the heavens. "What on Earth am I supposed to do with this? I don't know anyone in the film industry!" And that was truly so. I had also broken contact with most everyone in Nashville that might have been a few degrees separated from a person that could help me enter into the film industry. In Nashville I was always one degree separated from anyone I wanted to know. You just never knew which one of your friends would be that person since privacy was always respected above all else.

At the exact moment I said that prayer aloud, my phone buzzed. I had just received a notification that an old friend from Nashville wanted to reconnect via LinkedIn. It was an old friend named Darra who I had not spoken to in nearly three years. Not to derail this story, but we first met because she lived in my same apartment building in Nashville. We became good friends almost instantly during those days. I would later go on to discover she is related to me via our Greek heritage. In fact, she is one of my daughters, but she doesn't know that yet either. In hindsight, it explains our connection so well now. But back to the present moment...

## CH14

I immediately reached back out to Darra, where she subsequently called me. I knew there was a purpose. This is how this stuff always works. Ask a question to the heavens, receive an answer (if you know how to listen). I answered the phone and we began to chat. After the "How are you doings?" she told me that I had been on her mind and she wanted to reach out. I asked her what she had been up to as of late.

She said, "Well, you know I was in the music business. But over the last few months, I've decided to start my own production company and produce movies. So far, I've raised about $25 million to begin my productions." My jaw hit the floor. Not because of the money. Rather it was the fact that my prayer was being answered in real-time before my eyes.

I said, "Wow. You won't believe this, but I am writing a screenplay right now!"

In hindsight, I think that was the wrong thing to say, but in the moment, I was so excited to see that my prayer had just been answered. This is how it always works for me. Quite simply, ask and listen. The answer will shortly follow.

So that is how the screenwriting began. It would turn out that this particular screenplay was completed in exactly forty days and was given to her on September 23, 2015. It should be of no surprise that this particular date turns out to be Yom Kippur on the Jewish calendar... the Day of Atonement and is the date considered to be the second time Moses returned from the mountain with the Ten Commandments. I didn't realize that at the time either. This would again be one of those Divine gotcha moments. Actually, every action taken during that writing would turn out to be in complete syn-

## CH14

chronicity to the Jewish observances of the days surrounding the holidays.

*Cut to close up of Jonathan looking up to the sky and pointing his finger.*

...
I see what you did there, Big Guy.
...

# CHAPTER 15
# The Battle for Saratoga Continued

Returning back to Saratoga Springs, New York, it was now early October of 2016. I still found myself at a loss for what I was supposed to be doing there, but I had found peace in knowing that I had figured out that Saratoga Springs was where I was supposed to be in the great state of New York while I was beginning the pursuit of bringing this screenplay to life. Lots of driving, prayer, and trying to navigate by energy and faith alone led me there. There had to be a purpose.

When I began location scouting, I found joy. I saw a creation taking place. I saw a way to bring this message to the world. I saw where the Great Wedding would take place. Yes, this movie has a pretty darn big wedding involved. Hera, I told you that it was about us.

As I journeyed to locations, I would meet people like the manager at a train station that I thought would be perfect for the train station in the screenplay. Then strange coincidences started to happen. I was of course still listing items online for sale to maintain some type of income while I was there. In my Jeep, I made sure to pack photography cameras, lenses, music gear, the works! Anything I might be able to sell until I was able to get settled in was tucked into my Jeep. I'd just list them for sale on eBay or Craigslist in order to keep some sort of cash-flow when my funds began to dwindle.

But suddenly I started noticing that my anonymous listings on craigslist were attracting the very people I was crossing paths with while location scouting. Case in point, the manager at the train station. He reached out via the listing to purchase the Canon camera I had listed for sale. When we met, I knew who he was immediately. We only talked briefly at the train station a few days prior – and I do not think he recognized me due to the number of people he saw on a daily basis – but this was one of the handful of people I had an interaction with in the previous days. It wasn't a coincidence. And this experience wasn't the only one. I began to notice that various people I interacted with were somehow intimately tied to the next step of the journey. All I could do was keep moving through the process and observe it all as it played out in some sort of divine synchronicity.

Then the unthinkable happened. As I journeyed around the surrounding areas in search of additional film locations, it started to get late. I had quit paying for data on my phone to conserve fund which meant I was mostly reliant on wifi and Starbucks when I needed internet. So, suddenly, getting lost became a real possibility in a world of Google Maps, Apple Maps, and navigation systems that would normally prevent that from happening. But that is just what occurred.

## CH15

I got turned around, lost in a darkened countryside. In the process of getting lost, my phone died. And I don't mean the battery died. I mean my new, advanced iPhone just died. Croaked. Completely. There would be no life support. There would be no recovery from Apple. In fact, the coroners at Apple would pronounce the phone dead with no capacity for resuscitation several days later. The mighty Apple doctors were also unable to provide a diagnosis even access any part of the phone with their special tools.

So as I found myself lost in the New York countryside, I eventually found my way to a rural gas station. Inside I asked for directions (by the way, I discovered you get strange looks these days when asking for something you should have access to on your phone). I was told I was in a village called Bethlehem.

No. I am not kidding. Bethlehem. It would turn out it wasn't even on a map since it was more like a township than an official city. So, on a darkened night, lost without any idea where I was going, I found myself lost in the township of Bethlehem. I didn't miss the symbolism. I knew it was another great sign.

*Cut to a montage of "Am I Jesus thoughts..." Cut back.*

The following day I returned to Starbucks to attempt to copy the location photos for the screenplay from my phone (I had taken hundreds of photos). I hoped beyond all hope that my phone's memory would at least be accessible. As it would turn out, it wouldn't be possible. Not only that, but as I sat at Starbucks trying to resuscitate my phone, my MacBook Pro

## CH15

died. And I don't mean the battery died. I mean my somewhat aging MacBook Pro just died. Croaked. Completely. There would be no life support. There would be no recovery from Apple. In fact, when I took my MacBook and iPhone to Apple on the same day, they were without an explanation as to what could have happened. I certainly didn't know (even though I was quite technologically savvy). All I knew is that any hopes I had of accessing any files related to my screenplay were no longer possible.

I luckily had the screenplay backed up in several cloud locations. But, as for anything directly related to the work I had poured my life into during the months of living in my car in Saratoga Springs, New York – well, that was all gone. Toast. So there had to be another purpose... I hoped. Otherwise, I was about to throw in the towel at this absurd situation I found myself in. I did not know how many more days I could take sleeping in my car, going to the gym first thing in the morning for the sole purpose of showering, before making my way onto the coffeeshop/free-wifi circuit for the remainder of the day. I was now down to my iPad as my sole source of connection to the internet and outside world, while quickly losing patience with the journey.

If there was an upside to finding Hope in these moments, I had come to learn I was in the location where the "turning point of the civil war" took place – as well as there for the anniversary of the event... The Battle of Saratoga. At a minimum, I knew this was my battle taking place right now. This was my spiritual Battle of Saratoga. I had to persevere. There was a purpose. This was apparently a war in which I was deeply entrenched, attempting to bring about change, to find Love, to find Hera.

As a general on this great spiritual battlefield, I was not privy to the full battle plan. I was only given orders that I could choose to continue to fulfill to the best of my ability, or I could go A.W.O.L. from my assignment. My resolve in this entirely absurd Earthly situation was that I would not lose this battle. No. Not on my watch. I would not be the reason why Love did not win in the ~~End of Days~~ Days of Ascension. I still didn't realize it was Hera's Love I was fighting for. I only knew it was the strongest Love I had ever known.

...

Hera,
I was fighting a war for you. I quite literally was fighting The Battle of Saratoga.

...

## CHAPTER 16
## Victory In Saratoga

A few weeks after the MacBook/iPhone/Bethlehem incident, I found myself trying to look inconspicuous in my Jeep as I sat parked in a hopefully-non-policed parking lot during the first major snowfall of the year. It was getting really difficult to stay warm at night, bundled up under three blankets while trying to not crank up the Jeep and burn extra gas... because, you know... the whole money thing was a severe issue at that point. I'm not gonna lie. It was getting bad. It wasn't beggar-worthy yet, but I was running low on options with no solutions ins sight. I had a few dollars to carry me through, but not much more. It was the middle of November and the first snowfall was pouring down around me as I slept in my Jeep. I prayed for help. I prayed for a bailout. I prayed for anything to get me out of this blasted situation. And then another miracle happened.

Around 2 A.M. I awoke – freezing of course. I pulled out my iPad and decided to kill some time. But to my surprise, when I pulled up my web browser, a single apartment website was pulled up. Now, it should be known that earlier in the night

I began looking for apartments, but I was only on one of those aggregate listing pages. This was not a page I had been to, nor was it an apartment that I had seen earlier in the evening. Of course, a sign right? The whole money thing? Well, I'd have to figure that out later.

The following morning, I met the realtor and viewed the apartments they had available. I should not have been surprised that the apartment number that was available was #304. This was the exact same number of my condo in Fort Lauderdale that I moved to sight unseen. I knew this was my sign. I decided to go sign the paperwork.

Now, this part I have no explanation for. During my divorce from years prior, my credit rating went from perfect to, well, basically the worst. That was explained in *Gravity Calling*, the first book of *The Nine*. So, ultimately I knew that chances were slim that I would be approved. My sword in battle up to this point was being able to pay for an entire year upfront. That wouldn't be the case here. My checking account balance? Somewhere in the neighborhood of $44.

Yet, while the apartment manager seemed a bit confused at my background check, she gave it a once over and then – magically – I was approved. Score one for the Big Guy. Then, the second gift came. Rather than pay first/last/deposit in order to move in, the response was, "Your first month is free due to our current promotion. Your first rent payment will be due next month. Oh, and you do not have to pay a deposit." Score number two for the Big Guy.

I went and enjoyed a Thanksgiving dinner alone at Denny's that evening. The snow poured down. There would

## CH16

only be a few more days of this and then I could move in. Thanksgiving. How symbolic. Without any money and with only a few belongings remaining with me, I moved into apartment #304 a few days later.

Now, I want to fast track through these next parts to keep the flow of the story and get to the important part of how I would go on to discover the Love of Hera was what I was chasing all along. So, just know everything that is about to be mentioned happened in similar divine order as these previous examples. Every step was soaked in divine waters as I proceeded to take leaps of faith that would defy any Earthly logic.

Here is a summary of events that subsequently happened after this divine moment:

In the days following my move-in date, I received a call from a past client. I had quite a number of shares in his private company that I had tried to cash out before leaving Fort Lauderdale. Originally, I had taken a reduced financial contract in lieu of additional shares in his company because I believed in his family's work, their mission. I still did (and do!), but I increasingly saw my shares as one of my best-chance financial lifelines. However, it was very obvious to me a year ago that he didn't want me to divest anyone from their company.

That viewpoint all changed with this phone call. His company was going through a restructuring and they wanted to buy back the shares. However, where I had hoped to see a six or (potentially) seven figure payout, the reality would be two four digit payments spread over the course of several months. I wasn't in a place to negotiate, nor were they in a cash position to make my dreams a reality. So here we were again... a lifeline granted. I had been gifted the ability to pay my bills while figuring out why the heck I was in Saratoga. I was actually able to buy a bed to sleep on instead of the blankets I had piled up during those first days after moving in.

In the days following that moment, I was introduced to a man named Jim Charles. It would turn out he is the current incarnation of Elijah. It is important to say that while I was in Saratoga, I never once discussed my books much less said anything about fulfilling a prophecy since I was still having the whole sensitive Jesus/Messiah questions continuing to percolate in my head. The only thing anyone in New York knew about me was that I was a screenwriter doing some location scouting. Yet, here I was. I was being introduced to a man who would tell me he was Elijah and subsequently tell me the most important piece of knowledge I would come to learn while in Saratoga. I'll get to that in just a moment, though. This wasn't the first time something like this had happened to me. Oh no! So at least I knew how to handle the situation this time.

*Flashback to Florida, June 30, 2015*

In the aftermath of being kicked out of the church and finding myself in the face of frustration with sharing my books to the surrounding churches, I spent a lot of time on the beach... paddleboarding, then sulking. Rinse. Repeat. One day, I was approached by a man I had never seen. He sat down next to me and we began chatting. It turned out he lived a few building away on floor seven. The symbolism caught my attention immediately – especially in the fact he wanted to tell me that specific detail. I learned his name was Jeff and another soul I will always believe to be an angel-incarnate upon Earth.

During that conversation, he shared with me that he was led to approach me and tell me a number of things I needed to know. He asked if I wanted to go get lunch. I obliged. So we began a mile long walk up the beach to the restaurant he suggested. It was during that conversation that he told me very directly, "You are the Christ."

I had so many questions. Why would he feel the need to tell me this? What would prompt this conversation? How did we get here? Was this a joke? What did he know about me? I didn't know anything about him...

I didn't want to believe it actually. It was a question I wanted answered, but I still wanted to reject hearing any real answers because that would mean I would have to face a very difficult truth. How would the world view me? They already were laughing at me with the whole "fulfilling a prophecy" thing. In fact, I would guess only a handful of people had heard the full story. I was usually kicked out of meetings with pastors and church elders before I made it that far into the conversation. But most of the time, my meetings were simply cancelled or courteously wrapped up shortly following our introductions... Either that or the church elder just didn't show up.

But here I was, being told I was the Christ. I pushed further as we continued on the walk up the beach. "Does that mean I am the Messiah?"

"Well yes!" Jeff said smiling.

This was a very real conversation that took place. We had lunch and I returned to my sulking/paddleboarding routine (now with greater internal conflict) on the beach. I didn't know if this was some grand cosmic joke or whether it was really the path I was upon. Was it a test? The answer would only come to my attention later that evening when I read a news article about the celestial event that was taking place that day. On that day, June 30, 2015, the Star of Bethlehem would return to the skies above Earth. It was the first time in over two thousand years. The last time? Well, that was when Jesus walked the Earth. True story. Here we go with that whole Jesus thing again…

Chills.

However, what I did not pay attention to that day was the significance of just *what* the Star of Bethlehem was. I can only laugh at my virgin eyes from that moment. As I write this, I'm actually tearing up. And non-coincidentally, while I am writing this, I am just now truly recognizing the gravity of the moment that took place that day. The song that is currently playing over my headphones while writing these words is "Shout to the Lord." The specific words being sung as I recount this story? *"Power and majesty praise to the King. Mountains bow down and the seas will roar at the sound of your name."* And no, it wasn't on my playlist. It was randomly selected by Spotify in this exact moment. And no, my playlist had nothing to do with spiritual or religious songs either. This is just how this spiritual communication thing works. Believe it or not.

So just *what* was the Star of Bethlehem? You see, the "Star of Bethlehem" was a conjunction of Jupiter and Venus. And what would be important to see in hindsight that I didn't see on that day? Well, Jupiter is… well, it is pretty significant to the whole Zeus story that you know on Earth. More or less, Jupiter is another name for me. Yep! I just didn't quite get the grand hint that day. Jupiter is the planetary representation of me. Venus is the planetary representation of Love.

On that day, June 30, 2015, Jupiter and Venus converged at 23° ascending to form the Star of Bethlehem in the skies overhead. On that day, June 30, 2015, I was told by an angel in human form (whom I had never discussed any of this information with) that I was the Christ, the Messiah. I should have understood it then, but I didn't quite grasp it yet. It seems obvious in writing it... but there was still a lot to learn from that point. I also could have caught the symbolism from the release of the movie Jupiter Ascending earlier that year... but I missed that big sign, too.

*Cut back to Saratoga conversation with Elijah*

As you can see, what I am about to tell you about the Saratoga incident would not be the first time that I had been told something I didn't necessarily want to hear through an inexplicable, divine moment. And when I say I didn't want to hear it, I really *did* want to hear it. It was just the point of absolution that I was fearful to embrace. Couldn't the answer just result in something magical? Indescribable? Impossible to dismiss through coincidence rather than the gray area I felt caught up in? But, oh it was! I was just scared. I admit it. There I said it. Ol' Zeus was scared.

So returning back to the whole Elijah thing. Yep. Here I was in New York, no longer living in my vehicle, having miracle after miracle happen, looking for a reason for being there while slowly whittling away potentials that were not supposed to be part of the New York journey. All roads seemed to have been leading to this moment – this one encounter.

It was on that day that Elijah told me my higher self was Melchizedek. It suddenly all made sense! Everything came flashing back to me. There was the moment from several weeks prior to me moving into my apartment when I had been shown a vision of Melchizedek speaking to me and I awoke to his name written upon my leg by the moonlight overhead.

How could a name be written upon the body in the moonlight? I have no Earthly rationalization. All I know is that I awoke from this vision in the front seat of my Jeep to a full moon overhead. I looked down to see something that looked like a small shadow on my thigh (I was wearing shorts and had my leg propped up against the door). My first thought was I was seeing a shadow. But as I moved my leg, I realized the shadow moved with it. After I realized this was something being shown to me from the heavens and had been written upon my thigh, I took a photo of it and proceeded to try to unravel the mystery of the symbol.

It would turn out that the shadow symbol contained the ancient Hebrew letters of Melchizedek's name: Namely "Zedek." The image slowly faded from my leg as I came to the understanding of what was written. I just didn't know why at the time! Silly me. And while I did not realize the Melchizedek (Translated: King of Jupiter, King of Salem) relationship to Zeus yet, I was aware of the name from antiquity. These would become the days of remembrance for me.

## CH16

*Cut to a black screen with the text: "On his robe and on his thigh he has a name written, King of kings and Lord of lords. – Revelation 19:16"*

Perhaps no one will believe these stories, but there was a photo taken that day. I've tried to document all I can to ensure that everyone knows these words are (and have always been) Faithful and True. Whether it is ensuring works have been published or timestamps have been captured on these events, I have tried hard to maintain proof for any questions that could arise.

In the days following – and with my newfound knowledge of my higher-self being Melchizedek – I began to unravel the whole Zeus thing. Really, it wasn't as if there was much to unravel at this point. I had thousands of pages of journals that now made perfect sense. I also had memories rushing back to me that I had never experienced in this Earthly life before – memories of my life, my past lives, my life with Hera. All of it. All new. All old. It was Ancient Love that has stood strong in the face of antiquity's tests. I fought the battle of Saratoga and won.

...

I won the Battle of Saratoga for you, Hera.

...

*Cue Pachelbel's Canon*

# CHAPTER 17
# The Wedding Medley

This new *knowingness* of my identity served as the greatest turning point during this Civil War for Love, for Light, for you, Hera. And while there were new truths flooding back to me, there were also more questions arising like a fire blazing on a parched desert-dry land. All of these new questions circled back to Hera. She was the only mystery left to unravel.

There were new questions I had of her spiritual identity, and of the identities of the "angels" I saw in the heavens. How were they related to my Bride? To me? Hera certainly had never identified herself by that name if indeed we had ever interacted in the heavens. Beginning in the summer of 2015 I thought I had begun to have interactions with "My Bride" and "My Wife" in my heavenly travels. Was that Hera? Would she be in human form on Earth, too? Was this just a spiritual/metaphorical thing? How old would she be if she was on Earth? What would she look like? What would her world look like? Had we ever met before? Would we ever meet? It may not seem like I should have had questions about any of that, but I

## CH17

did. I was treating this with the eyes of a child. No assumptions. No stone left unturned.

However, before we move on to answer these questions, I desperately want every reader (and especially you, Hera) to see the world through my perspective. Just for this moment – to see the world through my eyes.

As I was completing the writing of the previous chapter, Victory In Saratoga, I experienced such a beautiful and divinely timed moment. Again, this involves a song, but it is important to see it through my eyes. Imagine you are me for just a moment. Imagine (despite whether you believe this story to be real or not) that you have been on a desperate quest to find Love, to return Home after a grueling, difficult, and impossible-to-believe journey. Believe it to be a fantastical fiction story if you desire. Either way, you want to see your Love again more than anything – more than you think anyone could possibly imagine. You are overflowing with Love.

Now imagine you are writing the very pages you are now reading in this book, knowing that you now *truly know* exactly who she is in **both** human form and spiritual form – that she will soon be reading these words being written on these very pages – that this will be the Love Story for the ages, the grandest of introductions. It is a Love Story written specifically for her, one in which you are pouring out your soul. Now imagine that you have endured and survived the experiences from Saratoga (the greatest turning point on this journey) and now you are recounting that emotional victory here in this story for her to read. Now imagine writing the final words, "I won the Battle of Saratoga for you, Hera."

At this point, the song playing on your headphones transitions to a violin and cello duet. It is Pachelbel's Canon, the most widely used song for weddings. It is precisely why I wrote "Cue Pachelbel's Canon" at the end of that chapter. That is exactly what happened. The song again was a total surprise, but there was a greater surprise in store. The song playing turned out *not* to be Pachelbel's Canon at all. It had the intro to Pachelbel's Canon, but suddenly familiar words were being sung. It was a medley of sorts. All I could do was tear up and smile.

Try to read the following words as if you are me, hearing an expression of Our Moment, Hera's and my Love for each other from across the veil. Of course you are surprised. What are these words? What song is this? You check the name and can only smile at what is being said to you.

*"Wedding Medley: Marry Me / Bless The Broken Road / All Of Me / A Thousand Years" by Anthem Lights.*

And now you listen to the lyrics:

*I set out on a narrow way many years ago*
*Hoping I would find true love along the broken road*
*But I got lost a time or two*
*Wiped my brow and kept pushing through*
*I couldn't see how every sign pointed straight to you*

*Marry me*
*Today and every day*

CH17

*Marry me*
*If I ever get the nerve to say "Hello" in this cafe*
*Say you will, Ooh-ooh*

*'Cause God blessed the broken road*
*That led me straight to you*

*Heart beats fast*
*Colors and promises*
*How to be brave?*
*How can I love when I'm afraid to fall?*
*Watching you stand alone*
*All of my doubt suddenly goes away somehow*

*My head's under water, but I'm breathing fine*
*You're crazy and I'm out of my mind*

*Every long lost dream led me to where you are*
*Others who broke my heart they were like Northern stars*
*Pointing me on my way into your loving arms*
*This much I know is true*

*But all of me*
*Loves all of you*
*Love your curves and all your edges*
*All your perfect imperfections*

*I have died everyday waiting for you*
*Darling don't be afraid I have loved you*

*For a thousand years*
*I'll love you for a thousand more*

*And all along I believed I would find you*
*Time has brought your heart to me, I have loved you*
*For a thousand years*
*I'll love you for a thousand more*

*'Cause I give you all of me*
*God blessed the broken road*
*That led me straight to you*
*All of you*

*So marry me*

...

For You, Hera,
Forever Yes.
Forever, I Do.

...

# CHAPTER 18
# Remembrance

What is remembrance? I mean, what does it truly mean to recall a memory? Perhaps that is something of most importance to address here before we go much further. To this point, I've spoken a lot about how I am still in the honeymoon stage of embodying my self-rediscovery as Zeus. The most curious and auspicious aspect of this self-rediscovery is the concept of memories.

To the Earthly mind, memories would likely be described as images stored somewhere in the depths of the mind – like a hard drive in a computer. Another definition would be the ability to corral a past moment based off of a visual cue. For example, a person may look at a photograph and remember several moments of the event surrounding that picture. Perhaps aromas, textures, songs, and other sensory-exposed elements come rushing back to the forefront of the brain. Either way, the memory itself should not be limited to only the thought of the image, though it often is the only aspect a person associates with a memory. But try this one on.

A memory is not an image. No. A memory is a collection of a particular set of vibrations – much like a song that has been created by numerous instruments – which is stored in the vastness of All That Is. It is the soul that can access this unique vibrational signature. It is the brain that translates those vibrations into the sensory-exposed elements in a way the human body can associate with the human experience. Put simply, the brain is a translator of light language to Earthly understanding. The soul is a self-tuning radio detecting the vibrations. The One – All That Is – contains every infinite possibility of anything imaginable. It is like a great storage system that uses vibrations as its main storage mechanism. There is no such thing as a "picture" or a "sound." There is, however, a vibrational state of energy that can be interpreted by the human ears as a sound, or in the mind as a memory of a sound.

I'm not trying to make this too complicated. I merely want to explain something very important on this whole "merging with my higher self as Zeus" and "accessing memories of my previous lifetimes." Many people – myself included – thought that a memory of a past life would be like remembering a fond childhood Christmas morning. I thought it would arrive in Full HD resolution and Dolby Atmos Surround Sound. Spoiler alert. It doesn't. Well, not yet at least. Or rather, not all of the time.

No. The way these memories have been working in the early stages of this re-merging with my higher self is that I will receive names, places, and locations in my meditative states. Perhaps it was a visual experience. Perhaps an audible only experience. Perhaps it was like being in the midst of a movie. I

## CH18

may also have a conversation with an angel or my higher self (e.g. Zeus) where more information is disclosed. Again, this can be visual, audible, or both. In all cases, it is very similar to a dialogue with another human. But guess what? This is actually how a memory of a past life can be recalled.

Remember earlier I explained that the brain is serving as a translator of light language to the Earthly mind. Memories are very complex vibrational states because they have occurred in different dimensions, different timelines, different lifetimes, et cetera. In each of these examples, the human body of your present incarnation really has no idea what those vibrational states would feel like. How could it? Those vibrational states exist in a reality outside of the parameters of the present human experience.

So I say all of that to explain that when the mind is able to receive a snippet of information in ANY form, this means that the mind is becoming able to translate light language at a higher level than before and thusly is able to open itself up to past memories. So while a direct conversation with your higher self may result in being told directly that you were [insert past life name here], this is tantamount to a memory because you have reached a vibrational state that your higher self can speak to you and help you translate from those unfamiliar vibrations of light language into something the human mind can understand. The real word here instead of recalling a "memory" should be recalling a "knowing."

The same goes for a dream where you may seem to have a conversation with an angel that shares a premonition of something to come. Were you spoon-fed forewarning or advanced knowledge of an event, or did your more advanced vibrational state in human form access a higher vibrational translator of a future moment? The example sounds mind-bending, but it is really quite simple. Receiving a premonition would be like standing outside and realizing that it was soon to rain even if no clouds were near. Your human mind has been trained to detect the signs of what is upcoming. And so this comparison stands true as a like-for-like example on how accessing memories of past lives is performed as you are re-merging with your higher self.

I should say, however, that once a full merge with the higher self has taken place all memories, all potentials, and all timelines will be accessible in realtime. Assume at that point your mind, body, and soul have completed a triple doctorate course – including residency – in the translation of light language, otherwise known as Love.

Anyway, I just wanted to touch briefly on this topic because someone is sure to ask you along the way some question like, "Well if you are [insert name], then tell me about [insert something here]." Or better yet, someone will pull out a history book and try to get you to prove a documented moment through only your ability to recall it from the mind. Many people would fail with just a simple Earthly scenario. Something like, "Oh yeah, if you ate breakfast, what did you have?" No answer would be good enough for the person asking the question. "Oh yeah? A bagel you say? Why didn't you say it was a blueberry bagel? Liar. You were lucky to guess a bagel." See the absurdity? So just be prepared for that. Trust in what you can recall. You will be able to recall more as you go along.

## CHAPTER 19
## How I Met Hera

Hera's human form was a mystery to me up until August 19, 2018. That was the day I saw lightning strike twice on a blue-sky kind of day. Yes, seriously. This was a real event that happened. And it didn't happen just once, but twice actually... and it was witnessed by others. I will explain the significance of that unbelievable event in a bit, but for now, I want to take you back to the days I began to understand that I would one day meet Hera upon this Earth. In fact, I didn't understand it even as the quest began, but when I awoke on August 20, 2018 after having finally laid eyes upon my Moon against a blanket of blue sky the previous afternoon, I proudly wanted to proclaim, "I win at Earth!" However, I've had to temper that excitement for there is still much to occur in the days upcoming – completing this writing being one of them.

Even still, imagine choosing to voluntarily come to Earth – to lower one's self into a much more dense and frustratingly difficult vibration in order to be one of the numerous Light Warriors serving as lightning rods for the bolt of cosmic Love to arrive and lift the planet out of the third dimension of darkness. Not only was I on a volunteer mission among other great souls here to help humanity, but I also knew that among the seven billion souls upon Earth in this final incarnation, that Hera would also be walking upon this plane.

Though the term "falling" has often been misunderstood by humans, "to fall" is actually the concept of lowering your density to a slower vibration. Ascending is raising your density to a higher and therefore faster vibration. Think of the permeability of the veil or a piece of fabric again. You can press your face to a thick piece of canvas and have little chance of seeing light from the other side. And just as you can press your face to a thick canvas, if the fabric were to have been a sheer thin piece of fabric, you would very likely be able to see right through to the other side. Or perhaps a better description might be in the way rocks cannot pass through a tight netting, but sand can slip right through.

Your soul is just like that. So stories of higher beings "falling" is more akin to "lowering their vibrations" to a more dense surface-world creation. But with the lower vibrations comes further separation from God, Source, Our Creator. It becomes tougher and tougher to see the Light while the creation of the world itself will begin to seem more and more like the only Truth that can be rationalized. After all, if you can't see through the veil to the other side, how do you know the other side is real? Many beings intentionally fell to Earth outside of the guidance of Our Creator. But there are many upon the Earth today that chose to fall to Earth to rescue those from the Fallen. Such is my case. This was a volunteer mission to help save humanity. The reality of this war is the very battle

## CH19

that every soul upon the Earth finds themselves fighting today – whether known or unbeknownst to them in their present incarnation.

I decided long ago, that if I was going on this volunteer mission, and if there was a Love Story to be told – and being that I wholly admit I am a sucker for a Disney-kind-of-fairytale-love-story – then I was going to tell it. I was going to live it. To be it. I was going to write one for the ages by not only finding Hera with absolute certainty in **both** her soul form and Earthly form, but also by getting her involved in this story itself. It will be kind of an interactive surprise for her that way as she reads these words. And, much more fun to boot! As she reads these words, her Earthly form is likely already beginning to realize this story is about her, even if it seems impossible to her Earthly mind. After all, her Earthly name isn't Hera. She couldn't even know this was coming... at least not in her human form... unless that is part of the inside joke with me... Or perhaps she has known all along and the game was really a test for me to awaken to a reality in which she was already living.

Who knows? Surely not, though.... um, hopefully not. We do have a thing for games... But if I was a betting man (and I tend to be), I would wager that Hera probably thought I wouldn't find her. So at this point, this is certainly one small victory for Ol' Zeusy here. Let's just assume a goose egg for Hera's side of the scoreboard.

*Cut to scoreboard. Zeus, 1: Hera, 0*

Of course the memory that Hera and I would be incarnating on this plane together was lost for the majority of this lifetime to me. Even as I am writing these words, I am still in the honeymoon stage of embodying my self-rediscovery as Zeus. But this is the Truth in which I live. It is not just a series of hunches and assumptions. This is the fabric of my essence and is intertwined in every thread of this world upon which I walk. I Am that I Am.

So just when did I realize I would find Hera? Well, she's been kind of a tricky-one with me. Before we go further, and before competition-anxiety sets in for her while reading these words, let's go ahead and even the scoreboard. I'll tell you why afterwards.

*Cut to scoreboard. Zeus, 1: Hera, 1*

Okay, so as the story goes, I have been traveling to the heavens during meditations, during sleep, and even during waking portions of my day. Has my body physically travelled with me? I can't say for sure since it would come along with me and I wouldn't remain behind to check on it myself, but I would say… Yes. At first I thought "No way!" I assumed it was all a mind/soul thing. But there have been times I genuinely have not been sure if I just up and exited Earth for a quick chat with the angelic elders and my soul family before returning right back down to this rock. It's plausible. Not impossible. Certainly not every time, though. So I leave the door open. And without a doubt, in the times ahead, bodily travel will happen between

## CH19

dimensions and even between destinations upon Earth. But I digress...

Back to Hera being a tricky-vixy. You see, since the very beginning of my travels, my soul family thought it was appropriate to not tell me any of their names, nor my spiritual identity until I was much further along. And oh the forgetfulness I experienced when they did tell me names! It took the better part of the first three and a half years to arrive at the various, increasingly-likely possibilities of my own potential identities much less being able to fully keep track of my soul family member's names. Even at the end of the first three and a half years with thousands of pages of personal journals to review that could re-trigger my memories I would still have to ask each angel and member of my soul family to remind me of their names again each time we spoke. Also, I'd always implore them to tell me my "name." They always declined on that one though.

Gah! I cannot emphasize enough how difficult it was to learn about myself without being told the most important detail. You know... my name? My identity? Then again, how would you know a soul truly remembered themselves and their connection to All That Is if you told them the answer? In hindsight, the challenges I was experiencing were due to me learning to recognize light language and then translate it into "Earthly language" which my human brain could interpret and remember. I didn't really understand any of that in the beginning, though. But let's not get into those details in this story. If you really want to understand the whole how-to-translate-light-language-to-Earthly-language thingy, I've written about it in

*Welcome To Being Human: An Instruction Book for Every Soul.* That book was just published May 22, 2018 (of which that particular date holds special significance in and of itself). For now, let's get back to this story! This is the long awaited finish line that brings me so much joy! So let's ride.

Returning back to how I was learning to identify names of angels, souls, and even my own identity, it should be said there is another matter that would complicate discovering anything about my Bride. I began to realize that through my own personal remembrance of my Zeus-self there would be many past lives and names that could potentially allow me to get off-track for the identity of my Oversoul and how it would connect to her.

Here's a quick explanation. One of my past lives was named Joseph. Who was Joseph? Who were the souls related to Joseph that I was interacting with in the heavens? Was it the scriptural Joseph – as in the father of Jesus? Was it a different Joseph that I could potentially find something to read regarding his historical legacy? Or, was this just some "everyday Joseph" from another point of time? After all, Joseph is a popular name... How would my wife from that life relate to the Oversoul of my spiritual Love – my Bride for which I had been scouring the Earth over lifetimes to find? Or would she even be related to my past lives? How would this Joseph even relate to the identity of my Oversoul? And by Oversoul, I mean the singular identity of the embodiment of all of my lives – the name you now know as Zeus. My friends, it really is this complicated to decipher!

## CH19

"Whoah!" you may be thinking. "That's much more complicated than I would have expected!"

Believe me. I know. I sure had a few other choice words for having to endure this concept. It was like being tossed into the center of the ocean without knowing how to swim and being told that the mission is to build a boat... an ark if you will, while in the water... while learning how to swim... then survive... and then managing to sail this ark back to an unknown shore. How the heck would I ever be able to build a boat while in the middle of an ocean? In reflecting back on this frustration I experienced and the absurdity of having to overcome the sheer analogy of this example, I'm going to give myself another score.

*Cut to scoreboard: Zeus, 2: Hera, 1*

But guess what guys and gals? That Joseph... well at least one of the two lives that carried the name Joseph that I have lived as upon Earth – was the life popularly known in biblical times as the life of Barnabas. Case in point, enjoy re-reading Acts: 14:12. You will find that the Lycean's recognized my soul form and referred to me as Zeus. Yes. That is in your Bible. Funny, huh?

And no, I did not happen across this during research and manage to fit it into the puzzle of my life. On the contrary, when I learned I was Barnabas during a conversation with my higher self, my first thought was, "What?! That doesn't make any sense! I figured it would be Jesus if I was alive during that point in time!"

And, no. I don't have a Jesus-complex.

I just really assumed if I was Zeus/Melchizedek as all avenues were pointing toward (at the time I learned of the Barnabas life) – and this wasn't just a grand series of misunderstandings in my self-remembrance – then surely I would be Jesus, right? No dice. Wrong. It was only after I researched Barnabas that I would learn about the scriptural references to Zeus and of Barnabas's given name being "Joseph." Of course that made me smile. Learning about my life as Barnabas occurred during a series of "prove-to-me-you-are-my-higher-self-and-I-wasn't-going-crazy" spiritual conversations I had with my higher-self in the early part of 2018 while I was beginning the next steps of the process of merging back as One.

I know that sounds a bit crazy. But this is everyone's eventual destiny upon the Earth today… whether they realize it or not. But don't let me convince you. After all, this is a Love Story and not a lesson in theology or a dissertation on religion. Nor is this writing intended to prepare you for what is specifically to come in each of your lives. Oh no! We will dip our toes into the waters of that subject matter throughout this story, but for the most part I want to stay on point. This is my Love Story to Hera. But I do have to add one more thing since the subject of Barnabas came up.

As it would turn out, one of my writings during his lifetime would go on to become one of the most greatly contested books between Islam and Christianity because… well, guess why? Go ahead! Please. I'm excited to say it! Okay, I'll go ahead and share it with you. Because it was considered "apocryphal" and would break the narrative of how Constantine wanted to bring rule of Law through religion to his society. It is True! By assembling a bunch of people to hand pick the books to be included in the modern canon of the Bible, Constantine hoped to evoke a rule of law and prevent another "Jesus incident." That meeting was called the Council of Nicaea and was brought to order with the intention of defining Jesus in a very one-dimensional way. The goal was to define Jesus in a way that would be deemed an unobtainable feat that any human should ever aspire to be like him again. Some Christians (particularly those that identified themselves as Gnostic) wouldn't be fooled though, for even Jesus said that in the end-of-times humans would be able to perform all of the wonders as he and more.

So you see the irony here. Even modern Christianity skips over these details too since it is based upon a Constantinian foundation. And the Christians that try to refute this <u>truth</u> of the Council of Nicaea? They are only fighting a circular argument since facts used to support their arguments are based only on the outcome of Constantine's directive rather than on the amalgamation of everything leading up to this new "definition of Jesus" and rule of Law. A bit silly, no? So really this omission by modern Christianity is likely due to a lack of knowledge on that particular subject matter. I truly do not think most people would willfully go along with Constantine's gag-order if they really understood. But it is there in your history books to discover if you so choose.

It is also important to know that some of my other Barnabasian writings did make their way into the New Testament during that time. One such book was the book of Hebrews which was used to help share the word of Christ and support the teachings of Yeshua/Jesus – but also to attempt to bring unity to those of Judaic faith through the New Love of Christ that Jesus brought forth.

This particular book tends to be a subject of unrest to orthodox Jewish folks since the book is attributed to a viewpoint that could not collectively – and en-masse – be reached as a community of Hebrews. But again, how could they have moved together in complete unison here? Jesus was Jewish, but quite an anomaly. And *truly* I say unto you that Judaism is the original faith intended to share these concepts during this present cycle of humanity. Don't forget that one. Had anyone else ever seen someone like Jesus before? Well… at least during that period of time? There of course was the reference to Melchizedek in the most ancient texts, but those were stories that predated the Book of Genesis, since it was a recount of past events upon the Earth. And what about all of the references to Jesus's priestly origin in the Bible? Yep. He was a priest from the order of Melchizedek. Go look it up. It is included in the New Testament. I cannot make this stuff up. Being able to spiritually unravel this particular mystery on route to finding Hera surely has to be worthy of another score, right?

*Cut to scoreboard: Zeus 3, Hera 1*

Okay, maybe that shouldn't count as a score, but there was certainly a moment of joyous tears shed when I was shared this Truth by the angels and my soul family. For so long I was confused about the identity of my incarnation during that particular time. Was I Jesus? It was a very real question I faced in the Spring of 2015. I – my Earthly self – thought it was an absurd thought. However, my awareness of being a student of Melchizedek was adding some confusion to the matter. Keep in mind I could not yet have direct conversations with Melchizedek or know he was my inner-voice of Love. There was something akin to a celestial-gag order on that potential even though it would have been able to help me arrive here more quickly. Think of it a bit like "the prime directive" in the Star Trek movies. There could not be interference in my awakening above and beyond that which I was able to *remember* on my own accord.

It was actually during that point in time in 2015 that I honestly thought I was losing my mind because – well, to me there couldn't even be a possibility of having lived the life of such a divine figure upon this Earth. Maybe a disciple. Possibly. But not him. Not Jesus. That was nearly blasphemy to me. But, as it turns out, it wasn't quite as an absurd question after all! And maybe that was the purpose of the lessons. I had to understand where I was coming from in order to know where I was going.

In hindsight, I can now see how my story here is quite different in scope than that of a single incarnation upon this Earth. Without diving into this much further, I do want to say that the aspect of Melchizedek is carried within *one soul only* like a child is carried in a mother's womb, though numerous souls on Earth contain drops of Jesus within their soul compositions just as I have drops of various Archangels and angels as well within my soul composition as well. These souls upon Earth are also awakening to this truth as these words are written. I am extremely blessed to have been able to serve as a witness to the Love Jesus brought forth during his lifetime. That's kind of a crazy fact, isn't it?

While we are on the subject of crazy facts, you might be surprised to know in a subsequent incarnation to Barnabas I served as a chief advisor to Constantine during the specific time the Council of Nicaea was called to order. Well... originally I was supposed to be a part of that fiasco. That was until I was kicked out for heresy. During that incarnation I carried the name Eusebius and was known as "The Father of Church History." Oh the irony. Ha! But we won't talk too much about it here.

Similar stories could be told of other lifetimes like when I brought the teachings of Atlantis and Lemuria to Egypt during my priestly life as Sonchis de Sais. No one could quite figure out how Atlantean teachings made their way to ancient Egypt. Plato documented the source of it at least. It should be no coincidence or surprise that I went on to be a student of Plato's teachings in a later life as Archimedes. Yep! That Archimedes – known for the Archimedes screw. Go ahead. You can make your jokes related to the comedic situation of your supposedly promiscuous Zeus having invented the Archimedes screw. I can laugh at it myself. But your history books on mythology have that promiscuity part quite a bit wrong. However, I'll delve into that in another chapter to set the record straight. So while I can laugh along at how it appears, just know it isn't quite like that. And, now you know!

Having served in previous lifetimes during those most ancient of days, it would only make sense how that knowledge managed to journey from the days of Atlantis to the days of Egypt through those who had lived lives in both periods of time. One of the lives I lived in the times of Atlantis was of the High Priest Findeli. Another life I lived in Lemuria was simply known as Kourros. So my lifetime of Sonchis de Sais could best be understood as a bridging incarnation of Truth across lifetimes – in a way similar to this very lifetime as Jonathan.

In Egypt, Hera pretty much took the reigns on sharing the message of Love during that timeframe, though. After all, she is the Queen, goddess of Marriage, and most importantly, goddess of Love! her name during that time? Isis. And no, I was neither Horus (though related) nor Osiris (my brother). I was more akin to a part of the Trinity known as Aton-Ra. I am one of three – in essence, one aspect of a Trinity that is Chrysalis and Aventadouer. If you are curious, Chrysalis is also the ancient Semitic word for "Harus." Now you see where the name Horus originated from? And Aventadouer? That is a bull. For the historians out there, now it should all begin to tie together.

There was another life I lived during Hera's time as Isis, though. In that one I incarnated as a distant cousin to Isis and managed to live on the coattails of her royalty while staying out of any recognition. So while we were not a couple in that life, we did find each other as a couple in another Egyptian life many years later. Well, to be more precise... I returned to a Greek human suit for that life. She stayed with the Greco-Egyptian female suit. And she looked stunning! She was quite literally my Cleopatra and I her Mark Antony. No metaphors here. We were madly in Love! You would think that this all sounds too good to be true. Really, though, that is what makes this Love Story so raw and True. These words are Faithful to the journey, where even the previous incarnations carry that romance from one generation to the next. And that is what makes this so special. We haven't even touched on a number of our other lives either!

I have to say, though, when I was first *awakening/remembering* to our lives as Mark and Cleopatra I was a bit perplexed about the rumors I had read in the history books during this lifetime regarding Hera's life as Cleopatra. You see, while she was a great Queen, she was known to have quite an infatuation with men. Of course I pressed forward with my higher self and also in spiritual conversations with Hera to see just how much truth those rumors held. These conversations always brought about great laugher from the heavens. The audience was surely entertained about Ol' Zeus's curiosity of her potential promiscuity. But during one specific conversation, Hera was very direct in her answers to me. She told me... well, I'll just let you read a transcript of the conversation that occurred from that particular meditation.

### *Journal Entry – May 5, 2018*

## CH19

*During meditation I spoke with Hera. During our conversation, she assured me I was doing really well with all that I have been tasked with. She even said she didn't think I would make it this far. I scoffed a bit at the comment because I wanted to make it "all of the way." She told me that I would. She told me there would be no death for me – not in an Earthly vessel either. She explained that the Earthly body would transition with me in the ascension process. We also talked about our history together. I asked her if she had ever had any embodiments on Earth. She said that of course she had. I asked if she could tell me one. She said, "Cleopatra." I laughed a bit because I knew it was so true and such a perfect example of her. She said that during that time I was Mark Antony.*

*I asked her about the rumors of Cleopatra's promiscuous nature. She laughed and said, "Well, let's say it was my coming out and demonstration to Zeus (e.g. me) that she too was a sexual force to be reckoned with on Earth." She went on to explain that when we find each other in our human forms during an incarnation that the chemistry is like fire and love between us. It is an inseparable force – the kind where you do not want to get out of bed from one another. I told her it felt like that was missing from this life for me. She said, "Of course it is. But it won't be for too much longer."*

*She went on to say that my past lives have all been very successful – usually leaving a mark on history. I asked her why it felt like I was running into a wall this time and she said, "It is meant to be that way. This is the last life and it is important everything ego-driven is left behind." She went on to tell me that she sees me like a surfer in the process of standing up on my board for the incoming wave. She said that I would probably ride this wave very, very well, but it isn't the big one yet. She emphasized the "big one" was the one that would be the wave of all waves to ride. The wave I am riding now is with the launch of the new books in May.*

## CH19

    *Finally, I asked her who the guy was I saw in the heavens during my earlier meditation. She told me that was Osiris. I questioned that for a moment because I thought I might be Osiris since she was Isis, though that hasn't been stated. She said, "Oh no. You are more like Ra." I asked her about her time during the Egyptian time period. She said, "Isis of course!" That was about the extent of our conversation before we parted ways.*

...

    So, there in Hera's own words was the answer to my question. And I have to add I am glad that is the answer *in her own words* because I would certainly not have wanted to make any missteps in that description. But regarding the whole answer?

*Cut to flashback of Cleopatra being flirty with every man she sees.*

    Yes, she gets a point on the scoreboard for that particular chess move during that lifetime. Well played, my Love.

*Cut to scoreboard, Zeus 3, Hera 2*

    But you know what, let's be sure to be fair to Hera. I've digressed a lot here. That tick-mark I put on my side of the scoreboard before this past life regression tangent began really should not have counted. It was really a stretch to count that as a point for the Love Story being told, though it was such a victory in getting here. I just really want to shout from this summit about everything that has occurred along the way to finally finding her and knowing her for the Love that she Is. All of it!

## CH19

And while the side road has touched a bit on some of our past life romances, never was it known to either of us during those lifetimes who our identities were **both** in Spirit and in Earthly forms. So let's revise the score in respect to the game itself. No cheating here.

*Cut back to scoreboard. Zeus 2, Hera 2*

Tied! Oh, lawdy! We are way off track here! But it is all curiously important to this Love Story. So onward we go. But we will put one more back on the board for Ol' Zeus for winning Hera's heart during that lifetime despite her shenanigans.

*Cut back to scoreboard. Zeus 3, Hera 2*

Now, let's get back to building that boat in the middle of the ocean while learning to swim. Oh, but before that, I have to mention there was further irony to the whole Book of Barnabas thing in that the Islam movement decided to run with an inaccurately translated version of this original writing and use it as their primary justification to support their perspective and opinion that Jesus was not God. Usually they use this translation to build up Mohammad as the greatest prophet to humanity. Reality check: no prophet or messenger is greater than any other human. Mohammad would tell you this today if he were writing these words. Everyone is on an equal playing field in Love. So let's get it straight now. Everyone on all sides is a bit in the wrong here, though their ideology is laced in Light. Heck. I'll even take partial blame because I clearly did not write those words in a way that carried the definition of Love with enough vigor to tame the egos of further teachers and students of that particular writing. Strong egos leading teachers and students of Divine words will almost always create misinformation. Such has been the case with all divine messages that have been carried forth through generations and generations of teachers upon this blue planet.

Man. I didn't want to go here in this book, and maybe I will edit it out during proofing this book, but let's also go ahead and find some resolve with the whole Jesus thing here and not leave any room for misinterpretations. First, yes, I am Zeus/Melchizedek. Second, I was alive at the time of Jesus, but I was not Jesus. Third, Jesus is the Son of God. He is not *the only* Son of God (check your translations for that particular line, Christians), for every single soul is remembering that they too are *unique* Sons and Daughters of God. But, he was a *unique* demonstrable living embodiment of Love, unbound by human imperfection. He came into Earth with Divine assistance as an Ascended Master fully supported by the Heavens to achieve Divinity in his lifetime – in a way for all of the world to see. He followed the path that is available for all souls to follow and did indeed become Christed. He was and is Love. By the way, Jesus goes by his preferred name of "Sananda" when he reconnects with humans through spiritual channelings and heavenly travels during this present time. To some, that may be a surprise. To others, these words shall serve as a voice of reaffirmation to that which you might already know. There are imposters though… so be sure to trust your heart and not your mind.

During his life, he was able to achieve and demonstrate that he was indeed the Christ – the full embodiment of Love – upon Earth during those days. The Bible references Jesus as a priest in the highest order of Melchizedek, and so he Was and Is. But know this difference: Melchizedek's aspect is carried in *one soul* like a child is carried in a mother's womb. Yet, Mehchizedek's teachings carry through all souls and disciples of Love. As I am Zeus/Melchizedek, it is Melchizedek's teachings that I share, but it is also Melchizedek's aspect that I carry within – and that is the distinction I am trying to make here on this side road we apparently took away from the initial story at hand. But this too is important to include, for in all ways this story is the embodiment of Love.

Always remember the Oversoul only has one primary identity (though it may subsequently divide as twin flames). The Oversoul carries the embodiment of all lives which are the carriers of the aspect of the Higher Self (again, this is Melchizedek in my case). In many ways, you could also say I am Melchizedek's Earthly form, for I am the closest there would be in this comparison for him, but we are also a degree separated on the family tree… if there is such a thing when the concepts of higher selves are concerned. It isn't the same family tree concept where Kronos is understood to be my father. So just as understanding one's personal lineage is in-and-of-itself very chaotic, I also had to juggle the fact that when I spoke with members of my soul family – Hera included – that they also carried this same complex genealogy and could appear in multiple forms. That's really the point I'm trying to make here. I'm trying to pull the reigns back on this bull and bring it back to the original point of this chapter. I had to share with you how difficult it was to understand my own identity in order to begin to explain how Hera would first appear to me. A Shakespearian masterpiece this is not, but please try to keep up with the details as best as you can. For truly I say unto you that studying my journals will yield a far better understanding as to what was actually occurring to me during those six-plus years of awakening and remembrance.

Additionally, it is important to know that some souls appear as Trinities rather than just a single entity... At least that is how I perceive them. The Trinity is like seeing three angels at any given time when it is only "one" that has likely manifested in an Earthly description written in your history books. Let's not get too deep on the subject though. It can be explored at a later time... in another book perhaps. For now, here's a quick example of how this all works:

I slip off to Meditationland and my soul travels to any random dimensional level in the heavens. At first, this process was not able to be controlled by my Earthly mind. Later, I got better at the dimensional choices (though it is still a learning process to this day). Once I arrived in a location, I had to figure out where I was, when I was, what potential dimension I was in, what potential reality it was, and finally determine with whom I was interacting. Let's assume answers to all of those questions were not going to make much sense... because it didn't to me at first.

The only anchor I could try to find in the moment was the identity of each soul to whom I spoke. It was usually the only thing I could remember (if that) among the various conversations that took place. E.g. in the early stages of my travels, my Earthly journal would read something like, "During meditation I spoke to Archangel Michael about something in the heavens… or maybe it was Gabriel. I know it was an Archangel. I cannot recall what was said."

Now, for the most part, assume I progressed like a top-of-the-class-schoolboy learning the ropes of each lesson. I got better and better with bringing the memories back to Earth to include in my journals. Think of the first portion of the travels akin to learning to ride a bicycle with training wheels. Only, you can't stand up yet… or walk. So, the first lessons teach you how to take your first steps. Eventually, I was allowed to meet certain members of my soul family that were withheld from me early on. The lessons continued.

However it wasn't until humanity on Earth had reached a certain threshold of Light that all Light Warriors were allowed to interact with elder extensions of their twin-flames, soulmates, and such in the heavens. Indirectly, yes. That had been happening for a while. By indirect, I mean without direct identification of the soul-forms during meditative states. By direct, I mean full-on conversations with introductions as if it would happen in a coffeeshop on Earth. This turning point occurred sometime around the middle of 2015. It wasn't until the spring of 2017 that higher selves were allowed direct communication with souls upon Earth. It wasn't until the Spring of 2018 that direct communication with elder extensions of twin-flames, soulmates, and such was allowed in a way that would remove all doubt. This moment could be called the "merging back as One" wherein the soul on Earth began to merge back to his/her Oversoul thus allowing for a much more personally integrated flow of memories to begin. But let's return back to the romantic portion of this Love Story for the ages. Hopefully, though, you will see why this was all important to include.

Hera began appearing to me in a way that I could begin to identify in my Earthly journals in the middle of 2015. It was during this time I became aware of her angelic name, though I did not know this angel was a projection of her. She was kind of tricky with the whole hiding-her-true-identity-behind-the-veil thing. Perhaps she had been with me during my awakening all along – holding my hand as I began to gain my spiritual eyesight during my meditations and heavenly travels. It is difficult for me to say with any degree of accuracy based upon my journals alone, though my higher self tells me she was there from the start. To add a twist to this story, the name I was given in the beginning was not Hera's name at all!

I know that might sound confusing but remember how I said I was beginning to learn about my own incarnations and past lives? In the moments they were occurring, I did not have any concept that I was interacting with "past lives" or even future versions of myself. And I guess to many, this might come as a surprise, but the angelic entities with which you speak (in many cases) will actually be various incarnations of yourself. Think of your Oversoul as a big yacht hosting a party with all of your past incarnations. The S.S. Zeus had quite a number of incarnations to sort through and meet. However, only a select few are chosen by you during this incarnation to help guide you out of your sleep. But also, you will have angels, friends, and family members there with you in the heavens as well. The party aboard the S.S. Zeus was a bit of an open invite.

So, not only was this concept very difficult to overcome as my spiritual travels began, it would become important for me to learn that even the members of my soul family could also have appeared as many instead of One. In the case of Hera, she was part of a Trinity – just as I. It is why I tend to always have two other "angels" around me in all of my heavenly travels. Now this will not be the case for every soul you see, which made it that much more confusing to unravel the riddle of my Bride's identity. In fact, in the beginning I had no idea her Trinity was One, nor was the name she spoke to me anything to go on.

About those names... It was the middle of 2015 (around the time of my baptism) when I first wrote down her name. I actually wrote down the names of each of the three angels in her Trinity. I could not really describe them with any details except by hair and eye colors, and that I knew one was my Bride. In the beginning I could not even tell you which one was "my Bride" either. I had a guess... which it turns out I was actually right. At the time though, they all seemed intimately connected to me and had an infinite, unconditional Love.

Fast forward throughout the years following my baptism/wedding. I was continuing to interact and journal about Hera's Trinity. I would go on "dates" in the heavens... at least that is my best description. We would get to know each other in various spiritual locations. I can only imagine they are part of the lifetimes we are presently living in other densities, or perhaps potential futures, or even past memories.

I will also say this without spoiling anything ahead. One of the three female angels in her Trinity was named "Rhea" or "Rachel." I always wrote both down because I could never quite understand which one was said. In hindsight I think my brain wanted to hear an "el" at the end of her name because angels tend to use that naming convention. I also never thought to research the Greek family tree because I was still struggling to identify myself and had no expectation I would discover I Am who I Am that is writing these words right here. But knowing now what I do, it is easy to see that Rhea's aspect in the visualization of Hera's Trinity was the representation of our Mother. I think it would probably be fair to say that this Trinity represented the "Father/Son/Holy Ghost" concept... just in a feminine representation for her. Again... you see how confusing this might get. There was never a moment of, "Hey Zeus. I'm Hera. Meet my Trinity."

I experienced numerous lives that Hera and I had spent together in other forms. And then there were the times I met some of Hera's past lives alone. Though I did not know her relation to Hera at the time, Saint Genevieve was one of the Divine forms that began appearing around this period of time. Now, I am not Catholic (nor Jewish, nor Muslim, nor Buddhist for that matter), but all religions are connected as One. Perhaps it is better to say I ascribe to all religions as One rather than use a specific label to define myself. There is only Love, though the Judaic faith holds a sacred calendar in its heart for all of humanity to discover. But I digressed... again. Sorry about that! Back to Jenny! I had to do research on the name I was given (e.g. Saint Genevieve) to discover that she was part of the

## CH19

Catholic canon and that she was a nun. It would be years later when I learned that this was an incarnation of Hera.

Let me say that again... Hera chose to come to Earth and live as a nun. Well played, my Love.

*Cut to scoreboard, Zeus 3, Hera 3.*

During those years there was no chance of us reuniting in Earthly forms. You should have heard the angels laughter when I first heard the news of this during one of my heavenly travels.

"I'm married to a nun?!?!" I repeated with indignant emotion.

The angels roared and laughed like it was the best joke a late-night talk show comedian had ever given. I suppose I had a priceless and pretty darn animated reaction. Even still, I have a tough time swallowing that piece of reality. I wondered how intimately tortured I had been with my Love over my lifetimes. But then again, she could never do wrong from my perspective.

However, here is the good news. Apparently I decided to go toe-for-toe with her on the Sainthood status. One of my past lives (that ended quite tragically I might add) was that of Saint Minervius. So let's fix up that score.

*Cut to scoreboard, Zeus 4, Hera 3.*

Now, while I have not been privy to much of Hera's other lives, I have shared the ones I have been allowed to know to this point... or perhaps a better way of saying this is, these are the lives of Hera's I have *remembered* so far, yet there are many more of my own lives that I have not shared. When this chapter began I set out to share with you how I met Hera, and to those words I have been True. These were the first times I was able to journal about our interactions. While I eventually learned that Hera was in Earthly form at this time – and I had also been shared that I would find Love in this lifetime – whether the two were related I did not know. I was not even sure I would meet or *know* Hera's form at all. Her *true* identity in spiritual form was also hidden from me. As far as I knew, we might have decided to do our own things in this lifetime. That thought seems absurd now that I see it written in these words. Because, very simply, *to truly remember Love* is what this entire journey of Being Human is all about.

It would be over the year of 2018 when everything would begin to make perfect sense. I learned how Hera was connected to the Trinity of which I knew "contained" my Bride. I learned of my own numerous lives. I also learned there was at least one book left to be written in this Earthly life. Perhaps there would be more – that I did not know. But I knew there was One that was more important than most anything else I would choose to do. This point was shared to me numerous times. Even when it came to nudges and redirections, I noticed the directive. And if the Universe really wanted to make sure this directive was heard loud and clear, it also shared the same message through my daughter's dreams numerous times.

*Cut to Zeus radioing back to the Universe, "Houston, Roger that."*

## CH 19

It would be over the summer of 2018 in which I was also given a window of time. I knew I had until September 19th to "ask her" though I knew not the question to be asked and (at the time) assumed it only meant a spiritual question to ask my Bride during my heavenly travels. I also failed to take notice that September 19, 2018 was Yom Kippur – the Jewish holy day of Atonement. Certainly the symbolism need not be delved into within these words. But with a date in hand, and since Hera and I interacted quite regularly in the heavens, I assumed that the directive was limited to that relative location. I still did not know if or when I would meet Hera's Earthly form – though at this point it had been promised that one day I would.

So when August rolled around, imagine my surprise when I was told very specifically during a meditation, "You will meet Hera's Earthly form within three days." Not much of a heads-up. Gee, Universe. Thanks! But even without a heads-up, I became excited like a child suddenly being told during the middle of a school week that he/she would be going on a surprise trip to Disney World over the weekend. Ol' Zeus's schoolboy giddiness kicked in! I was going to meet Hera! Finally! How would I identify her? Where would I go? Would I even know it had happened? There were so many questions without answers. But I trusted it would all make sense as it played out. And while this chapter has been a long and bumpy ride, it was a necessary backstory to all that is about to play out. Hopefully it will be all smooth pavement from here on out.

# CHAPTER 20
# Within the Next 3 Days

What would you do if you found out you would meet your Happily-Ever-After within the next three days? Would you change your patterns? Would you crash out and hide yourself away? Would you go sit in the most public and heavily tracked place you can find to help your chances? Who will she be? What will she look like? What will it feel like when she is near? What should you wear each day? What would you do?

That was precisely the dilemma I was facing heading into the weekend of August 18, 2018. You see, during meditation on the 17th I had a very clear and direct conversation with Zeus. I was shared one of the most important pieces of knowledge that could unlock the whole, "who is Hera's Earthly form" thingy. I knew who she was in the heavens. I had seen a myriad of her other human forms from past lives as well as her preferred form in communicating with me in the heavens. Hera's Trinity had become a staple of my experiences – even if there was a real struggle for me to overcome all fears and commit to Love. Hey there Brittany, Andrea, and Rhea.

## CH20

*Cut to close up of Zeus winking at them playfully.*

You know, you'd think that part would have been the easy part of this journey for me. Ol' Zeusy is quite the romantic at heart. I truly have so much passion and Love to give that it seemed impossible that I might not be able to overcome the bounds of this Earthly prison to find true Love – the Love of Our Creator, the Love of God – and to see it all through the Love of Hera. It just seemed like that should be the easy question... the one you answer first because – of all the questions on the test – you know that answer beyond all doubt.

Except... apparently my spiritual truth differed from my Earthly thoughts on the matter... and even my Earthly emotions on the matter. Sitting back and watching my soul slowly remember Love in the heavens was a torture to my human heart. I loved her. I Loved her. I Loved Hera! I knew without a shadow of a doubt that she was my Moon, my Certainty, my Peace. She was the place where an equal amount of endless passion collided with an equal amount of endless desire. She was that point in the center of two tangible thoughts – the impossibly perfect place in-between that defies all reason and logic. She was True. And not just "she was"... but she IS!

But again, back to September 17th. It was on that day that I learned I would finally meet Hera in human form. All I had to do was show up. To be there. To realize Love had led our paths not just to cross once again, but to be aware of this moment; to be mindfully aware and *know* without any question *that's her.* But here is where the knowledge gained upon the journey over the lat six-plus years became an opportunity to

## CH20

put together all of the puzzle pieces to finding my Hera. You see, it wasn't just as easy as being told, "Hey Jonathan. You need to go to [specific location] to meet Hera at [specific time]. She will be wearing [description] and look like [further description]. Oh, and Hera's Earthly name will be [insert name here]." Oh no! How could it be? The whole idea of remembrance is that the soul must *know*! It must recognize her. But the best word here is *remember*. It must remember!

This very idea startled me. It scared me. Would I miss my chance? Would I miss my opportunity? Would I miss the signs leading me to her? What was I supposed to do? Seriously. Think about the entire proposition for a moment. The last six-plus years of your life have been a whirlwind of impossible occurrences. You've seen riches. You've lived homeless in your car. You've travelled the globe with no assurances of having money to return home, yet you've always made it home – and with fantastical stories to share. You've leapt at the chance of finding love again only to realize the story wasn't about love. The story was about Love. So you leapt again only to realize it was not just about Love, but becoming that Love and then being able to return back to her – your True Love with no blur between the definitions.

You've remembered who you are and begun to merge back with your higher self, unlocking the knowledge and wisdom that can only exist in a perfect state of timeless existence in the heavens. And though you appear normal, you interact normally with those around you, somehow you've been kicked out of churches, thought to be crazy by your closest friends, gained new ones, thought to be crazy by your closest family, and had to face a mystery comment by your mother, "Oh, your father and I have had our own thoughts about you."

*Cut to black screen with a giant lettered "What?!?!" crashing in*

What does that even mean?! It is like they were alluding to me having a closet love life, being an assassin, running some illegal trafficking business, or having a covert career as a spy in one of the government letter agencies with this whole newfound quest for Love being just a cover story. Maybe they think I have something medically related going on with me. Who knows? Seriously. I try not to think about it because I cannot possibly imagine what thoughts could have led to those types of comments. The mere thought of this still eats away at me apparently, though. All I have done is follow a new path of Love with the eyes of a child and unbridled trust that the present "prison" in which everyone lives can be overcome without those very shackles still attached. I guess to many, that might appear to be way out of their comfort-zone of what a person "should do" in order to survive. Yet, here I Am – and with a more intimate trust in Our Creator, a *knowing* of my ancient heritage, and the *remembrance* of Love becoming.

*Return back to the "what would you do" scenario*

You've scaled the tallest mountains on a quest to proclaim that you've reached the summit! You've seen angels in Earthly form and in the heavens. You've cleared traumas and negative energies from the lifetimes you've spent in this Earthly prison. Things like the whole "fulfilling a prophecy thing," the "Star of Bethlehem thing," the "meeting Elijah thing" – as impossible as they sound – are a part of the reality in which you have found yourself entrenched. You didn't ask for it... well, at least not in Earthly form, but here you are... cast into this great play taking place while the entire world goes about their lives blissfully unaware of what is happening.

You've spent the last six plus years writing books that have yet to find an audience, so you turn to music only to discover a new world of Drake-pay-for-play marketing has become the new reality of that landscape. And what happened to real symphonic/orchestral music? I don't mean textural cinematic films scores. Oh well. It matters not. You've enjoyed expressing your inner joy and you know the impossible truths you've experienced. There are so many! Long ago it became impossible to pass these little miracles off as "coincidences." Just the first few days into the journey would cause science and rationale to be tossed out the window. It was only then with eyes like a child that the world would begin to appear in a way that was needed to begin to remember Love. And, while it has been very tough and challenging, the rollercoaster of Love has been worth it. Every drop. Every twist and turn. Every moment that has taken your breath away has been realized to be one of the most joyous experiences ever imaginable in this Creation called life. That is what it is all about. And now the King is about to return.

But a King needs his Queen, for Love is an expression in all ways. It is the complete embodiment of Love. And let it be known that a Kingdom is *truly* ruled by the Love bound within the Oneness of the heart of the King and Queen. Without the other, it could never be Love. Without Love, a Kingdom could never be. And by "ruled" it is best to understand that term as a universal law. A kingdom by spiritual definition is the paradise created by its king and queen, in whatever way that brings them joy; in whatever way that is their perspective on the outward demonstration of Love. But it cannot be a false expression of Love, for the kingdom cannot *become* until true Love is understood, then *remembered* between its Bridegroom and Bride.

So you should be able to see why this moment of meeting Hera's human form was so big to me. It wasn't about crossing paths with another human soul, or finding a romance in another. It *truly* was about all of the fabled stories and fantastical fairytales that have been written. To see Hera for the first time in Earthly form would mean I saw her for who she *truly* Is in her spiritual form. And maybe **"Is"** is an appropriate word since her most revered incarnation on Earth was as the goddess Isis. It is no coincidence that name is the word **"Is"** times two.

To say hello to Hera would be the moment we cross a spiritual threshold in the heavens – a dividing line drawn across the sands of the veil. On Earth, even if it appeared to be a passing smile, a nod, really just any type of acknowledgement of each other being alive upon this planet, that would be enough to kickstart the greatest part of all that is to come.

So what would you do?

I decided to do the only thing I knew how to do. I would go about my day as normal. I would drive to the coffee shop where I normally went to write each day, and just try do

## CH20

the same thing I always do. I'd of course need to pay attention to the spiritual signs that normally entered into my life. That part I could handle. Did I mentioned I had returned to St. Simons Island, Georgia?

...

Hello Hera. I am guessing that about now, you are starting to realize this Love Story is really about you.

...

# CHAPTER 21
## Wake Up

I cannot tell this story of meeting Hera without first telling you more information about the coffeeshop that I headed to that day. And, I suppose, you might even have questions as to how I was able to do my writing at a coffeeshop after my laptop was pronounced dead in Saratoga Springs, New York. Rest in peace my previous writing compadre!

You see, there is a very special place where I find my joy in writing while I have been located in St. Simons Island. Actually, if I'm being honest (and of course I am!), I have to say that I was desperately trying to exit out of this spot on the map since I arrived back here after my trip to New York. It would only be this particular coffee shop that has saved me. It served as a safe haven among the storm I had been weathering since I arrived back in this coastal town. But, here I was – the third time in my life I had managed to find my way back to this city despite my attempts to never return.

I can see now how there was always a purpose. It is all too clear as I sit here today. And while you may think that purpose was solely leading me to Hera, it was a bit more compli-

## CH21

cated than that. I was discovering how the entire fabric of this location was threaded into my very existence. I was innately tied to this destination regardless of how strongly my brain wanted to take me to other locations. But before we talk about that coffeeshop, let's rewind back to how I got here.

*Flashback to my final days in Saratoga May 2017*

    Nearly six months into the newfound comfort of my apartment in Saratoga, I was approaching a new pivot point in my life. The funds I had received from the buyout of my shares of my friend's company were about to run out. And while I had attempted to find other sources of income – even employment (I know. Surprise. I was flirting with giving up. Yep. Really.) – every attempt to find an answer was met with an inexplicable "No." There was no rationale. My work resume was top notch. Despite the crazy adventures in this book, by all outward appearances, my life appears as you would expect a normal person's life would look. Regarding outward appearance, I'm actually very confident in myself – albeit not vain. Just confident. I like myself, "the skin I am in," I guess you could say. I can wear my designer suits, $700 shoes, and fit in with the upper echelons of society. I know I interview well – that has always been one of my strengths. I certainly keep my hygiene in check. Case in point, I had no problem setting up dates with any girl I would desire to meet. So I knew it wasn't appearance. But you know something is amiss when you do not get any callbacks for unpaid volunteer work. Score another one for the Universe. It was divinely keeping me in check and I took notice.

# CH21

...
Hera, the Universe was always leading me back to you.
...

So when I found myself seeking answers to the next steps of my journey – whether that was just continuing on in Saratoga or taking a new opportunity – I had to take notice when my Earthly father called in the middle of that very prayer. Literally. I was praying for a sign, then my phone rang. In that call, my father offered to pay me a small monthly amount to come back home, to live in the guesthouse and help him renovate his home. Three to four hours a day was all that would be required of me. To him it was a wonderful gesture. I saw his pride, his Love in the offer. I do not want to take anything away from his gesture, for that was a wonderful expression of Love... and I saw it. I acknowledged it. I knew they did not have the finances to pay a full contractor while they were juggling retirement and getting a newly purchased farm up and running. I saw what the Universe was presenting.

But... Ugh. I did not like this proposition at all. I just didn't want to return home. However, I knew this day would one day come. My parents were about to retire. My father had purchased a farm nine hours away in Alabama and was spending twenty-eight days out of the month there getting it ready for cattle. Not to mention, he was also helping his parents tend to their own farm and family-owned businesses in their elder age. Yes. I truly am blessed to have all four of my grandparents still alive and doing well in this lifetime. I'm from a family that lives long and prosperous lives full of Light. Again, the symbolism is not lost on me.

The renovations though... that was the part I was dreading. Before my father purchased the farm, he had begun to tear apart their existing home on St. Simons Island. Even though it was a nice home, the inside had been an interim state of renovation for years. For years, the kitchen cabinets were absent of doors. The yard was overgrown. New exterior siding was in a partial state of completion. Some of it was primed. Some of it was painted. Some of it had rotted since it had been replaced due it not having been primed or painted. It was a general image of the worst kind of labor to me. But, I had to listen to the signs. In the midst of a prayer asking my Father what was next in my life, my Earthly father called and offered up a solution on a silver platter.

*Flash-forward a few weeks later to St. Simons Island, Georgia*

In late May of 2017, I found myself beginning to labor away at my new duty having returned back to St. Simons Island. The upside? As much as I wanted my daughter to experience New York for the summer with me (and she was so excited to!), it was again wonderful to have her be able to spend most of the summer with me while simultaneously be able to see her grandparents and cousins, too. I found peace in the decision I had made to return... for the summer months at least. It was the time period following the summer that really got to me.

My twelve-year-old daughter sensed it, too. She is very spiritually aware of the world and knows me all too well. Did I

## CH21

mention she is also part of a rich Greek history too? I haven't spoiled it for though. That's for her to fully remember on her own. I do think I mentioned this already, though. Either way, let's move on with this story. On the days my daughter is back with her mother, we always FaceTime. It was during a conversation in February of 2018 that she felt led to tell me that I needed to go to a coffee shop and work on my screenplay. She was emphatic that I had to return to writing and return to my screenplay. She felt confident this would also help me eventually return to my film scoring/music joy. She said very specifically, "you will meet someone when you go the coffeeshop on Friday."

Now, up to this point, I had not ventured out a single day to do any writing since returning to St. Simons Island. I figured I was just there to do the task at hand… only comically to have hurricanes destroy the work I had completed, to do it again, to have tropical storms destroy it once more, then repeat the cycle all over again. I can't be certain, but I am fairly confident that I had not even been to a coffeeshop a single day at all during the nine months of my return.

"Friday?" I asked.

"Yes Friday. You will meet someone. I know you will. I feel it." she said confidently.

"Can it be Saturday?" I asked. "I have a lot to finish up for my parents on Friday."

"Yes. It can be Saturday." she said after thoughtfully considering the options.

"And I will still meet this person?" I pressed.

"Yes. You will." she said.

As you will soon read how this situation played out, it would also not be the first time she had told me something similar and it had come true. And not only did the previous experience play out exactly as she felt led to share, it happened in divine Elijah/Jeff/Brian/Baptism/Bethlehem/Star of Bethlehem fashion. But let's review how this current type of situation had presented itself once before… in a *very* similar way.

*Flashback to Saratoga, April 2017*

After being led to begin writing a new book that went on to be called *Welcome to Being Human: An Instruction Book for Every Soul*, I was facing a tough challenge. Due to the style of writing, I wanted this new book to have fun illustrations to accompany it. I knew it was going to require several hundred playful images that assisted the story. In fact, I had written three children stories that I hoped to accompany the main adult version. The goal was to have the book be a reversible book – to have the adult version on one side and the three children stories on the other.

Since on Earth it seems to be fairly common to hear people exclaim, "Well, life doesn't come with an instruction book!" when difficult decisions have to be made, the book was intended to serve as a guidebook "for every soul." Imagine, before you came to Earth, you wrote a book that you would one day find after you arrived on Earth. The book would serve to unravel life's mysteries and bring unity to all of the chaos going on during the time it is found. For children, there would be three stories: one bedtime story for parents to read to a child,

## CH21

one for a child learning to read, and one for a child to read to his/her parents so that parents could hear a very child-like perspective to an otherwise long and detailed adult book. Anyway, not to digress, the point to be made here is I needed to figure out a solution for the art that would be required.

In a conversation with my daughter, she told me specifically to go to a specific Starbucks on a specific day and time. This was the first time she had ever offered such a specific premonition of things to come. And truthfully, she has only done this one other time... the time we will return to after this flashback is finished.

So, with date, time, and location in hand, I took my iPad to her chosen Starbucks and sat down to write. Within moments of me sitting down, a mid-twenty year old Asian man sat down next to me. There was no delay from the time he sat down until the first words left his mouth.

"Writer?" he asked.

"Yes. I am. You too?" I replied.

"Yep. Me too. But I like to draw. I do all of the artwork for my books." he replied confidently.

And while it is unimportant how the remainder of that conversation played out, just know that we spent hours at that Starbucks, went and grabbed dinner and continued the conversation until early evening. My daughter had been correct! And while he did agree to do the drawings, the end result was that I ended up having to complete the drawings myself a year later. I did allow for an entire year to pass for him to complete the drawings. However, I only received the initial sketches before contact with him went radio-silent. I'm really not sure what happened to him after those first few months passed, though I did continue to reach out to check on him. Regardless, the point here remains. My daughter shared a premonition of things to come. I believed and followed suit to discover she was absolutely correct.

*Cut back to St. Simons Island, February 2018*

Taking my daughter's advice, I set out on Saturday morning to work on my screenplay at Starbucks. While she did not specify a location, it was the only place I really knew existed for coffee on St. Simons. So, that part of my new mission seemed like a done deal. But oh was I so wrong.

"Closed for Renovations." That was the sign I was met with when I arrived at Starbucks. The entire building was being gutted and remodeled. Already it was clear the Universe was again at play. Where would I go? Having decided to voluntarily give up my phone a few weeks prior, I was now without any digital ability to find another coffeeshop, so I set out like Indiana Jones on a quest to discover my Holy Grail.

*Cut to image of a car slamming on the brakes*

Wait. What about that phone thing?

Well, even though it was not related to anything financial at the time, it probably would seem like that could be the only reason a person would go without a phone. But not me. This was again one of those extreme spiritual tasks I was led to follow. Much of the disconnection process began in the first year of this journey. It just became more extreme as the years passed. I had already disconnected from the outside world by removing all social media accounts (except for one used for marketing purposes), quit reading any news sites, and was without a data plan for my phone anyway.

My phone had seemingly already been systematically removed from my life in Saratoga before I decided to replace it. (Yes, I know… I wasn't ready to listen just yet). And, even though I was able to use a backup iPhone I still had laying around when I returned back to SSI when I could access my old personal belongings in storage (I had owned every model up through the model that died in Saratoga), the Universe took it upon itself to cause that phone to die as well. This second iPhone death occurred just after the Universe decided to invoke an initial death threat to my iPad immediately upon switching out sim cards to this backup iPhone. True story. So I took the signs and decided I must need to fully disconnect from the cellular world. So I leapt… again. I terminated my phone service and, honestly, it has been the most liberating decision I have made along this journey so far.

I now meet people in real life at places pre-planned, or by chance. Everything always works out when you are in sync with the Universe. That was the lesson and oh how fun it has been to experience this flow!

"How do I speak to my daughter?" you may ask. "What about the FaceTime thing?"

Well, I still manage to iMessage and FaceTime via my iPad, iMac, and MacBook Pro (Didn't it die? Yes. And we will get to that in a bit. This is a new baby.). So even though I have been untethered from a phone, I still have the ability to communicate when needed.

*Cut back to the main story as the car starts driving again.*

After driving around the island looking for any place that might be an inviting place to write and serve coffee, I pulled into Redfern Village – a small shopping area on the island. Success. Coffeeshop spotted. I pulled into the only available parking spot near my destination. As I pulled in I looked up to see that I was parked directly in front of a clothing store called Ariel. I smiled. There are no such things as coincidences.

Over the years, I had learned just how closely Archangel Ariel and I were related and just how much she was part of my life. In Earthly terms, she would be considered to be one of my guardian angels, though there are much more intimate, spiritual reasons for this. For one, my soul-essence contains drops of Ariel. She is a part of me, as I am a part of her. But there isn't need to discuss that further here. It is a good story though.

However, since I like having fun taking the side roads, you should take a moment to re-read the lyrics to that Train song "Drops of Jupiter." It was a notoriously popular song of the 2000s that was also universally agreed upon to contain more-or-less gibberish lyrics. Yet, truly I say unto you, that song contains more divine truth than most songs have ever known. And… it is about Jupiter to boot. Take another point on the scoreboard, Universe. Well done.

But back to Ariel. She was also one of the very first angel names given to me when these experiences started in 2011. Very specifically, Ariel and Anael were the first two angel names that were spoken aloud to me, though it was in an unfavorable context at that time. Apparently I had done something to upset them in my early spiritual travels. But again, in those early days of learning to meditate, to speak to angels, I had no clue what I was doing or what was even real. I did, however, feel crushed for months after I heard that comment. It carried an inexplicable weight for someone who was so innocent to those new light-blinding experiences. This was also written about in *The Nine*, so I won't belabor the point here.

After pulling into the parking lot, I acknowledged the symbolism and walked up the stairs to the coffeeshop. Perhaps I had been there once before, but this was the first time I was seeing it for the first time. This was all new to me. It would turn out that Ariel was adjacent to my coffeeshop destination... a destination that carried perhaps the most memorable name of all. You might wonder if this is the eventual location I first saw Hera. After all, I was supposed to meet her within the next three days. But let's not get ahead of ourselves just yet.

...

The name of that coffeeshop?
Wake Up. No. Really. That's its name.

...

## CHAPTER 22
# I Got Hit On The Head With A Hammer For You

The name of the coffeeshop should be enough to see just how intertwined the Universe is connected with each step a person takes. For me, it was a fabric in which my soul was intimately intertwined. Had this journey never began, I would certainly never have been in St. Simons Island, much less the situation I was in. I never would have seen the symbolism. Ariel? Wake Up? Really?!

"Wake Up Jonathan. Love is! Love is! Love is!" the Universe was shouting.

I thought I was looking for it. I thought I was doing all I could do. I thought I was awake! Surely... by now? Six years into this crazy battle? Obviously it was going to take a few more overtly obvious incidents to get my attention. It was like I was going to have to be hit on the head with a hammer to figure this out. Actually, check that. I was. We probably should talk about that before we get any further into the story. Don't worry. We will return to why I arrived at this particular coffeeshop and

## CH22

what happened once I arrived. That's all important, too. But so is this hammer thing. So let's visit that circumstance.

*Flashback to a couple of weeks prior. Jonathan is sitting on the edge of the roof of his parent's house. A ladder is just out of reach from his feet below. He is stuck.*

Yup. That's me. Sitting on the edge of my parent's house. I should have seen this part coming. After the summer passed, every effort I took to perform the renovations of my parent's house was being met with greater resistance from the Universe. The hurricane and subsequent tropical storms should have been the first obvious signs. They weren't. But, literally. Every task. Case in point: the ladder I used to climb onto the roof was now in an impossible position to climb down. No one was around. It would be hours until anyone would arrive home that could help. And yes, I had already terminated my phone service at this point.

That circumstance was the first of two dealing with that blasted corner of their house. There would probably have been more following this incident, but it would only take two for me. This was the first one. After the second one, there would be no more. It should only have taken one, though. In hindsight, I wish it had only taken one… well except it allows for a good story. It wasn't like these were the only signs I had received. Oh no! Not at all. This was just the most comical one that immediately preceded the final one.

What's more funny than the almighty Zeus being stuck on a roof because a ladder has shifted its location? How about the almighty Zeus being hit on the head with a hammer. How's that you say? A hammer? Did Thor come down from the skies above? Oh no! That's what makes it hilarious. Thor/Odin and his mighty hammer is just another embodiment of the mighty Zeus. It was the Universe that decided to throw a grand sign at me – it actually threw a physical hammer at Zeus.

These were the days I was just beginning to more intimately reconnect with my higher self. I was now acutely aware I was Zeus, but I was still in the midst of rejecting the idea. I'm sure that got under the Universe's skin. I also was acutely aware that I was not supposed to be doing the renovation work and instead was supposed to be focused on finishing the book I had written in New York as well as additional writings – the screenplay perhaps, or even this book. But I kept working on the house, ignoring my spiritual tasks at hand. I assume that was the final straw for the Universe. It needed to deliver a grand wake-up call to me.

I know you probably think I'm a stubborn student, and oh I suppose I was and am. But remember, I'm a Taurus – a bull of metaphorical origin. It is not a justification, rather a celestial warning for those around me as to how I am inclined to act. For better or worse, it will almost always be hard lessons that teach me the greatest strength. In this case, Love is the greatest strength of all. So, of course there would be difficult lessons in store for Ol' Zeusy. I just didn't see the hammer coming.

Literally.

And metaphorically.

CH22

So how did this hammer incident happen? Well, fast-forward to a few days after the whole getting stuck on the roof incident.

*Flash forward a few days days to the inside of Jonathan's quarters as he is getting ready to go work outside.*

Rains had subsided from the days prior and I decided this day was the day to work on installing a gutter. There wasn't much of a gutter to put up... maybe twelve feet of it at most. The only problem was that it was going to have to be installed on that blasted corner of the house that was at war with me. I didn't care. A gutter seemed harmless enough. I got dressed in my work clothes and headed out the door.

I'm not sure my rationale for the next decision, but in my infinite karmic wisdom, I decided that I didn't want to damage my hearing even though I would only be using hammer and nails rather than airguns and such. I wasn't going to be using any loud power equipment either. Nope. Just a simple hammer tapping away at a few nails. Nothing would be loud enough to justify ear protection, but my brain was telling me otherwise.

After heading out the door, I turned around, went back inside, and grabbed my sound-cannon headphones. You know the kind. These are the ones worn by runway operators at airports. They are meant to reduce the sound of a jet engine to a level that won't completely damage your hearing. It was a strange decision for me to say the least. I suppose I might have just wanted to silence the world in order to hear my own thoughts in a muffled cocoon. But either way, the decision would result in me wearing these monolithic cups around my ears while a fat, padded headband wrapped itself over the crown of my head. This decision, as bizarre as it was, might even have saved my life that day.

I set out wearing my sound-cannons and began work on the gutter. After getting the first set of nails placed, I climbed back down the ladder that was now in the location that left me stranded on the roof in the days prior. But this time, I reached the ground without a hitch. Win.

I began to fold up the ladder so I could try to move it down the house a little ways further. It was at this point the hammer I was using fell from the sky. This wasn't a tack hammer. This was a heavy duty claw hammer for framing nails which I had managed to leave sitting on top of the ladder before climbing down. Once I began to fold the ladder up, the hammer slid from the top and to the ground it began to fall.

The only problem? I was standing between it and the ground. I also had no idea it was heading my way. Clunk! Man down.

That really happened. The claw of the hammer hit my skull directly on one side of the padding to the sound cannons. The head of the hammer hit me on the other side of the padding – square in the center of my noggin. While it felt like the only part of the hammer that the padding obstructed from a direct hit was the handle, I have no doubt as I type this today that I might not be sitting here had that padding not been there. My strange karmic wisdom of wearing sound canons to protect myself from the "sound" of the hammer managed to

## CH22

save my life that day. But it wasn't about the sound... it was more like a karmic wisdom that I needed protection from the hammer itself. I just didn't understand why I might need protection from the hammer. Hindsight is always 20/20.

I was concussed and would be out of commission for a couple of weeks. I also had a gnarly, lumpy, sensitive, scarred up skull to heal. That was the final sign I needed. There could be no greater signal from the Universe to get my attention. Zeus had to be hit on the head with a hammer to realize he needed to change directions. I can laugh at it now because... well, I survived, right? The Universe must want me to stay alive, so I decided to hightail it out of my situation and move forward once again into the unknown... you know, incase the Universe decided to quit giving me lifelines due to my bullheaded ways.

It would take over a month until I felt like my head completely healed up. That first week was a woozy one! The second week was a painful one. The weeks after resulted in a super-tender scalp wherein I could barely wash my hair in the shower. Of course I did, but there would certainly be no swirling of the shampoo around to scrub my scalp. It felt like every hair upon my head was connected to an individual nerve ending. This was the sign required to get me to right my ship. It was listing heavily to one side, but I was now determined to straighten her out so I could catch a full sail of wind after the storm subsided. Though, in the immediate moment, the task at hand was weathering the storm as I was tossed about at sea.

The questions that remained in front of me for the next part of my journey would seem fairly obvious. I had a few days to contemplate them as I listed in the storm. 1) Where the heck was I going to get money to pay my child support and such? 2) If I was supposed to get out to coffeeshops and write, how would I do so without a laptop? My iMac kept me bound in my prison cell known as my parent's guest house. My iPad was a no-go for finalizing any writing projects. 3) And if coffeeshops were part of this equation, how was I going to even afford a coffee? I had just walked away from an income that was barely keeping me afloat. Yes. Finances were that tight.

And while I would have more questions like whether or not I was supposed to move, I was terrified to ask. Any rollercoaster similar to the one I had just ridden in New York nine months earlier was not one I wanted to get on again at this point... at least not while concussed. No. There still had to be a purpose for me being in St. Simons Island. I wouldn't be in this situation if it wasn't meant to be. I had to again saddle up and prepare for whatever came next. In divine fashion, my prayers began to be answered. Guidance was offered and I learned I was where I was supposed to be for the immediate moment.

The doors that opened were, of course, amazing. Within days of the hammer incident I had a small project I was asked to do by an acquaintance in Saint Simons. Of course I had to wait until I had recovered from the hammer thing before I could do her project, but it eventually afforded me the luxury to buy a new MacBook Pro to continue my writing adventures out in the real world... in a place furthest removed from the prison cell that was my parent's guest house. Now don't get me wrong, I was extremely thankful for the living arrangement I had at the time – the roof, the shower, the bed,

CH22

and all that comes with a normal state of living. It just felt like a metaphorical prison isolated like Alcatraz from the social life of the world.

Even as I write this, to this day every financial obstacle that could be presented had been overcome... albeit at the time of this writing I do only have $1.39 sum total between my two checking accounts. Throw in about $30 in a PayPal account and a little bit of cash in my pocket for gas and ordering tea at the cafe. Now we have the reality of my daily life. From wealth to... this. But I have a laptop to write, the bills are paid, a hot tea in hand, and Hera's identity is no longer a mystery. Life is good! Perfect actually. Well... it soon will be.

It might seem like this would be a scary ride, but really it is just another rollercoaster I voluntarily boarded (though it is undoubtedly the *final* rollercoaster) before receiving the grand prize and exiting off stage right on Oscar night... you know, the part of the stage where all of the behind-the-scene interviews take place and the world gets to hear the unbridled truth of the ups and downs of the journey for each victor. In a way, these words embody much of what will be recounted in that interview. But really, consider these words more like the notecard containing just a few of the noteworthy moments tucked in my jacket pocket in hopes my name is called when the nominees are presented. Oh, I know I am a nominee. That's been shared with me. And really, that is enough.

No. I'm kidding myself. I want to win! Who doesn't? So I will continue forward like a bull racing toward red, digging my hoofs in until I have given every last drop of my being for this battle of Love. Red is my destination.

...
Red is Love.
Hera, I'm running as fast as I can toward you, my Heart, my Moon.
...

## CHAPTER 23
## Christian & Noah

I suppose anything should be expected at this point in the writing. Certainly the stage has been set for the seemingly impossible. Still, that never stops me from being surprised and filled with a childlike joy on Christmas morning each time the Universe sends a token of its unbridled faith in my journey. Maybe it is just my personality. I am a jolly guy. Or maybe the Universe just likes to laugh along with me as I continue to prance around this playground in comically clumsy fashion. I'm having fun though, so either way... whatever.

*Cut to Jonathan shrugging his shoulders*

I enjoy the hurrahs and cheers from the grandstands... especially like what happened the day when I walked into Wake Up on my daughter's recommendation.

Most of the seats were taken that day except for a couple of bar-top seats facing out a window near the front of the store. Not ideal, but I could work with that. I ordered my coffee and sat down. I pulled out my iPad which now had a large crack across the glass because… well, remember that death threat I mentioned when I exchanged sim cards in my iPhone? This was one of the wounds left that day. The other resulted in my bluetooth keyboard kicking the bucket in divine style. I was now on bluetooth keyboard numero dos for this iPad.

Anyway, looking like a woefully unsuccessful writer based on writing tools alone, I began to re-read my screenplay (titled *I Am We*) to search for places I could possibly improve it. At least I was dressed nicely and didn't appear too much like a starving-artist… not that I should have cared. But I was new in this place and impressions do count.

No sooner had I pulled up the screenplay on my iPad – and I mean no sooner – than I heard someone say, "Writer?" This voice was not coming from just anywhere. There was a guy standing directly over my shoulder looking down at me and my wounded iPad.

Now I have to say, that over the thousands of times I have visited coffee shops to write, I have only had a handful of experiences where someone has approached me directly to speak… well, aside from girls who are just being friendly/flirty. But never does anyone approach for a random conversation. The only time this ever occurs with me is when it is divinely purposed – like the time in Saratoga with the writer/artist I met when I followed my daughter's guidance.

Sure, there are always other circumstances that can present themselves that create conversations. However, I'm talking about the stand-out moments where you sit down and suddenly have a human being breathing over your shoulder asking you if you are a writer. To some people, it could feel like a bit

## CH23

creepy. It is always startling if you are not expecting it. But to me, this put a big smile on my face. I turned around.

"Why yes I am." I responded. "And you?"

"I am." said the man standing upon this divinely appointed moment on the Universe's look-what-I-did-for-you timeline. "A screenwriter and author actually. It looks like you are working on a screenplay? Mind if I sit down?"

Of course I obliged. That was the beginning of a several hour conversation. We, of course, talked about writing, books, screenplays, music, my desire to score films in addition to writing. It was a wonderful conversation. It would only be in the final moments of the conversation that we would formally introduce ourselves.

"I'm Jonathan." I said.

"Nice to meet you Jonathan. I'm Christian."

*Cue the image of a record scratching to a halt.*

I could only laugh at the situation I found myself in that day. Having not been to a coffeeshop in the nine months I had been in St. Simons and only after being hit in the head with a hammer, I followed my daughter's advice and again found myself in the midst of something impossible to script. I was talking to a man named *Christian* who wanted to work with me on films, music, and writing. He filmed documentaries for Discovery Channel, was working on a new screenplay, and was also in the process of promoting a new book that CNN's Anderson Cooper was heavily promoting. Despite my quite negative viewpoint on CNN and news in general, it was great to hear (and see) substantiality to this man's career as our conversation progressed.

Our meeting wrapped up on great terms. A few weeks later I would make a trip up to New York City to bring Darra (my film industry friend) and Christian together. There were many reasons for this meeting, but the major point was that I hoped to continue building a network of beautiful souls that would desire to bring Light and Love into this world together through film. That trip was another one of those, "how am I going to pay for this?" type of moments where I wasn't sure if I had the gas money to get back. Yet, I made it back. Barely. I survived again. To boot, the meeting with Darra and Christian inspired me to write a television pilot for a sitcom about a group of demigods who have awoken to their true identities while in their Earthly forms, though absent of their powers. Most people think they are crazy, but they know their truth. They still find themselves in comical situations like Zeus living in his parent's house and such. The pilot is called *True Confessions of a Demi-God* and perhaps may even be the end result as to why Christian and I were led to cross paths to begin with. Or, maybe it was just a giant exercise to help *remember* and embrace these truths that I now hold to be self-evident. Anyway... I apologize for the side road again.

When I returned home I was literally down to less than $5 when one of my mother's friends asked me to repaint the new home she had just purchased. Ugh. I hate painting! I really do. If it isn't on a canvas, it isn't anything I would ever want to do. But I saw the gesture the Universe lobbed up at me like a softball. So I took it with all of the joy in my heart. Truly, I

## CH23

found joy in painting walls. Surprisingly. A few weeks later, I managed to be able to buy the MacBook Pro I now use to write. This all transpired a week or so before my 37th birthday, so I considered it a birthday gift from the Universe when my laptop arrived in the mail. I had to wait a few more days until my case arrived. It was at that point, I was ready to head out to the coffeeshop circuit and get back into the writing swing of things.

On my birthday and with my brand new writing machine in hand, I set out to finish my quest in editing the last book I published as well as to begin work on a couple new screenplays I had begun. One of those screenplays was simply called "*Hera.*" Yes, at this point I now knew the name of my Bride, though I still had no idea when I would ever meet her. I had been assured countless times that she, too, was in a body upon the Earth. I was even given an age range and a few other tidbits of knowledge. Nothing gave away details. It was more like hearing a sales-pitch from a friend's girlfriend who wanted to introduce you to her girlfriend. It was all lovely, fascinating, yet still seemed like a bit of a pipe-dream to me.

Anyway, not to digress. I would not see Hera that day... well, not to my knowledge at least. Instead, on my birthday I went to Wake Up, ordered a green tea, then sat down at a shared, community table. I had not even had the opportunity to take my laptop out of its case before a man sitting diagonally across from my seat said, "Writer?"

"I am. You?" I replied back, now used to how this type of divine interaction was taking place. It was like a cosmic passcode question-and-answer dialogue that was about to unlock a new message. I looked in front of the man and there was a stack of paper. He was handwriting something... all of his pages were handwritten on unlined paper in landscape orientation. I had not seen anything this ancient before. This surely was going to be interesting.

"I am." he said. "What's in the slim case? Is that your laptop?"

The conversation progressed as one would expect. I told him I was there to work on a screenplay. He told me he was working on one as well. In fact, a screenplay comprised one of the stacks of paper before him. Needless to say we hit it off really well. This conversation lasted for a couple of hours before any identifiable details really came up from either one of us regarding our work histories. Up to this point, I knew he was a writer and artist who seemed to be involved in film in some way. Then I heard it. I heard the one word I needed to hear and the only tidbit of knowledge I needed to hear to understand this divine encounter.

In a very nonchalant way, he was talking about a dialogue he once had with an un-named director. In the process of recounting this conversation, he managed to mumble out the words "when I was working on a small film called Noah." He continued on without touching upon that subject matter again.

"Wait. Did he just say Noah?" I wondered to myself. Of course I immediately associated it with the Russell Crowe film from a few years prior. If that was the case, that "small film" went on to make several hundred million dollars at the box office... hardly anything small by Hollywood standards. Then again, maybe it was some indie flick. It can be difficult to tell whether someone is being humble or really trying to not draw emphasis to a B indie movie that carried the name of a much larger grossing summer tentpole Goliath. I assumed it had to be the former. Then he mentioned the director's first name and I knew we were talking about the same film.

Don't get me wrong, this was not an "oh my gosh he works for Hollywood!" moment for me. Oh no. I always found myself in the company of friends and acquaintances that had flashy careers and dropped names. It is just how it was for me. So this wasn't anything new. I always found myself among the most precarious situations that many in life would dream to find themselves in. I always knew "that guy." Just as an example... Do you want to go to an NHL hockey game and sit in the best glass seats in the house during the biggest game of the year? There are only four of them – two sets of two along either side of the crease on the home offensive side. Most people don't realize those are the most prized seats in all of hockey. But yep, that guy was my friend and I went to dozens of hockey games that way. I think those seats were $20k a year for that pair of particular season tickets. I never paid for them though. But that was how my daughter saw her first hockey game and why she was given the game puck afterwards. I didn't orchestrate that part. Put another tick mark on the scoreboard for the Universe.

*Cut to shot of daughter being handed a game puck at the end of the hockey game.*

That was just a great surprise. The Universe always put me in the social situations that would open the best doors for me. Need an entire set of sixteen box seats for a concert free of charge? I knew that guy too. No favors required. NFL seats and hang out with the cheerleaders after? How about a date with one? She likes you. Yep. Same concept. It happened all of the time, yet it was never something that pulled me in. And about that cheerleader thing… Keep in mind that my heart had a granite casing over it. I often wonder how many sledgehammers the Universe was trying to throw my way in an attempt to take a crack at opening it up. None managed. I ignored most attempts. One girl got a good whack at it however. All in all, I share this to say that these situations were just a doorway I had the opportunity to walk through from time to time. Noah-guy would be no different.

Wait. I just realized… I Noah-guy once again! Haha. Anyway. That was a terrible joke. Hmf.

*Cut to shot of Jonathan unable to hold back a smile.*

Actually, that was a really good joke.

Now, I will say that staying in touch with anyone from those days had long been tossed from the boat of opportunity as I weathered the storm. I just wanted to share those details in this writing to demonstrate that it wasn't the Hollywood landscape or the person I was suddenly awe-struck over. It was the choice of the single identifiable reference that this man chose to drop in the midst of our conversation. We had not even exchanged names or contact information. No. The way he chose to identify himself was through a single name. It was the anchor he tossed to shore. That anchor, that name:

…
Noah.
…

Wake Up coffee had already served up a divine meeting with a man named Christian. Now I was sitting across from a man who I later found out was the storyboard artist for Noah among a long list of other Hollywood triple-A tentpole movies. If this were L.A., NYC, or Nashville, it might not be as surprising. But here, in the armpit of the South, marooned on a sulfer-smelling-shark-infested-cloudy-brown-water-definitely-not-paradise island which was located somewhere in a place farthest-from the film industry, I found myself in the shipping lane of miracles. Wake Up had delivered once again.

Think of how these situations might have looked if they had occurred in a dream. If someone told you about a crazy dream they had about going to a coffeeshop called Wake Up which was located next to a store named Ariel you would immediately be able to see the bold and obvious symbolism. In that coffeeshop your friend then managed to meet two people – one named Christian and the other who identified himself by the name Noah – both in the film industry. You see what I mean? You see where this road is leading? Results of these meetings in real life withstanding, the fact that Hope, Inspiration, Light, and Love had been served up like it was an all-you-can-eat crawfish boil in south Louisiana should warm anyone's soul... and I was born in New Orleans so it should have done so for mine. Except, I'm vegetarian... so maybe it isn't a perfect metaphor for me... or was it? I'll have to think on that one... Hmmmm.

Anyway, in seeing the significance that this particular place called Wake Up was beginning to mean to me, it should have been easy to see why this place might just play a significant role in the future days of my life. Possibly for Hera, right? Believe it or not, Ol' Stubborn Zeusy could still not wrap his brain around the heavenly vortex that surrounded this little cafe. Yes, I saw the obvious headlines that scrolled across my screen. I just didn't think I would need to consider Wake Up like a television channel. If you want to watch sports, tune into ESPN. If you want to watch news, tune into [Nope. I'm not going to support listing any news station here. You get the idea though]. Want to watch a cartoon? Tune into a kids station.

That is what Wake Up should have been to me. Want a miracle? Go to Wake Up. It apparently serves up free samples all day long! And while I did not necessarily view it as such at the time, I can now see how crazy-bull-headed I was for not paying attention to the bigger picture. I only saw red, dug my hoofs in and charged forward. I never stopped to realize there was matador waving a red cape around... or that it moved as he was leading me in various ways about the arena. For that matter, I didn't realize I was in an arena. I simply saw red. If this were a cartoon show, there could have easily been an anvil behind the red cape. In fact, I am certain there probably was from time to time. I guess if there is any consolation, though, I

## CH23

should at least be thankful I'm not colorblind. I do have that part going for me. Yay Zeus. Red.

*Cut back to "the three days" beginning on August 17, 2018*

Back to the main story at hand. Knowing I now had a window of three days and no plan or further guidance given, I decided to just go about my day as normal. I drove to Wake Up, parked in front of Ariel again, and moseyed my way into the coffee shop. I ordered a tea, sat down in my miracle seat by the door (the seat where I met Christian and always seemed to have other little miracles happen), and began to work on the new book I had started a few days prior. Only, I couldn't write. I had the worst case of writer's block possible. So mostly I just stared at my screen. The upside? Because I was not buried in writing or deep in thought, I did not miss the single biggest clue that would be placed in front of me. Oh, you are going to laugh at this...

# CHAPTER 24
# Conquering The World With A Hip-Hop Song

Perhaps I should first share why I had allowed myself to get to this level of writer's block extremity. Typically, I would never allow myself to stay idle for too long at any task. If something isn't working in an artistic expression for me, I just move on to the next idea. Hence, if I was working on a screenplay and became stuck, I would jump over to a different screenplay I had previously started. Perhaps I'd even try starting a new one. Regardless, the whole point I am trying to make here is that I allowed myself to be caught up in a state of writing confusion for most of this day – but it had a reason. Did you also catch the little comment I slid in the previous chapter about starting a new book? Wasn't I supposed to be working on screenplays and chasing the film dream? This warrants an explanation because it, too, is an important detail of this story.

*Flashback to one week prior*

# CH24

On the heels of attempting to avenge my college-driven, hip-hop producer dream where I had a song stolen from me that subsequently went #1 on Billboard's Top 100.... Wait. Let's go back a few weeks further. That part is important too.

*Flashback further to the last week of July, 2018*

On the morning following the last day I would spend with my daughter before she returned back to her mother's to start school, I woke up feeling invigorated, ready to do something big. I didn't know what. It was just one of those conquer-the-world type feelings where you knew you would be an unstoppable force with whatever task was placed before you. In typical fashion, I decided it would be a Wake Up day of screenwriting.

I was only at Wake Up for a few minutes before my friend Raymond met up with me (Raymond is actually "Noah-guy." We had become good friends at this point). As we were chatting, I realized I was not going to be getting any writing accomplished that day so I considered my options. He must have realized I was contemplating my day while we were chatting.

"What are your plans for the day?" he asked.

Without missing a bead, I said, "I'm going to conquer the world today."

He laughed. That was probably a bit unexpected. Then he replied, "Oh, really? And how do you plan on conquering the world?"

"I'm going to write a hip-hop song and attempt to unseat Drake from the top of the Spotify charts."

Raymond nearly spit out his coffee. He was both humored and intrigued. To this point we had never discussed music aside from me saying I enjoyed scoring films. All he knew about my musical side was that I had a classical, symphonic passion. All anyone ever saw of me was that I was a writer on a deeply entrenched spiritual path. To add more humor to it, he and a number of friends who I had met through him often sought spiritual guidance from me. So a hip hop song was farthest-from anything expected to cross my lips.

"I'm in." he said.

And so that was that. Zeus and Noah were setting off on a hip-hop adventure. What is more funny than that image? Well, one of my 19th century past lives was that of Camille Saint-Saëns, a classical French composer responsible for works like Danse Macabre and Le Carnival Des Animaux. Understandably, you might not recognize his name unless you are a classical music fan, though you have more than likely heard some of his songs before. I never reached the status of Mozart or Beethoven during those years, but I did succeed in many ways during that lifetime which would go on to affect modern film scores of today. Oh, yeah. Then there was that other life I lived in the classical composer world as Johann Sebastian Bach. That one you might know. But anyway, not to digress. Back to conquering the world.

Raymond and I wrote a number of songs during the following days. Would they unseat Drake? I have no idea. But it was fun and great joy was had during those days. Raymond even storyboarded about 100 screens for a music video we planned for one of the songs. Our intention was to include the storyboards in a lyric video that preceded the filming of the full video in order to create a living resume for various skills we brought to the table. Yes. We had all of this planned out! Conquer the world, right? And no, we weren't going to be rapping in the video, though I did discover my inner Lil Jon along the way. The video was going to be a cinematic experience about a girl awakening to her true identity through dancing – an identity of diamond-like perfection within.

...

Hera? Are you taking note? I still did not know the video idea was a story about your physical life on Earth. You are a dancer, right?
*wink*

...

    If nothing else, at the time it seemed our efforts were a way we could each figure out how to build a film foundation with each other. It was also during this week that we learned just how many times the events from our respective lives seemed to be mirrors for each other. It became clear that the efforts to produce a hip-hop song were just another cosmic effort from the Universe to grab my attention. Did it have it yet? Not fully. This was also "trinity eclipse month," so I did not really know exactly what to expect.

*Cut to shot of a solar eclipse*

# CH24

Yes. Trinity Eclipse Month. During a six week period in July and August, Earth would experience three eclipses. Though these eclipses were not visible from North America, this type of cosmic even affects all souls upon the Earth. It is the movement of energy upon this sphere that is affected, an energy to which every soul is bound.

The effects of these eclipses upon the soul could be seen as tantamount to washing out a paint-filled sponge. You know the experience. Even when you think the sponge is clean, you squeeze it one last time only to see paint manage to continue seeping out of its pores. When paint is involved, it almost always seems like an impossible task to clean a sponge. But this analogy is exactly what was happening for every soul upon the Earth at this time. Even the souls who thought they had cleansed their past traumas, past emotional hurdles, past life issues, or any roadblocks to Love – all souls were experiencing this wringing out of the soul. Every soul. No one was excluded.

Many people experienced physical pains, sleep issues, relationship issues, job issues, etc. Whatever issues remained – whether dormant, buried, or in the forefront – were being brought to the surface. For me, apparently it was my hip-hop trauma which I honestly did not know was an issue from my past. But truthfully, it was… and it was apparently tied to a few other traumas. All of it was bubbling up before my eyes during Trinity Eclipse Month. I saw it as we were writing our Drake-topping future hits. Let me take you back to my college years.

## CH24

*Flashback to 20 year old Jonathan as a sound engineer for a hip hop show in an Athens, Georgia club*

Yep. That's me. As an aspiring music producer, while in college I took a job at a local club (and subsequently a local music studio) to learn the ways of sound engineering. But in this moment, I found myself cast into a landscape of hip-hop acts and jam bands... neither genre of which I really had on my personal playlists at home. But my job demanded the most of me and I enjoyed it. I was learning the ropes... and was quickly being cast into one celebrity interaction after the next. These were the days of Destiny's Child, before Beyonce would step out and become Beyonce. That show was one of the first shows I worked actually – but it was on a larger field rather than this particular club. Watching Beyonce trip and almost fall mid-act, only to share a laugh with each other over her priceless reaction mid-performance – those little things that happened while sound engineering... they made every day worth it even if the genre wasn't for me.

But returning to the club, I found myself building an engineering fanbase among Atlanta's growing hip-hop movement. These were the days of Outkast, Juvenile, Ludacris Petee Pablo, and the re-emergence of silly staples of rap's past like that song Tootsie Roll. And then there was Bubba Sparxxx. He was a "country white boy rapper." That was the marketing behind him at least. A gold album under his belt, he was fast-tracking up the charts.

He performed a couple of times at the venue where I sound engineered. I eventually became friends with his management and thus my journey into writing hip-hop songs began. While I was only asked to do a few remixes for him, I was a young up-and-comer hungry for stardom. I wrote three tracks (instrumental only) that I thought were worthy of sharing with him. I gave two of them to his management team for approval before they were to be directly shared with him. I was still perfecting the third one. I also had a number of discussions regarding my approach for his second album. I wanted desperately to produce him. Keep in mind that Timbaland (e.g. one of mainstream music's most revered producers) had produced his first album. I had absolutely zero chance of this happening for me, but I tried. Young Zeus tried his mightiest.

I gave Bubba's management team insight on the path he should take, how he should take the country roots a bit deeper in other ways and basically gave him the blueprint for his next album. Then, one day, they just vanished. The entire management team fell off the radar for several weeks. No replies to texts. No phone calls. Nothing. It was a bit disconcerting because all of my studio equipment was setup in his basement to which I suddenly had no access.

However, I did eventually hear back. It would turn out they had travelled to New York to record his next album. Nice. It would have been great to have gone along, but I soon came to realize why I wasn't invited. I played it off really well though.

"Oh. That's awesome. Who did you record with?" I asked curiously.

"Timbaland again." Chad (Bubba's assistant manager) said.

"Oh. That's cool. What is your first single going to be?" I asked somewhat disheartened.

Chad smiled. He handed me a CD with all of the newly recorded tunes. He said, "The one that sounds like yours."

I didn't think much of the comment at that particular moment. But when I listened to this new compilation of songs, it was more than obvious. It was clearly my song... just Timbaland-ized. Here I was, twenty years old with zero way (or financial ability) I could go about resolving this wrong. And not only was the song just taken without credit, it went on to chart #1 and help his album receive one of the highest aggregate critical reviews of any hip-hop album from that decade. And yes, the entire album was built around my blueprint and vision for his sophomore release. That song name?

...
Deliverance.
It was the album name as well.
...

It would be sixteen years later during the time of this writing that I would catch the symbolism of the song and album name. It would also be the trigger to releasing the last remaining trauma still haunting me during the cleansing period of the Trinity of Eclipses.

# CHAPTER 25
# Hallelujah

I can't make this stuff up. Sometimes I wish I could. It would only be during this Trinity of Eclipses that I would realize my whole "conquer the world through hip-hop" thing was the way I was coping with that particular past trauma. And, it was only as we began to write lyrics for our new songs that I stumbled back over the word "deliverance." It was then that I saw it... the overtly obvious neon flashing sign that in-and-of-itself was the most blatant symbolism of the musical side-quest part of this journey. I missed it for sixteen years. Deliverance. It was always going to be about Deliverance.

*Cut to neon flashing sign with the word "Deliverance"*

In the days of the Trinity of Eclipses I would find my release of this past trauma and discover a few others along the way. For Bubba, I saw the glory I was able to help provide him through both the blueprint for the album and the basis for his sophomore album's lead single. Sophomore albums are difficult, so I saw the goodness I provided to him, regardless if I felt

## CH25

wronged at the time. Truly a soul can never be wronged, for all humans are children on a playground. It is just learning to gain this perspective we are all in this together – including seeing myself as a child among other children – to finally be able to overcome the past hurt. Every step forward can then be built on the wisdom gained from that interaction, though the hurt must be released.

In hindsight, I now kind of wish I had given Bubba the third song I recorded. It was called, "Bubba's Hoedown" and had a complete hip-hop fiddle line-dance thing in the middle of it. Think about it... "Bubba's Hoedown?" Get it? *Hoedown?* Ha. I can only imagine the lyrics that would have been written to that track. That title makes me laugh today. There couldn't be a more appropriate double entendre title for a country-influenced hip-hop song.

*Cut to clip of Zeus line-dancing to "Bubba's Hoedown"*

As it would turn out, other past music-career wrongs bubbled up during this time as well. Around the time of the Bubba Sparxxx incident, I had also formed a band in which I hand-picked every player among Athens, Georgia's best. The music was along the lines of 10,000 Maniacs, starring an amazing singer songwriter I had recently discovered and began producing. Her name was Cyndi Harvell. Our band instantly had a following of hundreds per show (which was huge in terms of local bands). Within our first few months together, we entered the Battle of the Bands my club was hosting. And while we officially won, we were not allowed to receive the prize due to how it would look to the other competitors. So the award was given to the runner-up under the pretense that they won outright. And, really, they were *very* good! If we had not truly won, they were every bit the deserving victor.

However, my band became angry at me. Up until the moments it became evident we won the competition, I had been told by the club owners that it was of course possible for us to win. Never trust the words of a club owner. The venue owner just didn't expect our crowd or following to actually be big enough for us to win. That was a difficult conversation to hear. "Hey. You guys are the victors, but we decided that we can't give it to you." Record contract lost. Yes. That was what was on the table for the victor.

It wasn't long after that I was kicked out of the band, but it wasn't for drama reasons that you would expect or try to guess. Oh no. I was very close to Cyndi, but never desired to have a relationship with her. I did not know that our drummer, Brian (Yes. This was yet another Brian involved in a divine moment in my life), was falling in love with her. Love does funny things to people. The Earthly version of it causes humans to go into self-preservation mode, to eliminate any competition, to clear a path to the desired destination. That is exactly what happened to me. I was viewed as "competition" by him and subsequently kicked out of the very band I had created. Of course it didn't sit well with other band members. The bass player left shortly after. A few shows later and the band completely dissolved. Brian and Cyndi continued on as a percussionist, singer duo adventure. As far as I know, today they are married and still performing as a duo together.

# CH25

At the time, I was crushed. I held that anger inside for a long time. I thought I had overcome that particular trauma, too – yet it bubbled up during this Trinity of Eclipses as well. I took some time to seek out what there was to explore in that situation. It turns out I missed the most obvious part. Brian and Cyndi fell in love, got married, and lived a life together that was purely founded on their love in each other. They were happy, even if I was not. Considering the majority of married friends from my past were introduced to their partners by me, I didn't quite see the significance. I recognized I was a catalyst of sorts for Love Stories. It was just another part of my life, right? Yet another couple that found love. Why would that be important?

It turns out, I *was* still harboring a bitterness. Further soul-searching would lead me to the conclusion that this bitterness could only exist if I had yet to truly find Love (with a capital L), to *truly* accept it as part of my Being. I could not be upset at that incident. Those two lovebirds found love! But, I was on a quest for more than that. I was on a quest for the most Ancient Love. I was on the quest for the Love of my Bride. I thought I had found it, I thought I had found her in spirit – and perhaps I had, but I was wincing at the brightness of the Light of her Love as we stood on the grand stage. My eyes were still closed causing me to nearly forget where I was standing. While my lips were locked in the tenderness of hers I was just now beginning to realize what was really happening. I'm locked in a kiss? Really? Oh yeah! My Bride! Where am I though? The Wedding? I was just beginning to overcome the Brightness of the Light from that moment. Forgiveness found.

And then came the release of the incident of my foray into country music. Just a year or two following those incidents, I was married and living in a condo on St. Simons Island. I know, this place again, right? What is it about this place?! Anyway, my brother-in-law came by late one night and asked if I would be willing to record a fellow caddie of his (they worked as golf caddies at Sea Island). He explained this person did not have any songs recorded and he wanted me to record one song to take with him as his demo to Nashville. I learned that I would only have the evening to work on the song since his friend, Kip, would be moving to Nashville first thing in the morning. So, of course, I accepted.

Kip came over, I recorded an acoustic song. That is all he wanted. He just wanted an acoustic version of his tune. I told him I'd deliver it to him before he left town in the morning… and oh I did. I did not sleep at all that night as I plowed through a full production of his song. I was determined to sign him as my first country artist to produce. I was willing to double-mortgage our condo and leverage any financial position I could to see it through. I saw his Light.

He rejected the contract offer (probably smart in hindsight), but was thankful for the recording. A year later, my wife and I would move to Nashville to continue the chase of music. I'd go on to reconnect with Kip there, write songs with him, record, and produce songs for him. I helped him in any way I could… actually so much that it became an issue in my marriage. Even though I was only spending a few hours a week during my non-slave-working hours to pursue this dream, those hours proved to negatively affect the relationship with my wife (even if she claimed that she wanted to see success in that avenue for both of us). So I respected her happiness before mine and told him I would be unable to further record him. I saw my situation as the 40+ hour work week being purely for her. I certainly did not want to be doing that line of work, but that was her request. So how could 3-5 hours of music for me be so wrong? Anyway, let's not blur the issues that arose here.

The story here is that Kip went on to be a successful country artist with #1 hits, a successful touring career, a five album record contract, and the life he always desired. I was always promised that once he got his record contract that he would put a song of mine on one of his later albums, and perhaps that will still happen. His career is far from done. But, I should say that he is sitting on a number of sure-fire chart toppers (not written by me if you are curious) should he ever decide to release them. I'm still not sure what he or his label are thinking there. *Hallelujah* is the first one that comes to mind. Gosh that song is… just chills.

But – point being – I apparently still harbored emotions from those situations too. Perhaps I wasn't ever wronged per se, but the emotional toll my soul had experienced from each of these life lessons in the music industry had scarred me from seeing Love for what it Is. There were no other artists I helped. It was only a handful (and a handful of times at that), and only ones that saw grand success. I helped Kip. I gave him the only song he had to pitch in his beginning days. I gave him albums worth of additional productions of his songs, and songs that were both his and mine. But above all, I helped him find Love. It is only today I feel at ease, but first had to come the release during the Trinity of Eclipses. The name of that first song I helped him record to kickstart his career goes oh-so-perfectly with the name of the one song I hope he one day releases. These two songs could serve as the book ends to this Love Story I am writing in these pages for you, Hera. I Love you so much. Those song names?

...

This Is How It Ends
Hallelujah

...

# CHAPTER 26
# Might As Well Address The Pop Genre Too

Following the release of traumas from the hip-hop, folk, and country genres, I suppose it would only be appropriate to mention that this series of events brought the release of a trauma from the pop genre as well. We will be quick on this one. I apparently had some built up frustration at Gavin DeGraw. Yep. Another well known name.

On the heels of my divorce that occurred a couple of years after the last Kip recording session, I sought out new music to help me cope with my sadness. I ended up purchasing whatever the name of Gavin DeGraw's latest album was at the time. I only knew one song by him, but took the leap. It was a great album. I listened to it non-stop. It was manly enough to not be judged by my friends while I was actually using it to cope. I never let my friends see me vulnerable – like when I would go watch the latest sappy romance movie releases on the Big Screen by myself on Sunday afternoons. But that was the type of stuff that I did. I admit it. Ol' Zeusy liked watching girly-movies like *Time Traveller's Wife* and *How To Lose A Guy In 10 Days*. There's one for the history books fellas.

That said, the album from Gavin DeGraw carried me through my new found rookie year of being single again. I rocked it out, windows down, songs blaring. Then came the day that my daughter and I were driving around town and I was listening to this album. She innocently had no idea what she was saying to me, so there was no anger or sadness from the emotions I felt within about her comments. But it was in that moment, she told me how much her mother loved that album. Apparently Gavin DeGraw was one of my now ex-wife's favorite artists.

*Cut to the image of a pin dropping, no sound of course.*

And that was that... or so I thought. I no longer had the desire to listen to Gavin DeGraw. But you know the Universe seems to have a way of bringing humor to any situation that involves Ol' Zeusy. This would be no exception. It just wasn't obvious at first.

As I began the rookie year of my one-date-and-done dating life escapades where I would not even kiss the girl (No, there would be no Disney song with Sebastian and Flounder singing along to a couple in a canoe while flamingos danced alongside crocodiles on a romantic moonlit night), I began to notice something very curious occurring in all of my dating scenarios. Two names always came up in conversation. These names: Denny Hamlin (the NASCAR driver) and... Yep! Gavin DeGraw.

# CH26

"Why were these two names coming up?" you may wonder. I know I did. Surely that seems like a curious combination of people to bubble up in conversation over and over again with the girls I would take out. Okay. So in order to remain Faithful and True, I should say *most* of the time these names came up without reference to the other. However, there were the exceptionally well-scripted moments by the Universe where both names would come up in the same conversation. I began to realize that every girl I went out with would always mention one of these two people.

*Pause.*

*As I write this, a Little Mermaid medley started playing in my headphones. You've got to be kidding me, Universe! No I do not have anything relative to Disney on my playlist right now that could have triggered that recommendation. I suppose this is due to the medley I added to my playlist from the other day (you know, that Wedding one that popped up while I was writing?). But Little Mermaid? Really? Just after that reference above? Okay. Let's return back to the chapter at hand.*

"What was going on with those dates?!?!" Well, I will tell you. Somehow the Universe thought it would be funny for me to find my way to the exact same dating pool that these two individuals swam in. And nope, they did not live in Nashville. This was one of those moments that could only have been orchestrated by the Jolly Man himself. Apparently America's most eligible bachelors were Gavin DeGraw, Denny Hamlin, and Zeus… only everyone knew me by my Earthly name, Jonathan. No, I am not trying to demonstrate any arrogance in saying this. Oh, farthest from it! I just have no other way to humorously explain the situation of finding myself – a fragile, broken, freshly divorced technology consultant, living in a farm-town north of Nashville – in the same dating circle as two other men with celebrity status who did not even reside in the area. It was like a great cosmic prank was playing out in real-time. It did not make any sense to me then. Keep in mind my spiritual journey had not yet begun either.

It got to the point that when I would decide to pursue dating a girl beyond the first date, conversations would become more surreal. Here is an example... no exaggerations, no embellishments:

"Hey. So I will be out of town next week, but when I get back, let's go to a hockey game." the anonymous girl would say.

"Awesome. Sounds good. Where are you headed?" I'd ask.

"Oh, an old friend of mine that I met when he was in Nashville invited me out to California for the week." she'd say.

"Oh cool. Anyone I know?" I'd ask blissfully unaware where this situation was headed.

"Well, do you know [so-and-so]? No? Oh. Well he introduced me to Gavin DeGraw and we've been friends since. I think he likes me, but we are just friends." she'd say.

At first, I laughed to myself at the comedy gold taking place. Then it got to the point where I could fill in the blanks with the women I took out. I even tried to head off the eventual train-wreck that was coming. On first dates I'd pretend to know someone that was friends with one of those two guys.

## CH26

"Oh you know Gavin?" she'd say. "We dated for a while, but it didn't work out."

Or I'd hear, "Oh yeah. Denny! I love him. He always invites me out to his races."

Universe – this is my message to you. Ha. Ha. There. I've laughed at it now. Gavin? Denny? To both of you two men, I tip my hat good sirs. We at least seemed to identify the same melody and heartsong of these women. I will however say that these incidents did contribute to my eventual abandonment from dating in Nashville as I allowed the granite casing over my heart to further set and harden. Granted, I would much rather have experienced these types of moments rather than situations like when an NFL Titan roofied me because he wanted to talk to the girl I was out with. He wanted to take me out of his field of competition and quite literally did. Oh, what a rookie year it was for me! I have so many "remember when" stories to tell from those years, but let's skip those for now.

No, the irony of the Titan is not missed by me now. How could it be? It is so obvious in hindsight! However, I couldn't quite possibly see the irony at the time. Tennessee's NFL football team was named the Titans. A Titan went to war with me. Remember that whole Titans vs Olympians story from mythology – you know a little something called the Titanomachy where this here Zeusy overthrew the Titans (of course with great assistance from my fellow Olympians)? Yeah. So it only makes sense I had to release these parts of my past as well; to see them for what they were – part of the humor and wit the Jolly Guy wanted to write into the script on my quest in becoming Love once again.

Music Industry, your points on the scoreboard were numerous. My score remained a goose-egg... blanketed by your incessant will and cosmic pranks. Well, at least that is how it would appear right now. But I have found forgiveness, release, and joy again. I found Love that is stronger than the blows dealt to me along these squabbles on the battlefield for Love. Just wait and see the outcome brewing in these words. Oh, you will see. You will see.

...

Hera,
This is getting back to you. I promise. The stage has to be set for you to see what is to come.

...

# CHAPTER 27
# From Music Avenger Back to Author Then Back to You

    I know it may seem like a bit of a detour down memory lane with all of these side-stories about music, but they are of most importance. You see, every past experience builds the present moment which, in turn, will go on to build the future. Too often people assume that a simple "I forgive you" or "Oh, it's okay. Don't worry about it." will serve as the release from hurt and pain. But *truly* I say unto you, every negative emotion felt is *truly* an emotion founded upon a past hurt that has yet to be released. Think about it. How could a person who has become Love ever be hurt? The only possibility could be if Love has been wronged to such a degree that Love has to counteract the negative force at hand. Jesus flipped a table, right? This doesn't mean that anger is okay or appropriate. But True anger can only arise in the defense of Love (true Love with a capital L). And this type of anger will never bring harm to another. Oh no! This anger is only an immediate awareness that your Love has to shine brighter and more strongly than it ever has before to extinguish the darkness trying to creep into your world. No force or harm can be brought upon another in Love. And this is the tricky part. It is only when you reach a state of knowingness and re-mergence with Love that this state of Love can *truly* be understood.

So you can see that the release of any past trauma would be important. In my case, I was a music avenger returning back to being an author, which was leading me back to you, Hera. But… Oh. Hold up. We were still in the midst of explaining why I had returned to writing a new book rather than working on the screenplays I had already begun and chasing the film dream. Remember? Before we took the music-avenging side-road, we left off with me experiencing writer's block at Wake Up, sitting in my miracle seat, knowing I had a window of three days before I would meet Hera's Earthly form.

That writer's block? Well, it came in divine timing… of course. But while I was sitting there experiencing it, it felt like a giant question mark was blinking at me from the cursor upon the digital white canvas blinding me from my laptop screen. Why was I even trying to write a book again? What led me to this moment?

*Flashback to a week prior to August 17, 2018*

On the heels of avenging my college-driven, hip-hop producer dream, I thought I had finally emerged from the cast of any remaining shadows encumbering me. I felt as if I was basking in the full glory of the morning sun. Even though more work would be required on the music I had worked on, this feeling was raw. It was new. It was the feeling of release. The content of the music did not matter. The results did not matter. The exercise had only been an exfoliating scrub of my soul, complete with a facial and cucumber eye peel. Throw in a laser rejuvenation process as well. I felt reborn.

It honestly felt like I had won the lottery. I was racing toward Love as if there was nothing but red in sight. But, of course, the wit and jolly of the Universe came to play again.

"Dream big!" the Universe said. Seriously. That is what it said.

So I did. I knew I was being led to start taking the next steps on my journey in a similar way to how my transition to Fort Lauderdale took place. Perhaps it would be in an even grander style. There would be no more New York suffrage-like moments this time. This I knew. I had been shown the general location in the United States where I was being led. And while it is a place farthest from the ocean, I found joy in knowing this was my next location. Maybe it was even my final destination. After all, I knew that the end of this seven year battle could only last until November 24, 2018 at the latest. This was certain. I knew there was some form of an Event brewing for all of the world to see and experience. There could be no alternative as far as prophecies go. Everything else had played out without question. In this I have no doubt. A beach soul I may be, but this next place I was being led was the music in my soul returning me back to where I belonged once more.

So when I was asked to dream, I did. I searched online for houses beyond my wildest imagination. I hunted through locations just as I did before my transition to Fort Lauderdale.

There were a number of houses I found that seemed perfect, but one stood out above the rest. I couldn't put my finger on it at first, but it would take a day of prayer for me to see just what it was I saw in it... Love.

Of all the houses I found, this one was the embodiment of Love. It was warm. It was soft. It was everything I could ever desire for a family. And, oh yes, the cost was exorbitant. I had an anemic bank account, terrible credit, no job by any lender's standards, and no reason this should be a consideration. It mattered not. I was instructed to dream big, so I did. I studied the pictures. Every aspect of the house was built on a foundation of Love. I saw it. Even the living room had a large painting that said the word "Love" over the fireplace. I saw myself standing with my Beloved Hera from the heavens. We were happy. I hoped this house was the place we would spend all of our days forward should I meet her on Earth. I could see my daughter with us. I could see a future family running throughout this great structure of Love. It was everything for which I could have ever dreamed. And then, as I was closing out the web browser before laying down to meditate I saw the address: 5304.

If you've learned anything about me over all of the books I have written, you certainly will know the significance of the way I see the Universe's communication to me through numbers. Humanity's destination is the fifth dimension, aka heaven, aka Love. To see 5304 was a sign of the divinest kind. 304 was the number bestowed upon each location I had been led with each previous adventure (as discussed in the earlier chapters). I knew this house was for me. So I did the only thing

I could think of. I prayed. I meditated. I committed three days of my life to a near-constant state of meditation. It was my commitment to the Universe in learning how to receive and how to manifest. For nearly three days I stayed in a state of euphoria as I saw my life in this house. I lived a life in this place. I was convinced the answer would arrive at the end of these three days... at least that is what I had been shared from my higher self. It was only in the final moments of the third day that the dream started to collapse. It was something I could only describe like the scenes from the movie Inception. Everything that seemed so true, so real – everything I thought was to become my Earthly reality started to crumble around me during the meditation. I couldn't stop it. I felt helpless.

All of this was a new experience to me. The three day meditation concept was new. I had fasted for three days before. But this was the first time I spent fully in prayer. The manifestation of a dream thing was new. And certainly, the crumbling was new as well. No, there were no drugs used. These are how experiences are for me. Truly meditations had become much more intense in these summer days. However, there were also many days that I couldn't find a calm point for meditation at all. But the moments when I did, however brief, were becoming more intense. So why was it crumbling?

I heard Zeus's voice. "You did well, but you should dream bigger!"

I was stumped. Miffed. I brought myself out of the meditation and casually checked my email. I noticed I had just received an email from Zillow that corresponded with the exact point in time the crumbling began in my meditation. I scanned through the email. Then I saw it. "Homes no longer available." There was my house listed – *the house*. It had not sold, it had just been suddenly taken off of the market. What the heck was going on? It seemed so perfect, so divine. There was so much Love in that particular house. I felt it. I wanted it. I could see it. What did Zeus mean by saying, "dream bigger?"

By all Earthly standards, I couldn't afford an overnight stay in a Motel 6. The house I had found was not only worthy of a successful CEO's salary, but it would likely require five or six times its value in extra cash to produce enough annual interest earned to cover property taxes, maintenance, and home expenses. It wasn't a measly dream at all! But I did see the symbolism. The house was Love, the house was me. The house represented everything I desired within this human form. This wasn't just about a physical house. This wasn't anywhere near the biggest or best house available of the lot. It was just the one that embodied Love. To me, that made it the best... no questions asked. But to the voice of my higher self, I could go bigger in my dreams.

Crushed and confused, I spent the afternoon deep in thought. Had I compromised at all? If so, where? What was I missing? What limit had I placed on my dream? The last questions turned out to be the best one to ask, but it took some time to ask myself that very question. I chatted later that evening with my daughter. I explained to her what happened to see what she had to say about it. She's so beautiful with her answers. I explained that this was definitely part of my "final exam" on this graduate course on becoming Love, to see Heaven and Earth merge as One. She agreed. She knew this too. It was something she and I had both been shared in various visions and experiences. She also had been blessed to witness countless unbelievable stories when we were together.

My daughter said, "Well, if this is your test, maybe there is still a final question."

"What do you mean?" I asked. I truly couldn't fathom an answer that would supersede the reality that I saw vanishing away before me.

"Well on my tests, I usually turn over the last page and there is a writing prompt."

I stopped her. She didn't know what she had said, yet it had been said. The truth was undeniable. To her, she was describing the "dream big" questions I had been given during meditation as tantamount to the questions that would be answered just before flipping over the test to the final page. And then she said the big one: "writing prompt." Her wisdom is beyond her age.

I don't even think she realized the significance her words meant to me. Or maybe she did. She and I had each received countless visions over the course of this year regarding "one more book I would write." Though they are all great stories to recount, I'll just share a brief overview of Georgia's dreams here. The others you can read in the journals I will eventually release from the time period February 8, 2015 to present day.

### March 31, 2018
*Georgia had a dream that I published a book in August.*

***April 7, 2018***

*Georgia dreamed that I would publish a book in August. She saw that I had an overdue fee at a library of $3000. This fee was charged at $0.14 a day since I was so late. What is interesting about those numbers is that works out to about two and a half years, which is roughly the amount of time since I wrote and published my last set of books.*

***[Summer]***

*Georgia dreamed that I would have a book written on 8/8.*

So, you can see how even if I claimed experiences were Faithful and True solely from my side, the Universe had seen to it that I would hear these truths through the voice of another as well. Now, you may think it might be a self-fulfilling prophecy since she shared this ahead of time, but as of August 7, 2018, I had no expectation of starting a book. It would take the completion of the hip-hop avenging sessions on 8/8 to be the trigger for the "dream big" meditation weekend. which would in turn trigger her to make the comment about "the writing prompt" as the final question on the exam.

Good thing there was someone there to ask for help I suppose. Right? I took her advice and immediately began an effort to write about the experiences I have had since the last books ended. I knew it was time to bring this six plus year journey to a conclusion through one final book. I did not know how. I wasn't quite sure how this book would be written. Even in the beginning it felt like throwing literal darts at the wall as I began to write the chapter "Darts" which showed up near the

# CH27

beginning of this story. And then came the moment I was shared I would meet Hera within three days.

Of course writer's block set in! Why wouldn't it? Did this book start correctly? How was that meeting going to fit into the context of all that I had to write? If I was going to meet Hera, what was I supposed to look for? What would be the signs? Would I get it wrong? This had the potential to be the very worst question that could possibly be asked. What if I thought she was a blonde and she was a brunette? What if she was twice my age and I didn't pay her any attention? What if she was half my age and I certainly did not pay her any attention? You can see my conundrum. On August 17, 2018 I set out to write in my miracle seat on at radio station Wake Up hoping to hear a divine message served up like public service notification.

Hang on to your hats folks. This is where it starts to get really good. For, as I sat there staring blankly at the cursor flashing on my screen, she walked in.

No. Not Hera. But this "she" was going to be important. Follow along.

## CHAPTER 28
## Save The Date

I paid her no attention initially, but at least I took notice. Who was I talking about? Who is this woman that entered into my life that was going to lead me to Hera? Well, remember how I voluntarily became a passenger in my "miracle seat" hoping the Universe would give me a divine sign? Well, it could only have happened in this miracle seat. Let me tell you why.

The seat I chose was the seat closest to the entrance to the coffeeshop. At times, it was the type of situation you would find yourself hopping up five or six times in a row to open the door for people who were carrying packages to and from the kitchen. Sometimes, an elderly person would need help. Then again, on other days the seat was just a silent cocoon, perfect for writing. This seat was situated at a bar-top window-sill so the outside view of Redfern Village could bring inspiration to a writer's mind. I often found it more inspiring to stare out the window while thinking about the next words I would write rather than stare at a flashing cursor. This was one of those days.

## CH28

I almost would have missed her if it were not for the fact I was sitting by the door which, in turn, gave her three separate chances to catch my attention. Who is *she*? Actually, I still don't know. Let's call her Agent Mikayla who works for the Secret Angel Service. I consider S.A.S. to be a good acronym since the Universe seems to be full of sassy wit and humor with its grand gestures. So, let's go with that.

As I sat engulfed in writer's block, staring hopelessly out the window, Agent Mikayla walked up and stood next to me. Why? I wasn't sure at first. I assumed she was going to strike up a conversation. That was really the only option. It was a situation that seemed to almost always present itself when I sat in this seat. Instead, though, she reached down on the ledge of the window sill and picked up a hand full of post-card sized marketing flyers. She studied them for a moment, then put them down rather boisterously. I figured she was trying to get my attention. She had it. Was this Hera? I heard the voice of Zeus inside.

"No. That's not her." he said.

I promptly went back to "ignore mode" as I tried to overcome writer's block. But, she wasn't leaving. She picked up the post-cards again and fumbled through them. She was obviously trying to get my attention. Maybe she wanted me to speak to her. You know the game. The girl stands near a guy long enough and finds reason to linger, sending off every social queue imaginable so he will certainly say something to her.

Nuh-uh. I wasn't budging. I was going to pass my test. If she wasn't Hera, she wasn't for me. This wasn't even a challenge mentally or emotionally. I had not even pursued dating anyone at all since my Wedding Day/Baptism nearly three years ago. I was faithfully waiting for Hera, though back then I never knew if I would ever really see her in Earthly form. I decided to increase security and man-up the defenses to my heart's fortress for these three days as I awaited for a divine sign. But here was my sign and I was sitting there clueless what was occurring. Yay Zeus.

She once again put the post-cards down. She picked them up once more and repeated every action again as if I was witnessing a real-life instant replay. Rinse. Repeat. Once again she picked up the cards. This was the third time and now it was getting awkward. Not budging, I figured she would get fed up with the chase due to my non-reactions. She forcefully placed the stack of cards back down one more time. This time, though, she tapped her finger on the stack of cards three times to get my attention before she walked out the door apparently flustered at my inattention.

At this point I was slowly considering that this girl may have been one of Radio Station Wake Up's local deejays. Deciding I had missed an opportunity due to my obstinance (bull, remember?) and feeling my immovable writer's block's foundation becoming even stronger, I decided to change locations. To Palm Coast I would go, get another hot tea and try to write from a new location. But, before I left, curiosity got the best of me. Of course I noticed the girl tap her finger on the stack of marketing materials three times. I think subconsciously I was really just scared to find the breadcrumbs leading to Hera. In the moment though, I was hunkered down in my fortress of self-preservation mode so I would not have to face the potential

## CH28

of this whole "meet Hera in three days thing" not really being true.

Why would I doubt? Oh, I didn't doubt. I was just fearful that even if I followed every clue over the three days, that I would wind up no closer to Hera. I feared I would learn in the days following that I missed her and would have to set out on a new quest again. Rinse. Repeat. I was getting tired of it, really. Anecdotally speaking, it would be like a straight A student (okay, maybe B+) cramming for the final, being confident in his studies, but choosing to stop at the door of the classroom, rolling himself over with his back against the wall, looking up at the sky and saying, "Please no. Please no. Please no. Please no. I'm afraid I'm going to fail." That was me. The sad thing is I knew it too. So, before I left, I decided to grab one of those post-card marketing materials for whatever reason this girl wanted me to see, slid it in my bag and headed to Palm Coast.

I pulled into Palm Coast, found a seat and began staring at my screen again. Now keep in mind I had attempted to write chapters for this new book over the previous days, so it wasn't like the entire document was blank. Flashing away the cursor went. I looked down in the bottom left of my screen. The word count meter read 6,666. Ugh. I really can't make this stuff up. I do not know why I did not notice this before. But here I was now being reminded about fear by its very numeric signature. Put another tick on the board for you, Universe. I decided to move the word count meter up and away from that devilish number. It didn't matter if the words were gibberish. I typed away for a few minutes then pulled the post-card out of my bag.

## CH28

It turns out Agent Mikayla had left her calling card. Actually, I am not sure if the girl standing there was named Mikayla or not, but the marketing materials had the contact information for a "Mikayla" printed on the bottom left corner of the card. At first I assumed that was her purpose in getting my attention and that I was right in avoiding conversation. But then I saw it. And, no, it wasn't the first thing I read on this card. Willful negligence I suppose. But there it was. In giant bold lettering across the top of the post-card – pretty much the entire intent of having this thing printed – were the words "Save The Date."

Now, clearly I tend to demonstrate a lack of acceptance in the signs the Universe tosses my way. I will create every reason why something isn't rather than accept that it Is. Then again, maybe this is what makes me great at this game called Earth. But now we were playing with fire. This was the final exam. This was connected to the red. This was Love at stake.

I studied the card. It gave a date of Sunday (two days away), a time (3:00 pm), and a location (the porch, Wake Up). Okay. Maybe this was just a marketing thing. Or, maybe it was a time and location I needed to be somewhere. At worst, I decided that I would go there if I had not met Hera by that point. At best, the deejay at Radio Station Wake Up served up another grand miracle… because, guess why? No really. Guess. The logic was not missed on me.

The *only* time a person person receives a formal "save the date" invitation is when it comes to weddings and baby showers. Clearly I wasn't having a baby, but even that analogy could still fit with the whole "baby being born" concept written about in the Bible. It was also an analogy I used in the third book of *The Nine*. As I spoke about the wedding taking place in that book, I talked about "the prince being crowned," and likened it to a baby crowning from the birth canal on its way into the New World.

So be it an analogy to a baby shower or wedding (I preferred the wedding analogy myself), a "Save the Date" invitation was the most obvious sign I could have received. It was as specific of an answer as I could receive. But you know Ol Zeus was going to doubt. He was going to look for any reason why it couldn't be that easy.

*Cut to black screen with bold text: "Spoiler alert: It was"*

Being imbued with a new potential for Love and new knowledge to boot, I was now inspired to write. I tried to plug away, but the Universe wasn't having it that day. While I listened to my music in order to drown out the table of older ladies gathering to celebrate an early Friday happy hour, my music suddenly cut out. Where did it go? I didn't know. I knew it was the Universe knocking again. I tried to keep typing, hoping music would once again fill my headphones. But it didn't. Not only did music not return, but the voices of the ladies became louder. Then the words came.

"My daughter just took a job at Lucas Film. She was working in the streaming side of Netflix, but was recruited over to Lucas Film. She's a huge Star Wars fan too, so that worked out well." said one lady who was obviously proud of her daughter.

Welp. Here we go again. This little island farthest-from Hollywood had once again sat another film-industry potential right in my lap. And, with the Hera variable still at play, maybe this was another sign for me to take. I did not hesitate. I took my headphones off and walked the three short feet over to their table and introduced myself while apologizing for the interruption.

They were wonderful ladies – apparently they either all worked or knew each other from the Club (a fitness club) on St. Simons Island. They were celebrating their 181st consecutive Friday night out together. That's impressive by any measure! They all radiated Light and beauty. They were all so happy. It reminded me of my heavenly travels where everyone is always so happy without any negative energies at all.

After a quick chat, I learned that her daughter's name was Jude. Her initials were J.K. which were my initials as well. But, it was the little point about her name being "Jude" that stuck out the most to me.

Did I mention my last incarnation upon this Earth was as John Lennon? I guess not. I was stuck on sharing the classical composer sides of me during the hip-hop avenger mission escapades. I guess I will share that briefly too. I assume you can see how this music side of me has been part of my very essence over the centuries.

*Flashback to 2012/2013*

It was sometime during the early stages of learning how to meditate that I began to have "memories" of a number of my deaths from previous incarnations upon Earth. At the time, I did not know these were memories of past incarnations. Past lives were not even a consideration for me. I assumed I was only seeing real-time interactions with angels and my spiritual family. I never thought twice about past-lives during that time.

However, when I did begin to have these experiences, they weighed heavily on me. I often woke up and combed the internet for obituaries that might match these deaths I was seeing. I searched the missing persons reports. I assumed that I was experiencing something like a psychic would experience when seeing the location of a murder, or being able to share the location of a disposed body from an unsolved murder. And, really I suppose some of those visions still could have been. Regardless, I always felt helpless receiving this knowledge since I figured, "who would believe me?" But the death of my incarnation as John Lennon always stood out. I can still see the image so vividly that I relived in my dreams, the woman who was by my side. I even saw the man who shot me in the back multiple times as I felt myself gasp at my last breaths on Earth.

It.was.horrible.

And while the name Lennon had come up numerous times in my heavenly travels, I always assumed it was a reference to my clothing choice. On Earth, white linen shirts are my favorite attire. I often saw myself in the heavens wearing white… So…? White…? Linen…? You see how I made the connection.

It took a while for me to come to grips with the fact I was reliving my Lennon memories. During the spring of 2018, as I began merging more closely with my higher self, these memories rushed back with greater detail. Not knowing when John Lennon died, I assumed our lifetimes overlapped, which would have meant I couldn't have been Lennon and be here in this body today. When it got to the point of there's-no-question-about-it status – and it had been confirmed by my higher self multiple times – I looked up his death. December 8, 1980. My birth? May, 9, 1981. I exited Earth and, just as quickly, entered the womb of my Earthly mother as I continued to mature as a fetus in that moment. Not only that, when I read about the description of his death and saw photos of the location where his murder took place, everything rushed back to me. It all made sense. I was reliving his death.

This newfound awareness of my past life answered a riddle I had long been unable to crack: *Where was I during the Love movement?* Well, apparently, I helped lead the Love movement in the 1960s before my life ended prematurely (or maybe that is how it was planned all along). I then had to return back to finish this adventure for these final days. Honestly, this missing piece of knowledge had troubled me for some time. If I was the mighty Zeus/Melchizedek, then why would I not have been leading (or have been a part of) the Love movement from the 1960s?

It sounds like a strange thought for a me to have. However, most of the Earthly messengers in this present day who receive divine spiritual guidance to share with the world seem to have lived through that movement and helped champion the cause of Love. If you don't believe me, search out all of the channellings that are taking place on Earth at this time. Find websites that aggregate these messages on the internet. At thirty-seven, I am among the youngest (if not the youngest) to have these types of experiences – and barre none, with the highest documented quantity. I'm pretty sure based on documentation alone, there is no other source that has written the sheer volume of experiences that I have been blessed to receive. Not that it's a competition. Rather, it is just something of which to take notice. Who are the divine messages coming through? What is their commonality? In almost all cases, the answer relates back to the the Love movement of the 1960s – be it children born during that time, children alive at that time, or adults leading the charge. It is also the movement that faced the greatest political resistance of the modern era. I guess you can see why now. And why would the political leaders in the United States really want to kick Lennon out of the country? The more you know... It all makes sense, now, right?

*Flash-forward back to Palm Coast*

Jude.

That's the name of her daughter. Hopefully now you can see the gravity of this moment. My music cut out only to hear the ladies next to me talking about contacts in the film industry, only to then find out her daughter's name was Jude. Anyone who follows the Beatles will know that Hey Jude was one of the longest running #1 singles of all time spending 9 weeks atop the Billboard charts. The final chorus had an amazing 36 piece orchestra recorded for the na-na-na-na-nas outro. It was the Beatle's longest running #1 single and was a source of many intriguing stories regarding its meaning and origin between Lennon and McCartney. I won't recount them here. For now, just know that hot on the heels of the confirmation of my past life as Lennon, the name of this woman's daughter was more than just a flag waving against a blue sky. What color was the flag, though? I did not know. It was just a flag.

We ended up exchanging contact information and I was instructed to wait a few days before I was to email Jude. Jude's mother wanted to give her a head's up first... which made sense. I would have asked for the same grace period or would have chosen to do a warm-introduction email. The end result of this not-so-chance encounter was that I found peace in knowing that – at a minimum – another film door had been opened. At a maximum, it was another breadcrumb leading me to Hera. Regardless, another node of God's Light Network had been connected. And while I will say that for a few days I held onto the possibility that Hera's name could be Jude, it would prove not to be the case. Oh I am sure this connection is part of the story being told, but the way I would meet Hera would be much more undeniable, unfathomable even. The encounter with Jude's mother that day? That was just the Universe nudging me along as you will soon see. Oh there is still quite the adventure in store.

# CHAPTER 29
# The Wedding Tree

The following day (Saturday, August 18. 2018) I awoke with a fresh wind of air in my lungs destined to see some kind of wonderful. At this point I had spent much of the previous evening and morning in meditation. Writing would not be as much the focus for me that day as just following the signs and and sailing wherever the winds blew. I was a ship tossed about the great ocean trying to find a headwind to help me navigate back home.

At this point I knew the "save the date" card was more than just chance. Prayer and meditation and a quick chat with the Big Guy Upstairs let me know without a doubt I had received a personalized invitation to my own Wedding Day. Keep in mind that time is relative. Yes, my wedding began on May 8, 2015. That was the day I emerged from the water. But as we have discussed, I blinked. I closed my eyes wincing at her brightness as my Father pulled back her veil just before my lips met hers. While measurable time would pass by on Earth – a little over three years – it was up to me to *remember* that I was still standing on the great stage with her that day. Receiving a "save the date" card was a pretty romantic gesture from the Universe I'd say.

Knowing this, I decided to return to Palm Coast to bask in the afternoon sun and complete more writing. I didn't quite know why I needed to go to that particular area other than the coffeeshop was only a block or two from the pier, beach, and park. I needed sunlight – something that Wake Up's particular setting did not offer. So to Palm Coast I went. Oh – I should probably add this here, too. There was another reason I returned to that location...

*Flashback to the day prior at Palm Coast*

While I was experiencing my writer's block at Palm Coast the previous day, a brunette girl that I did not know walked by. She seemed to recognize me and waved profusely at me. She smiled and asked me how I was doing as she passed by. I, of course, smiled back and said hello as she wandered off. Of course I racked my brain as to how I might know her. I really did not recognize her at all. I have to say that she was very pretty and – in the midst of this great quest for Hera – it was yet another interaction of questionable origin.

"Nope. Not her." said Ol' Zeus in the back of my mind.

Yes, these are the things that just happen to me on a daily basis. No rhyme or reason in Earthly logic, but all of the spiritual rationale is there. I often consider everyone in the world to be angels and I am the outsider looking in. When people interact with me it helps to think of them as being my spiritual guides in Earthly form pointing me in the correct direction. So when someone waves, I smile internally back at the Universe and acknowledge that I did indeed receive the sign. But I goofed on this one... again, in Zeusian style.

Oh I didn't goof on the first interaction. It would be about an hour later when I walked up to the barista to get a refill on my tea when she walked up again... and then I goofed. This time she stood within a foot of me, stopped, and fidgeted with her nails. Do you know what Ol' Zeus did? That's right. Nothing. Though your history books will tell you all about my womanizing ways (and there is some basis of truth to the stories, though the stories are quite the embellishments for the most part), this example is more like the reality of my Earthly interactions. Yes, I can recount these stories with style and humor. And when I want to talk to a beautiful woman, I have no problem doing so. But, I can't escape the fact that I find myself in the midst of these awkward circumstances that often do involve women. And while my "single years" after my divorce are full of stories for the ages, they almost always resolve with me searching for Hera rather than paying attention to the woman standing before me. I just wouldn't realize it was Hera I was searching for. Funny thing about this planet. Remembering Love proves to be quite difficult! In fact, it is why we are all here right now.

In this particular case, I felt bad for the girl I awkwardly did not acknowledge. You see, acknowledgment is the most important gesture a human can make to another. If I had just smiled and had a quick conversation, that could have made her feel special. It was why she walked up to me... at least that is what I thought her purpose to be. And you know what? I want to be clear. I do smile and talk to nearly everyone I meet! I acknowledge most everyone by name. And if they are wearing a name-tag while they are working, I certainly hope it is their real name because that is how I acknowledge them in the midst of our passing.

Heck. Then it hit me. I suddenly began questioning whether I had missed another potential sign like the "save the date" card from hours earlier. I tried to dismiss that thought. More potential answers meant greater potential for failing the exam. I returned back to thinking about my lack of acknowledgement for this girl and tried to place myself in her shoes. I would have wanted to have been acknowledged. Yep. There it was. I goofed. In a world of social queues, delicate emotions, and self-confidence issues, the polite thing would have been for me to have simply said hello. I didn't. And it ate away at me throughout the evening hours. But then I began to return to the thought of having potentially missed another grand sign from the Universe. I'd return the following day. That was my only resolve. If I saw her again, I'd say hello and listen for another sign from the Universe.

Long story short, over the evening hours I was told in meditation that I had not done anything wrong and that I should just trust the plan. It was emphasized from my higher self that the brunette I met earlier in the day (the one I did not acknowledge) was like a firecracker (or more specifically, one of those little snap-its that pops when you throw it on the ground) rather than a grand display of fireworks. Make no mistake, this is nothing against this brunette's character, soul, or essence. This is purely a metaphor for the emotions I would feel inside –

## CH29

very specific terms repeated over and over in order to help me understand how it would feel when I met Hera. My higher self wanted me to not question whether I might miss the signs, the feelings, the emotions. It was important that it would be fireworks. Let me emphasize this again.

...

Hera, you are like a grand display of fireworks to my soul.

...

*Return back to the present moment – August 18, 2018 – at Palm Coast*

With new knowledge that Hera would be fireworks, I set out to Palm Coast to write and redeem myself (hopefully) if I were to see the brunette girl again. I knew she was not part of the story, but I was still unsettled that I had been cold to another human being. That isn't Love at all, though it was a byproduct of my quest of finding Hera. Well… I thought the brunette was not part of the story, but as you will see, everything has a reason. This was actually part of the Universe's plan. It will all make sense in a bit.

I arrived at Palm Coast, and fought through a paragraph or two of writing over the several hours I was there. Ugh. It was another writer's block kind of day. But you know what? I was a little off kilter since I was going to meet Hera's Earthly form within 48 hours, so I gave myself some leeway on my performance issues. However, while I was there I did happen to see the brunette again. Another smile and a wave my way. That was good to see. My lack of acknowledgement from the day prior did not do too much damage. But, I still took it upon myself to find a way to make small talk with her when she approached me. Interaction saved. I could move on with my life. Having accomplished that mission, I decided to end my writing day and walk down toward the beach. My higher self simply said, "See? I told you everything would be fine."

When I walked to the beach, I was a bit taken off-guard. The park that overlooks the ocean and pier was very crowded. In the middle of the park were around 150 white chairs facing a giant oak tree. It was a wedding... or would be. It appeared like it was still being setup for a service that would take place later in the afternoon.

The whole wedding thing was a very curious moment for me to see. Obviously I saw the symbolism. And let me say very clearly in these pages that as many years as I have spent on-and-off again in St Simons Island, I have never once witnessed a wedding in a public place. I visit this location very frequently and this was a first for me. But here I was. Day two of this three day window into finding my Bride's Earthly form and now I found myself walking toward the empty seats for an actual wedding beneath a great Wedding Tree. I laughed aloud. I'm sure of it. I even wondered if I was going to see my name on the sign the wedding planners were setting up. So, I went to take a look.

I moseyed about the park and over to the seating area determined I would walk down this aisle as a physical acknowledgment of the Universe's gesture. Oh, I had too! If you knew you were about to experience your spiritual wedding day in Earthly form, would you not breathe in every moment leading up to the grand denouement? Would you not want to have said, "I even walked down the aisle of the wedding that day?" Of course you would… but few would probably actually do it. But Ol' romantic Zeus would not be stopped. Except, that I was stopped. It wasn't as if there was anyone around when I approached, but there was a single wedding planner tying ribbons to the chairs. She was firmly planted in the middle of the aisle. So instead of drawing attention, I just glanced at the name tag instead. Nope. Not Jonathan, Zeus, Hera, or any other name that pertained to my physical form. But, I did take note that the bride's name was Christine… get it? The female form of Christ? Of course it would have been. A perfect Bride's name.

 At this point I decided to head back to my place to seek further guidance. But as I neared my Jeep, I felt something pulling me back toward the wedding. So I took the cue. I decided I would just hang out and watch the wedding. There was quite a gathering beginning to build up and the wedding party was just beginning to take pictures a few yards away from where I would eventually be standing. I couldn't decide to run out on my own wedding! Ha. Remember how I said earlier that every physical gesture happens on the other side of the veil? The example I gave in that chapter was how physically cleaning a house would help you spiritually clean your soul. Your body is your temple, no? This would be no different. I wouldn't miss my own wedding. I wouldn't. I couldn't. I had one job. I was going to meet Hera within 48 hours. I had a "save the date "invitation (this was completely unrelated to this particular wedding by the way), and now I was witnessing a wedding donned in a deep azure blue. Even the color choice was not lost on me. This color is the Earthly representation of a color from behind the veil – the very color that represents the fifth dimension, heaven, etc.

The wedding took place and was a beautiful show of Love. While there were no storm clouds in sight prior to originally discovering that a wedding was taking place, by the time the ceremony was in motion a large darkened cloud rolled in from the West. There was not a single sound of thunder, rain, or lightning as it approached (and you could see it coming from many miles away). But as it neared the ceremony, it became obvious it was going to put on a show. I prayed it would hold off until the kiss. I thought that would be perfect timing. Above the wedding was blue sky, but the storm clouds were fast approaching.

As the Bride kissed the Groom, I turned to look up at the clouds that were now very close. Nothing. I was a little frustrated. I get to make these kind of calls right? God of Thunder? God of the Sky? What a disappointing moment. I let the Universe know that a divine sign here would have been a little better than nothing. At this point, the music played and the wedding Bride and Groom exited the ceremony. The bridesmaids and groomsmen followed suit. After everyone was escorted out, the master of ceremonies officially concluded the wedding. At the moment that everyone stood up, a crack of lightning shot out of the cloud… then another, and another. The thunder rolled. The storm played its song all the while leaving the blue sky overhead the park's pavilion where I stood and the wedding was taking place.

## CH29

Okay Universe. Well done. You played your symphony of the skies at the conclusion of the wedding rather than at the moment of the kiss. Symbolism noted. I forgot I was still stuck in my blinding, wincing moment on the stage. When I open my eyes again and allow my spiritual eyesight to adjust to the Light of my Bride, the ceremony will still be occurring. I wasn't at the end yet no matter how much I like to rush things. I was approaching the end, though – the grand conclusion, the grand denouement. The Universe showed me so. Day Two was done.

# CHAPTER 30
## A King Upon His Throne

As has been shared throughout the pages of this book so far, the last several days had not only been quite an Indiana Jones and the Quest for Hera's Love type of experience, but my body/soul had also been experiencing quite a thunderstorm of change. Before we get into what transpired on Day Three, it is important to also discuss the great change that was taking place within my body. If this were a movie, what I am about to describe would be written into the script like a parallel timeline to my Earthly existence. Don't worry. This isn't confusing or difficult to grasp.

In short, imagine that my Earthly soul had been in a process of merging with my higher self since May 8, 2015 (though, really, this has been taking place for every human over the course of all lifetimes. This particular date could best be understand as the most obvious point of acceleration in my series of lifetimes.). The body is merely the meat-suit of the existence. My soul is the life within the body you know as Jonathan. The soul has complete governance of the body, though the human mind often believes the body cannot be governed from within and instead must seek outside treatments and therapies to hammer it into health. But the soul is truly each human's life essence. It is my higher self that I *truly* Am. The remembrance taking place and memories rushing back were byproducts of the merging of my soul back to my higher self (Zeus/Melchizedek) before ultimately returning to One – to Love.

While this merging had been taking place, I was having moments where I would see two worlds laying on top of each other. It wouldn't appear like two landscapes per se. Rather, I would see two versions of the reality... though not precisely at once. For example, I might see a person in the perfect beauty of his/her spiritual form one day then, the following day I would see him/her in a more true-to-life Earthly version of the soul. The Earthly version of the soul could best be described as an expression of the energies they are carried with the soul at this juncture of their journey. Both appearances are closely related, but they were becoming very different in visible appearance to my eyes. I use that description not in a way of judgement or criticism. Instead, I have used it to portray the difference in the spiritual interpretation of all of the Earthly imperfections. Both are important, for as I've consistently said from the first book written, *true beauty* is found in the imperfections. Heavenly beauty is Divine.

Still, there is a difference between the great cosmic ideal and the Earthly form. Consider this visualization similar to how a person in Love may not see the flaws of a person because they are mesmerized in the afterglow of the Love they have found. Each perspective of the soul embodies the various energies the soul is carrying in their respective planes of existence.

These energies carried forth from their respective planes were bringing about the sheen of the appearances I would see with my Earthly eyes. In terms of the Earthly form, consider this description akin to the polish and detail to an otherwise roughly carved block of marble. The other forms I would see were more akin to their existences upon their heavenly planes (e.g. what you would imagine the end product of your marble carving to look like).

The internal changes to my body/soul had been considerable over the previous six-plus years, but there was a noticeable shift during the days the recent Hera Quest began. The shift of location of Zeus' voice in my head was now as if it was becoming a full aspect of me rather than just a phone call I could answer from one portion of my brain. Archangel Ariel's voice was sounding fuller, more encompassing, Loving, and warm (as if that was even possible!). And then there were the sleep issues, the pains within my chakra system that felt like pieces of a great puzzle being shoved together to fit into a position they perviously were not. Visually, I would see it like an animation of a complex safe rotating through the internal tumblers to unlock each progressive step prior to the safe door being completely unlocked, opened, and accessible. That's just how it felt. To illustrate this point in further detail, I wanted to include my journal entry from August 17, 2018. This was the first day the Hera Quest began in full-force.

**Journal Entry from August 17, 2018**

## CH30

  *Today is the first day that Zeus has fully merged within the base of my cerebellum – where my spine meets the base of my skull. Up until today, I had initially been receiving my communication in a particular part of my right hemisphere. But all of that went silent through the final storm of the triad of eclipses over July and August 2018. I was forewarned though. Hera? She was closer to the front and center portion of my brain. Caliel? She always appeared from the base region of my brain and filled my periphery. Ariel? She initially came from the left hemisphere – located a bit more left than Zeus was from the right side. And while I have just mentioned a few here, every angelic being I have ever communicated with has appeared in different portions of my brain. It would seem like a human could run out of spaces to describe these locations, but when these openings begin to occur, the internal map of the brain seems more like the map of the globe, where each of these locations is more akin to a country or a city.*

  *Channelers have described these locations upon the brain in more ambiguous terms like "the channel on the left side" and such. These descriptions are not wrong and I can certainly relate to these descriptions, but I also would express that these "channels in the brain" used to receive communication from all types of sources are more like a particular public phone location. These are important, for they certainly are places of significance. However, the places I am describing are more like private communication locations.*

  *I tended to not answer the public phone line ringing in my brain. Sometimes I did. They were always interesting phone calls. I entertained the communications. In fact, "entertain" is probably a good description since the conversations were a constant state of back-and-forth nonsense as I sought to make sure 1) I was not crazy and 2) to make sure my mind wasn't being mislead by a nefarious, negative being.*

So in the beginning, I was very protective of my communications. It was only the communications from the closest of my soul family that I would answer. Even then, it was probably a comedic conversation that consisted of me asking for proof of the voice on the other end of the call. I'd ask for an Earthly sign. I wasn't specific as to what I wanted to see, rather, I just had to learn to listen to the manner in which they could communicate. And I received it... surprisingly actually.

The communications I began to receive initially were not tied only to my brain. It wasn't like I would suddenly hear a voice that said, "Hey Jonathan! Go do [fill in the blank]." Oh no! It was nothing like that. I mean, once I managed to be open to a state of listening, I might have "heard" a voice spoken aloud once or twice, but that was a rarity and nothing like the manner in which communications actually take place.

So, if you are reading this and have yet to learn the inner workings of your galactic call-center of your brain, then you will certainly want to remove any pre-conceived notions as to how these communications must occur. Those notions are actually like static white noise preventing a person from hearing the phone ring. You would be focusing on the wrong sensation. You should actually be focused on your vibratory state... and locations of the vibrations.

For example, when Ariel wants to reach out directly, I feel a specific sensation in my naval area. It is different than when Michael wants to speak. Sometimes the vibratory state is in a different portion of my body – my heart for instance. Sometimes it may just be the acknowledgement of a full body vibratory state summoning a time for meditation and communication. And even as I describe this, it may be experienced slightly differently for each person. This whole thing... the connection to our Ancient Oneness... Yeah, that thing... Well, while it will follow a few similar principles among souls, the exactness of how each soul experiences personal com-

*munications will always be relative to their particular capacity to hear. More specifically, think of this capacity as each soul's academic level of spiritual communication that is measured on a soul level and not on a tangible Earthly level. Always remember that.*

*A doctor would never attempt to have a conversation about a recently written research paper rife with medical terms to a child learning not yet able to say "dadda" or "mama." Oh no! But as the child learns to talk, conversations will be had. And, if a doctor is truly knowledgeable about a very academic conversation point, he will be able to explain it in a manner the child can grasp. But again, just because a doctor may have finally been able to explain a lifetime of research and study of a medical topic to a child in a simple way for the child to understand, it does not mean the child would then have the full knowledge of that particular topic. Oh no! There would be so much missing knowledge that would be lost in the communication.*

*But the funny thing about humans is how they believe their relative awareness of life and existence must be similar to an eye-to-eye doctorate level when it comes to ability to speak to God and the galactics. This is very, very deceiving and where most humans fall into the trap of "well, prove it to me otherwise" rather than "seeking to learn the unknown for themselves." Hint: it isn't scientifically provable with Earth technology yet, but it will be one day.*

...

I'm not sure how we got so far down this side road, but it must be important to share for it is flowing freely from my heart to these pages. It is flowing like we are driving on a smoothly paved road, yet in the context of "staying on track" this is more akin to taking the off-road path. It is tricky, ins't it?

But, in short, when I started to receive communications in a manner more consistent with what will one day fully evolve to the term "telepathy" rather than just "divine signs, dreams, and astral travels," I would hear the phone ring in my soul via a tingly sensation arising in various locations of my body. To "answer the phone," I would then focus on maintaining a higher vibratory spiritual state in the moment or by taking time to close my eyes and meditate. In either method, it involved turning down the outside world to a near silence so I could then hear the internal communications within.

That was a terribly tricky state to achieve! For me it took years of full-on-100%-committed-to-pressing-pause-on-the-world-and-entering-into-trial-and-error tactics. In the beginning I would use blindfolds and headphones with binaural beats (among other methods) to bring my body into a meditative state and remove the sounds of the outside world and distractive inner thoughts. Introducing yoga into my daily routine would help. Exercise and improving my state of health was just as important (even though I *thought!* I was in shape). These days I am aware of the slightest changes to my vibratory state even if my weight shifts just a pound in either direction from my optimal form. Much of the learning process for me purely involved the sheer will to lay down without moving while managing not to fall asleep – all the while, trying to listen inside. To what? I didn't know. I just kept listening.

One day early into this journey when I was severely frustrated at the process, I simply asked God to shout at me louder than the outside world. Surely I could notice that! A tree falling or a siren cutting through the daily cacophony of sounds would certainly serve as a flag of communication. Instead, the world was silent... curiously silent that day. Nothing happened out of the ordinary except I felt as if I was in near isolation from everyone. No texts flowed back and forth. No phone calls. No work interactions. And then there was a simple divine interaction with one person that day that allowed me to see just how The Big Guy was communicating with me. Riddle solved!!! Asking for a divine shout above the human noise equated to observing profound silence while listening for simple signs. I then just had to figure out how to do this on my own in a state of noise and then learn to discern His Voice from everything else. The schooling continued.

    As I progressed in my lessons I found that little things such as changing my diet helped me get there more quickly. Every method initially was a brute-force tactic for what would one day become a more real-time experience for me. So it can be seen that even in the beginning, answering the phone wasn't as simple as picking it up and saying hello. Oh no! It was more like, not hearing it ring and then one day saying, "Did I hear something?" Eventually that turned into, "I hear a phone ringing, but I can't find my phone!" Gah. The exhaustion!

    Truly I say unto you, tell a person not to think of something and it will be increasingly more difficult to remove it from the mind. It is one of the most challenging parts of the whole process. So I suggest that you should just prepare for the full commitment to the process. Otherwise, it is just delaying the inevitable.

    So, returning back full circle to the beginning of this chapter when I was starting to explain the idea of how Zeus is now taking a seat where my spine unites with the base of my skull... it can now be understood how his voice began to feel like the wind filling my sails, propelling this vessel forward. It is as if his voice now surrounds the base of my brain between my ears. Perhaps this moment could be called "a king upon his throne," for there is not a more appropriate way to describe this particular seat that he has taken. There are so many metaphors I could use, but none serve a better comparison. In Truth, his voice is as much mine as it is his, though I would describe my personal voice and egoic decisions more along the lines of "my personality" whereas his voice is the connection to a wisdom most ancient. Truly there is no separation, though the words written here describe it so.

Make use of these words and descriptions in the form of another guidepost to help you. Depending on where you may find yourself along your personal journey, the ego can attempt to use it as a way to foster fear and separation from your True self. In the early stages of the journey, the mere chance the ego will twist the knowledge revealed within these words into such a way to maintain division between the worlds is an utmost certainty. So, be prepared for that. Tricky ego.

# CHAPTER 31
# Day 3 Began

Shortly after I awoke on Day Three of the Hera adventure, I was instructed by the Cosmic Director that I should not further delay before making my way to the cafe. True, I had been dilly-dallying around after I awoke. I journaled. I checked my email. I read my daily dose of spiritual blogs (there were not many for the day for some strange reason). I also fought the urge to go back to sleep. But, when I finally got my engine running, I suppose it would only make sense that I was urged onward with gusto. I have to state the only times I've ever received nudges of this type of intensity is when something truly great and noticeable was about to happen in my life. Part of me wanted to delay. I know that sounds absurd.

"Surely if everything happens as you say, then you wouldn't delay, right?" you might be thinking.

I know... I know... I know... But honestly, remember Day Three was tantamount to the final exam... and not just the final exam, but this one single day could prove out the course of the entire six-plus year journey. All of the completely out-of-the-world experiences I had been blessed to have still

# CH31

had a fragment of doubt remaining. The prophecy thingy? Oh, there was no doubt in my mind. But to others? How many other people on Earth have claimed [such and such] is the fulfillment of [such and such]? How many have been right? Why would this be seen any differently? People forget the handful of God's miracles written about in the Bible occurred over enormous spans of time! A miracle on Earth today would be forgotten and dismissed tomorrow. That's just how it is.

Humans love to try to prove prophecies despite having no proof. Others love to snuff out any hope. My proof? Well, I had journals of experiences, witnesses, publications timestamped and placed into the written record of Earth prior to events happening, and then there was that great earthquake in Nepal from 2015. Perhaps the earthquake was the most tangible proof others may see. Oh well. But now here I was standing on the Edge of Destiny. This time, I didn't care if the world would see it. It was obvious this story had one focus: my heart, my Love.

Maybe this moment would shake the world quite literally. Maybe this was "The Event" that has been spoken about for so long. After all, the end of this whole seven years of tribulation is fast approaching its conclusion. By my count, we just entered the fourth quarter of the final year.

*Cut to scene of Athens, GA. The UGA Bulldogs are playing a game and the quarter is transitioning to the fourth. All of the fans hold up four fingers. Cut back to this moment.*

## CH31

Any football fan knows the fourth quarter is where the game is won! One team plays their hearts out until the other team wears out. And here is a crazy thought: what if Zeus finding Hera is the fourth quarter moment that actually triggers Love across Earth? I could certainly argue how that could be possible. Everything else in my life has been in divine synchronicity with the Universe What if this moment is the only single thing standing in the way of the Heavens unleashing Light and Love across this planet in such a way that no human could deny for all time?

...

Then again, what if just these words might simply be that miracle?

...

Oh, it is so tough to figure out the closing sequence of the Great Writer's script! All I know is that I am on this journey like a bull on red. Case in point, I would certainly honor the request to head to Wake Up earlier than I had planned.

I got dressed and was ready to head out the door when the voice of Zeus spoke up inside. Apparently I wasn't wearing the right clothes. No. I'm not usually concerned, but I was clearly being instructed to wear a white linen shirt in lieu of the one I had selected. Knowing there could be any number of reasons for this, I obliged. I ironed a white linen shirt as quickly as I could and headed out the door.

*Cut to scene of Jonathan getting in Jeep and closing door.*

Once I sat down, I decided to fire up my Spotify playlist called "Screenplay." This list contained songs that either inspired certain scenes during the writing of *I Am We*, or contained instrumental music used as temp tracks for the pacing and the pulse of the dialogue. I had not listened to this list in years possibly, but I thought it was appropriate to fire it up. After all, I was pretty much living out the script of that particular screenplay, right?

I selected a song called "Stuck In The Middle" by Boys Like Girls. Even if it may not seem like it at first blush, this particular song is a very spiritual song about leaving the body and traveling to the heavens during meditative states, then returning to Earth. But let's just take the title for a minute. Stuck In The Middle. The Universe was not having it. The song played for a few seconds. I kicked my Jeep in reverse. Midway down the driveway the song jumped to an entirely different track.

"What? What just happened?!" I thought to myself. Nothing should have caused that to happen. But, I acknowledged the Universe's desire to play deejay before I was to hopefully receive my miracle at Radio Station Wake Up. The new song started playing.

Here. Let's put you in my seat. Read along. This is how I was hearing the Universe speak to me.

The intro began.

I recognized it immediately. The song was called "Loved" by Lucy Hale.

Keep going Universe. You've got my attention. Loved. I got ya. It felt like a warm hug across the veil in this moment. There isn't a more appropriate title of a song to send me.

## CH31

The lyrics began.

> *I don't need a hundred roses waiting by the front door*
> *I don't need a fancy house in the hills*
> *You could rope the moon and bring me all the stars in heaven*
> *It won't change how I feel.*
> *You don't have to be a modern day Shakespeare*

At this exact moment, my iPad (which was used to play these songs via bluetooth) suddenly beeped as if I had received an email or iMessage. Not being in wifi range, this was a bit baffling as I do not have a data plan on my iPad. Perhaps it was still processing something as I was leaving the house. No matter. I paid attention. My iPad literally said, "Hey Jonathan, you've got a message: You don't have to be a modern day Shakespeare." And, oh, Universe – make no mistake. I certainly have not mistaken myself for being a modern day Shakespeare. Oh no! I just hope that whoever begins reading these words will make it this far. Especially... well, Hera of course. But at this point, I recognize that writing may not even be important. The purpose may just be about saying that first "hello." The song continued.

> *You don't have to be anything you're not*
> *You don't have to give me diamonds to impress me*
> *Just give me your heart.*

> *Make me feel loved*
> *Make me feel beautiful*

*Make me feel dance around the room Cinderella kind of magical*
*Make me believe I'm all that you'll ever need*
*Hold me close and make me feel a million kinds of wonderful*
*Baby your touch, is more than enough*
*Make me feel loved.*

*It's the way you bring me coffee in the morning*
*and how you know just what not to say*
*I don't need you to try and fix everything when I've had a bad day.*

*Make me feel loved*
*Make me feel beautiful*
*Make me feel dance around the room Cinderella kind of magical*
*Make me believe I'm all that you'll ever need*
*Hold me close and make me feel a million kinds of wonderful*
*Baby your touch, is more than enough*
*Make me feel loved.*

*Make me feel loved*
*Make me feel beautiful*
*Make me feel dance around the room Cinderella kind of magical*
*Make me believe I'm all that you'll ever need*
*Hold me close and make me feel a million kinds of wonderful*
*Baby your touch, is more than enough*
*Make me feel loved.*

Now, there were several reasons this particular song was on my playlist. But first, let's acknowledge the message the Universe was sending me. Without a doubt, I was going to find my

# CH31

Moon, my Hera. I was even receiving a reminder of just what she would need.

However, the symbolism did not stop there. For one thing, the only reason I had this song on my playlist was because I thought Lucy might have been a potential actress for the lead role in *I Am We*. There were a few songs throughout the screenplay that might need to be sung, so I wanted to hear her voice as well. On appearance alone, she also fit the description for the main female character (Eden) – most notably due to her dark brown hair, milky white complexion, and affinity for bold, yet soft rose-colored lipstick. That was going to be important in the moments to come, but honestly nothing beyond the words being sung had entered into my mind as to the message the Universe was sharing with me in that moment.

"Wait. Brown hair? I thought you said Hera had blonde hair and blue eyes in you heavenly travels?"

And you are not wrong. Remember I said that Hera could quite possibly have any appearance (or age for that matter). But if I had truly been paying attention to the very screenplay I had penned (which was clearly sourced from beyond my Earthly mind), I would have taken note that the Earthly version of the lead actress (Eden) was different than her spiritual representation. On one side of the veil, she had blonde hair, blue eyes and was to be played by a completely different actress. On the other side, she had brown hair. This was an intentional choice, though I did not know just how much this screenplay was going to come to life before my eyes. And the name Eden? Well, that was a choice made because I still had no idea what my Bride's name would be. In *The Nine*, she is referenced as

CH31

Eve. In the screenplay, Eden. Now I know my Bride is Hera, but her Earthly name? Well, you will just have to wait and see.

 It was like a grand moment from the movie Inception except in this plot I was the lead actor oblivious to starring in the very screenplay I had written... which was actually being written by the Divine Author himself. Yay Zeus... again. I see where this is going now. But when Day Three began, I did not.

 Let's not belabor the point. Summary: I woke up, left the house in a white linen shirt, was promptly hugged by the Universe and reminded I was Loved while also being reminded just what kind of Love Hera's Earthly form would need from me. I drove to Wake Up, parked, and walked in.

# CHAPTER 32
# Wake Up, Day 3

Now, while I enjoy being cast as the lead actor of this play and laughing at the humor of the Grand Author's script as it plays out in real-time before my eyes, the twists and turns upcoming would be over the top – even by The Great Hand's standards. Seriously. Then again, if this part of the story was symbolic to reaching the peak of Everest, I would expect it to have a final tier of unexpected challenges. All great movies have their most unexpected sequences at the end. If there were no surprises, twists, and turns, it wouldn't seem quite as fulfilling, now would it?

I can only laugh at the situations the Universe has put me in along this journey. But, every time, I willfully play along, both curious and humored by the inside joke in which I know I am starring. It is like signing on to be the lead actor in a Hollywood romance only to realize the movie was more like a hybrid tragedy/comedy/drama as it played along. Script changes, hidden meanings the director wants to plant in the minds of the viewers, co-star changes while the movie is being filmed... nothing is impossible.

## CH32

    As the lead actor, I just look around at the landscape each directorial change creates, smile, and go along with the gag. Maybe the movie is more of a reality show that I didn't know I signed up for. You know, the kind. It is the one where the whole purpose of the show is just to see how I handle the situation? At times it feels like that.

    "Hey Jonathan (e.g. Zeus!)!" I expect to hear. "Look right over there! That's a hidden camera! None of this was real!"

    The crew of the television show will be all smiles with ear-to-ear grins, hoping I laugh a little... hopefully a lot! Somehow, though, even when I feel as if I have it all figured out, there will be another twist... one that I might even be suspecting yet cannot quite figure out before it happens. They've seen to it. Surely. Any crew worthy of this job would certainly have seen me catch on early into the filming and would have already written the twists and turns that I am now experiencing into the story. All the while, I'm just reading along – reciting the lines, showing up to the various shooting locations, laughing at the cosmic jokes internally while maintaining an actor's composure... all the while thinking, "Yeah suuurrrreee....this makes sense with the preparation you shared with me, Father..."

    Enter Day Three's cosmic joke. While Wake Up is normally a trendy place with people sitting at various tables regardless of time of day, rarely is it busy to the point where people turn around to leave and go elsewhere due to the volume of people already inside. Lines can be acceptable (and there generally is a line). By the time your order is made, a seat or table will probably free up. If not, you wouldn't have to wait too long. But Day Three... oh, Day Three.

    On my drive to Wake Up I had memories of what it felt like to be a giddy teenager who had recently secured a date to the dance with the most beautiful girl in the school. My heart was racing while I realized the similarities to those memories. It was a fun trip down Memory Lane. I had not felt this feeling in ages. On Day Three, I couldn't wait to see how the Universe's script was going to play out for me. But I didn't expect this.

    I walked into Wake Up to see an entirely packed house. Let me tell you... this was not a normal packed house. Oh, no. I looked around the room to see somewhere in the neighborhood of forty girls occupying nearly every table. The only guys in the room were the barista and a couple of (what appeared to be) tutors. I wasn't sure what I had walked into, but I could only assume one of two things. A quick look around the room brought my attention to the fact that every single girl was wearing something college oriented which at least helped me identify a relative age. I saw a number of sorority t-shirts and sweatshirts, so I assumed this must be the new undergrads at the local college gathering for a Sunday study session. Age withstanding, I found myself in a room with forty women and three guys. And no, whatever going on in this moment had nothing to do with the "save the date" event from the postcard. I was hours early. Also, that event was supposed to occur on the porch and involve jewelry and such (as best as I could figure out).

    I could only laugh at the situation. I had been to Wake Up probably a hundred times or more since getting hit on the head with a hammer and had *never* seen it filled with that many women. Ten? Twenty? Maybe of various ages. But not forty all in the exact same age group! And now, there I was. On a day I was supposed to identify Hera, I was surrounded by a sea of women. I ordered my tea and sat down at the community table – the only seat that was available actually. What a crazy start to that day.

It would only take a few moments to pass for me to understand why I was being pressed to get there several hours earlier than the time listed on the "save the date" card. At first I thought the nudge to get there early was to head off the potential of Hera arriving early. Or, maybe the time was unimportant on the "save the date" card and it was just the date that was detail of which I was supposed to take notice. After all, it was a "save the date" card and not a "save the date and time" reservation.

It would only take a few moments before I began to realize that I arrived on the frontside of the rush of women who were planning on attending (what had turned into) my own personal version of ABC's The Bachelor. Had I not arrived when I did, I would never have gotten a seat for my own show! It is true. Over the course of the next thirty minutes to an hour, there were probably another thirty to forty women of the same age range who entered Wake Up and subsequently had to turn around and go elsewhere to study.

The Universe's cosmic joke was in full swing. As I sat there, I prayed about how I would identify Hera. A new woman waked into the store. My laptop dinged with a message. Was that her? I heard the voice of Zeus laughing in my head.

"No, son, that is not her." he said.

## CH32

"Great. This was a celestially-televised event." I thought to myself.

Another girl continued to glance over at me and make unrelenting eye-contact. Was that Hera? More laughs from the voice of Zeus.

"No, son. Not her either." he bellowed.

I got up and went to the bathroom. Guess what? There was another group of ten to fifteen girls on the back porch. Wonderful. This was going to be tougher than it first appeared. If I was back in my rookie year in Nashville, this would have been a fun game. But on this Day Three, everything was now on the line. It wasn't just about talking, flirting, or finding myself among beautiful women. This was about finding One... remembering One... knowing One. I had not dated a single girl in three years... maybe four now? Five? No. Surely not that long. Wow. I wondered how long it really had been. And I have to be honest, I thought Hera would be a little older than the company of women I found myself among – at least that was the guidance I had been given, so this was a bit of a twist unless it was just a distraction.

On my return from the bathroom I walked by one girl who kept making eye contact with me.

As I walked by her I heard, "Wow!" exclaimed in that "I'm being flirty but you weren't supposed to hear it that loudly" kind of way. I felt her eyes scanning me up and down.

*Please note that I am not writing this play-by-play to entertain my own ego. This is honestly the situation I found myself in.*

"Nope!" said the voice of Zeus.

I laughed inside as I sat back down. What did I get myself involved in? I decided to just focus on writing and wait for a sign. That's how they've always happened. And yes, I am usually very obstinate in taking notice of signs, but I thought that Day Three would bring about a higher level of observation skills... I hoped it would at least.

After some further internal prayer while the sea of women made its presence known to my rickety vessel, I was led to focus on the details that I had been shared about Hera to date. Those details should be seen as tantamount to recalling the details of her memory. So that is what I did. And, if what I knew about Hera was to be true – unless I was really misjudging the women's age around me – this was just a cosmic, comical distraction of the grandest proportion.

If I was wrong, I felt resolved that the Universe would see my heart and know I was being True. In those types of circumstances, I would place my faith that Hera would manage to find me if she was in the room. My money was on her not being there though since I had arrived several hours early.

...

This was my final exam.
I circled "none of the above."

...

Hours passed. I stared at my blinking cursor trying to find something to write about. I did manage to start a couple of chapters which made their way into these pages, but mostly my mind was trying to find calm amidst the ocean of women surging around me. I wanted peace. I'm god of the skies! Surely I can command a metaphorical storm to subside and allow the waters to calm, right? So, I sent up a prayer.

*Father,*

*In Nashville, I once asked for you to help me be able to hear your voice above the noise of my daily life. On that day, the world fell silent. I did not receive texts. I did not receive phone calls. Even the work place was silent. I need that same type of intervention today. I need to hear your voice. I need to be able to see Hera through this storm.*

Just like that the storm began to subside. It was approaching 3:00 P.M. – the time mentioned on the "save the date" card – when the women in the room began to finish up their study session. Out of curiosity, I looked out on the porch, but no one remained. Tables began to open up. I received a text (iMessage via wifi, so there are no questions about how I could receive a text without a phone) from Raymond that he was coming by. I wasn't sure how I felt about having anyone affect my day, but I told him to come on anyway.

At that point I began to have flashbacks of a moment that occurred during the first book of *The Nine*. There was a particular circumstance where Lindsey was texting me and I knew if I engaged in the conversation we'd be hitting it off. If I took too long, it was going to be a missed opportunity. Just after I received that text, my friend Jason came by to tell me fantastic news about his plans for his engagement to his girlfriend. Despite me wanting to text Lindsey back, I gave my friend priority.

As much as it frustrated me, that seemed like the right thing to do. At the time, I viewed it as a cosmic obstruction to Love. Nope. That was just a lesson for today.

I realized that having Raymond come by was going to be a reprise of me reliving this exact same situation with Jason from years prior. I knew it. This was test time and here was the next question. The difference? This time everything was at stake. This was Hera, not just an Earthly flame. It would be a little after three o'clock when Raymond arrived. At this point, nearly every single person in Wake Up had left. A few people were still finishing their work, but would end up leaving not too long after he arrived. The people sitting at my community table left. The tables around me? Empty. Silence. This was the Universe at work for sure. I had just asked for this, right? I should also say, there was no event that seemed to be occurring on the porch. The card did say "the porch" for a location. That part left me baffled. Had I misread the card? All I knew, was my prayer had been answered.

...
The storm had subsided.
...

# CHAPTER 33
# Lightning On A Blue Sky Kind Of Day

After Raymond arrived, we chatted it up for a bit. It was impossible not to take notice of the emptiness in Wake Up. It was painfully obvious that something was amiss. Had I missed a sign? No! I would not question anything. The "save the date" card, the wedding from the day prior, the storm full of women subsiding upon my request... it could not have all been coincidence. To my heart I had to remain Faithful and True. I knew I was where I was supposed to be and I was determined to pass my test. Bull, remember?

Raymond must have sensed my attention drifted elsewhere when a stunning brunette walked in the front door. My heart was racing faster than it ever had. This wasn't just an excitement of seeing a potential suitor. Oh, no! This was different. This felt like the feeling from the heavens when I am around angels. To lesser degrees I've felt it among others on Earth. This was how I learned to identify souls in Earthly form early on in this journey. Each soul has a signature. But this woman who walked in, there was no denying there was a connection. But, was it *the* connection I had waited lifetimes to find once again? Was this my Moon, my Light?

"Focus! Focus!" The words seemed to be mumbled from Raymond's side of the table. I wasn't listening. Was he speaking? Really, that divinely timed? I didn't care. I was lost, caught up in the glow of this woman's radiance as she walked to the counter to order a latte.

"Focus! Focus! Are you listening to me? Focus!" It was now apparent that Raymond was actually saying those words as his voice slowly became more clear.

*Cue the sound of voices going from muffled to loud and clear.*

"Huh?" I had no idea what he was talking about, but my mind registered that he was telling me to focus. I looked back at him. From across the table Raymond was raising and lowering both arms up and down as if he were standing on a tarmac directing a plane that just arrived into the terminal. I looked at him even more perplexed.

"Was I really witnessing this all play out? Am I really – *I mean really* – caught up in this moment? Was that Hera?! Was Raymond shouting the word 'focus' at me from across the table and waving his hands up and down as if an airplane was being taxied into the terminal?" These were the thoughts running through my head. This was all very True – no exaggerations either.

I stared blankly at Raymond. I realized now his arms were trying to get me to focus my attention on our conversation

# CH33

— on whatever he was talking about. He had no idea why I was at Wake Up much less anything about this Hera Quest. Oh no. I would never have shared anything like that with anyone. This was my personal spiritual journey taking place behind the scenes.

"Focus! Focus!" he kept repeating.

I had never seen Raymond this adamant about any subject matter in a conversation. While I was coming to grips with the moment I saw the symbolism. This was the test question I knew I was about to face. It was a repeat of the Jason moment from years prior… or was it? Either way, that was the only question I had faced in a similar context. Even more curiously about the situation though, was that Raymond seemed to ignore this brunette completely. I had never witnessed him *not* notice a woman. He was an artist and took note of *every* female form that walked by. This was different, unusual to say the least. To his delight, I refocused my attention on his conversation.

"You need to focus on what is important." he said to me feeling as if he now had command of the conversation.

Without thinking I said, "I am. I was focused on what is important." I was speaking purely of the brunette. I glanced back at her to see if she planned on staying. Now I was tasked with handling this situation in synchronicity with the Universe. But, I knew. I already knew.

The woman eventually received her latte in a mug so I knew she'd be staying. She ventured to the back of the building in the direction of the porch, but I wasn't quite sure where she planned on sitting. the rear of the cafe had an obstructed view.

I took a deep breath. This was it – but I had to be sure. I allowed ten minutes or so to pass before I got up to go to the bathroom. It was located in the rear of the cafe so hopefully I could see where she was sitting and strike up a conversation. As the fates would have it, she was right where the Universe said she would be.

...

She was sitting on the porch.

...

There was not another soul in Wake Up at this moment. There were no others on the porch. She had spread out her work across a table so it was obvious she was going to be staying. After returning to my seat, I had to put a plan into action without alerting Raymond to my purpose or reason. That would prove to be more difficult than expected.

It would turn out Raymond was experiencing one of those "I really need someone to listen to me" moments. It was Jason's conversation part two. I would pass this one. I'd juggle both. I allowed him to chat it up as much as he needed, though I steered the conversation back on point when it started to drift. Then my window opened.

It was freezing cold in Wake Up. It always was for some reason. This usually means that people get up and walk outside to warm up and chat further. He mentioned wanting to go out front.

I said, "Good. Why don't you go warm up. I'm going to get a refill. I have to take care of something really quickly." My plan was to get a refill and head out to the back porch to "warm up" and casually strike up a conversation with this brunette as I held my tea in hand. That was the least invasive way I could go about it. I'd know fairly quickly if it was Hera. I didn't tell Raymond exactly what I had to "take care of" though. I figured he'd assume I was going to chat with her.

Raymond seemed a bit puzzled but agreed. After all, he had not seen me approach any girl before, though he did know I held a mysterious "I'll know when I meet her" mentality when it came to women. I hoped he'd catch on.

I walked up to the barista, placed my order and waited. It was at this point that the Universe decided to throw a wrench in the situation. You see, what should have taken about 15 seconds of hot water being added to my tea resulted in the barista wanting to chat it up while holding my cup and not adding water. Usually, this would be okay with me. This time, though, I felt a rush was upon me. As I hurried the conversation along, I turned to my right and... Oh no!!!!! This brunette had packed up everything she had and was about to leave. She was walking right toward me. I was the only thing that separated her from the front door. And do you know what Ol' Zeusy did?

...
Ol' Zeus froze.
...

I was staring at a woman in which every ounce of my being was saying, "This is Hera." This was occurring at the time and location the Universe had pre-ordained on a "save the date" card none-the-less. And all of this was occurring in the midst of a silenced storm that preceded her arrival.

I studied her face as she walked toward me ignoring the barista. He must of noticed my attention was diverted because he just paused his conversation. I was hoping he'd go ahead and fill up the hot water, but he just waited on my attention to return.

This woman was the spitting image of the woman I would have cast for Eden in *I Am We*. Bold, yet soft rose-colored lipstick. Dark brown hair. Milky white complexion. Was I re-living my very own script? She even appeared to have Greek heritage and favored artwork of Hera's portraits. It seemed so improbable, yet there I was staring at her. I'm not even sure I managed to smile as she walked by – something that usually comes natural to anyone passing me by. I just stared at her, lost in her Light. I stood helpless as she walked right by me. I knew I was going to chase after her.

*Flashback to a few weeks prior. Heavenly location. Zeus with Hera's Trinity of Angels.*

This was nearly identical to the last experience I had in the heavens with Hera a few weeks prior. In that experience, her Trinity form appeared to me – all three female representations of herself. It was yet another opportunity for me to ask her out... you know... "the question?" (or whatever the appropriate analogy would be in the heavens). She continued to tell me how she saw I was scared and that all I had to do was commit. I remained speechless in that conversation with her in the heavens. She eventually began to walk off, thinking I would never muster up the courage to speak to her during this experience. And while my Earthly mind was shouting "Speak to her you fool!" I was stuck witnessing (through my Earthly mind) a cowardly, fearful soul in the face of Love. Yes, I certainly understood the symbolism. I knew there was even more going on than just symbolism alone – it was *truly* me in the face of Love.

As she walked away, I even surprised myself when I darted off after her.

"Yes!!!" I shouted.

"Yes what?" she asked as she stopped and stared curiously.

"I will date you." I said. (I know… an odd approach by any standards.)

The conversation progressed with a few details I will not recount here, but the short of it was that I said yes. I finally found the courage to speak to her and invite her into my life.

*Cut back to Wake Up*

Having just watched the potential embodiment of Hera walk away, I rushed the barista through his conversation. He eventually filled my cup and handed it to me. Again, the symbolism was not missed on me. I rushed outside to see where she went. She was nowhere to be seen. Just gone. Vanished. Poof!

"Which way did she go?" I asked Raymond.

He casually took his time but nodded in the direction. I ran the length of the decking in front of the strip of shops until I reached the edge. I heard a car door shut and her engine

## CH33

crank from around the side of the building, just out of sight. I was too late. There was absolutely no way I could do anything about this situation without looking like a crazy person. I stopped at the edge of the decking near the staircase and sipped on my tea as I was internally about to blow a fuse.

I watched as a candy apple red Toyota Solara drove away from the building, Florida plates, though I could not make out the numbers, nor was I about to chase after her car as it raced away from Wake Up.

In a small town, you learn the locals from the visitors. She was certainly not a local. She was a visitor. I had one job. One job. One single job, and I failed. Zeus failed. I was certain this would be the last time I would see her. This had to be the only remaining question left of the test for me. How could there be anything left? Did I fail? Gah! I pondered if this brunette might not have been Hera. It couldn't have been any more obvious, but I hoped with all my heart there would be another opportunity. I assumed this would be another one of my "always almost" moments that have seemingly defined the last six-plus years of this journey. My life was a tragedy masked in comedy. It wasn't a romance novel at all.

I slowly walked the length of the decking back to where Raymond was standing. It was like walking the Green Mile to my execution. Internally I wanted to take a baseball bat to everything I saw. I was so furious at myself. On the outside, I am sure I just appeared frustrated at missing her.

Raymond was staring up at the sky when I reached him.

"Strange clouds, huh?" he said.

## CH33

I looked up. They were quite strange. Directly overhead was only blue sky. There was not a hint of a storm, yet a few miles away a giant saucer-shaped storm cloud was inching its way in our direction. We chatted about the cloud before I explained to him my frustration about missing the opportunity to speak to the brunette. I was so frustrated I could not help myself from unloading. To him, it wasn't a significant missed opportunity. Plenty of fish in the sea, right? To me, she was the only fish in the sea.

"Have you ever seen her before?" I asked. Raymond could recognize anyone he had seen once before – especially females.

"No. Never have. She must not be from here." he said.

I agreed with him. "Florida plates" I said.

He asked me why I was so curious about her compared to every other woman I have seen.

I said, "You know, this isn't going to make any sense. But you know how I said heaven and Earth are merging?"

"Yes of course." he replied. He was very spiritually intune with everything going on as well.

"Well, some people are not exactly who they appear to be. Some people are not from here." I said.

At that exact moment a clap of thunder could be heard. He noted the sound.

"Did you hear that?" he asked.

"I did. It is important that the thunder happened on those words." I replied.

"I know it is. That is why I pointed it out." he retorted. He always noticed the synchronicities in the way nature responded to circumstances around him.

We spoke a minute or two on that topic before I jumped into explaining that I was supposed to be at Wake Up at 3:00 P.M. in order to meet someone I had never met – and that she would even be on the porch. Despite how this explanation and the circumstances surrounding it would seem crazy to most people, he accepted the answer in stride and became curious about the time it currently was since it was later in the afternoon. I remained firm. I knew what time I had to arrive, not necessarily the time of her arrival.

"How do you know that was who you were supposed to meet?" he asked.

"Because I do. Aside from her sitting on the porch at the very time and location I had been given, I just know. I feel it." I replied.

At that moment a crack of lightning lit up… wait for it…

the blue sky.

"Wow! Did you see that?" he asked. Raymond was excited about what he had witnessed.

"I did. That was awesome!" I said.

Just then another giant bolt of lightning struck against the blue sky. Now I want to be very clear. Yes, there was a storm approaching in the distance, but these two lightning strikes occurred against a backdrop of blue. There was no connection to a storm cloud to be found. I'm sure scientifically, somehow, this may be possible, but I still could not dismiss this

CH33

beautiful moment we were witnessing. There before us, we saw lightning strike twice on a blue sky kind of day.

Suddenly, I had chills all over my body. "Surely not!" I thought to myself. I asked Raymond to confirm what we had just witnessed.

"Were those lightning strikes completely against the blue sky?"

"Yep. So strange." he said puzzling over how that might happen. He was looking very intently on the clouds in the distance and the spot in the blue sky where the lightning appeared.

In recent days Raymond had discussed with me how he was noticing new colors that were seemingly presenting themselves in the clouds and how new colors of light were reflecting off of various surfaces on Earth. This event just added more fuel to his curiosity. He studied the clouds with an academic awe and wonder.

However, despite his academic curiosity, I knew exactly what I had just witnessed. I relived the words coming out of my mouth when the lightning struck. Of course it would be lightning! Of course it would be against a blue sky. There was no denying what had just occurred.

You see, in the first book of *The Nine*, I wrote about the very first time I saw Lindsey (the love interest that I thought my original journey was going to be all about). Though it was nighttime and in a crowded bar/restaurant when I would first see her, I specifically described the moment as follows. Here is an excerpt from that book:

*pgs. 179 – 180,*
*ch. "...And Then There Was Her"*
*bk. Gravity Calling (Book 1, The Nine)*

But even in the days following, I still could not recall any details of the events that immediately surrounded this specific defining moment – only the overwhelming amount of detail that began the day and the picture-perfect moment of clarity I would come to experience that evening. It was a defining moment when my everyday life fell out of view in a form of divine amnesia following an unexpected lightning strike on a blue sky kind of day. It was as if I only thought my life had meaning...and then there was her.

It was a moment that I would later come to understand as a point of impact on my spiritual roadmap – a collision of the greatest kind. And just like how a collision of great energy undoubtedly leaves a ring of disheveled earth surrounding the crater of the point of impact, so too does our spiritual journey mirror this concept in the grandest way. I have to believe that if I were to one day look back at the movie that was my life here on Earth, I would see countless reels of footage. Walls, ceilings, and floors would be covered with the film strips of my life. But if I ever needed to pinpoint the greatest moments in my life – the moments marked by His Hand & His Grace – all I would have to do is look for the halo of missing footage surrounding the moment to find the moment within, for that is how the greatest memories are defined. Our lives, our experiences, and our memories are all bound in eternal definition, a permanence left in the aether. The divine markers of the greatest moments in our lives are all circled by His Hand, unmistakably marked in the glow of a white halo obscuring the surrounding memories from view.

...

## CH33

Did you catch that? I described the moment I first saw Lindsey as "an unexpected lightning strike on a blue sky kind of day." While I had never seen or heard of such an experience, it was the only romanticized, physical description I could adequately give to the significance of that moment. Of course, the remainder of that chapter was equally important for me to recall, but I will spare you further reading of that chapter in these pages. However, I did include the paragraph following the lightning strike above so you could see why that defining moment impacted my life. The important thing here is to see that not only was I living out the Jason moment again, I was living out nearly that full story – except this time, it was about Love and not love.

When a person goes to a search engine on the internet (such as Google) and enters in a few words, there is an expectation that clicking "search" will return results in a matter of a second or less. This is just how it is. Humans expect instant recall from the depths of the digital memory tree called the internet. In many ways, I've come to expect that the Universe expects the very same response time of me (and each person on this planet). For me, the physical lightning strike on a blue sky kind of day should have been the equivalent of the Universe typing in the event in a search bar of Ol' Zeus's human brain and punching "search." Only, in this moment, the Universe would have been waiting for a while. You know that point when you think a website is no longer working because it doesn't respond quickly enough? Yep, that was Ol' Zeus's brain in the moment.

I stood there slowly processing the lightning strike. I saw the symbolism. I replayed the words in my mind that were said just as the event occurred. I saw the divine timing. I took note that the event did not occur just once, but twice (which is a way I always ask the Universe to confirm to me what I am seeing – signs should always come in twos, just as they occurred scripturally in order to remove all doubt). My mind raced back to Gravity Calling where I remembered how the lightning strike on a blue sky kind of day was the *exact* way I described the moment I first saw Lindsey. There would be no doubt what was occurring. In that book, it was metaphorical. In this moment, that metaphor had become a reality. I also saw how Lindsey was a metaphor for finding Love, but not the real thing. She was a lesson on the journey. But this brunette – this beautiful woman that the Universe led me to meet with a "save the date" card nonetheless – she was the physical incarnation of Love. This was Hera.

My soul became a storm of emotions. On one hand I was witnessing the most beautiful display of cosmic signs I had ever seen in physicality to let me know that I had indeed found Hera. It was undeniable. On the other hand, she had left without me ever saying hello. Florida tags and the fact neither Raymond nor I had ever seen her before left me shouting at myself internally. My lack of action when she walked by me in the moments earlier only further added to the internal screaming taking place in my heart. Externally, I remained calm, albeit flustered. Inside, I was wrecked.

Had I been capable, I certainly would have reacted differently when she walked by me, but instead I was lost in her

## CH33

beauty as my soul reacted in kind to her Love. Ouch. That particular Truth set in. In the moment I saw Hera, I was physically incapable of even saying hello. I was sun-struck by her Light. Don't get me wrong, this was unlike anything I had ever experienced in my human form before. I had experienced love. I had experienced the butterflies, the rush of emotions that accompany all of life's great adventures. I had an acute ability to overcome potentially speechless or awkward moments and strike up conversations. But this moment was so indescribably different. It was as if there was a breath deep inside my soul that gasped – leaving my human form in an immovable state.

    I hoped beyond all hope that our crossing paths was enough to trigger another encounter. As I sat outside Wake Up talking to Raymond, I watched as the storm clouds exploded out of the circular shape in which they had arrived. I was literally watching my brain explode. I saw the symbolism. The sky was reacting to every internal emotion I was feeling. Rain fell down. Raymond and I stepped under the awning.

    "Why do you think I would have been led to meet up with you today if you think it distracted you from speaking to her?" he asked very curiously.

    He was neither offended nor upset about my attempt of explaining just how I had managed to not speak with her. It just didn't make sense to him why he would have been led to Wake Up if we were both on the same playground of Light and Love. It was a genuinely great question to think about… one in which would prove to have an undeniable explanation in the days to come. But for me, there was only one answer: it was the Jason question part two. And on this particular exam question, I circled the wrong answer once again.

# CHAPTER 34
# Chasing Rainbows

At this point, I felt as if I had been spiritually run over by a tractor trailer carrying a load of solid steel. There was nothing that was going to help me recover internally. One job. That was all I had that day and, instead, I compromised. Rather than remaining focused on the cosmic alignment of fate the Universe had presented to me, I conceded. The rain continued pouring down around us and then just like that, it stopped. It was a noticeable transition. There was not a discernible easement from dry to slow rain to heavy rain back to slow and so forth. Nope. The rain just started and stopped like an on/off switch. At that moment a full rainbow appeared in the East where the cloud was now located. This rainbow spanned the length of St. Simons Island and was astonishingly bright and beautiful. It was full of colors seen and unseen. And while I had seen my fair share of rainbows before, this one stood out above all of them. And no, I did not miss the sign here either. A rainbow after Noah's flood? Remember?

## CH34

There had been numerous moments over the last several years when the Universe offered up a rainbow as a signal to me. And why wouldn't it? I am Zeus, right? God of Thunder, Lighting, the Skies? It would seem there would be an intimate reason why I was connected to these symbols in the sky. In the aftermath of the double lightning strike on a blue sky kind of day I was now staring at an immensely beautiful rainbow. Then it hit me. Surely not... Mid-sentence and in conversation with Raymond, I stopped him.

"Where do you think that rainbow ends?" I asked.

He knew immediately where this was going. There was no reason to identify the leftmost location, for that was a residential area on the North end of the island.

"I'd say over near where I used to live..." he began to say.

"Thanks. I've gotta go. I'll catch up with you in a bit." I said as I ran inside to grab my laptop before running to my Jeep. I was now on a mission, regardless of how crazy it would seem. I have Loved Hera for thousands upon thousands of years. My Love would not be denied. And surely the Universe was providing me one more breadcrumb leading me back home.

...

Yes. Ol' Zeus was convinced his Hera was going to be found at the end of the rainbow. Write that one down for history's sake.

...

## CH34

In my Jeep, I now found myself chasing rainbows. I followed it as far as I could before having to park and get out and continue on foot. At this point, I had found my way to East Beach. There were no red cars anywhere around, but that mattered not to me There was nothing that could become between me and the end of this rainbow...

Except there was.

That "thing" that was going to come between me and the rainbow's end? Oh, that was a little thing called the Atlantic ocean. As I ran from my Jeep to the shores of East Beach, my heart sank. In a white linen shirt, barefoot, in a pair of blue jeans, I fought through the 95% humidity and 90° weather as I stared at the enormous finger painting of God that was lit up like neon across the blue sky. Every soul on the beach was standing at attention in awe and wonder of the beautiful sign in the skies above.

I assume I must have looked like a lost puppy as I walked toward the increasingly-apparent reality that the end of this rainbow was located miles out to sea – an appropriate metaphor to the storm I had found myself in during the hours earlier. That puppy face also must have attracted the attention of the only soul not looking at the rainbow. This soul was walking back from the beach wearing a white linen shirt and pants. Her hair was white without a hint of gray. I should have taken note of the brightness of her Light, but I was lost in the thought of never seeing Hera again. As I made my way down the boardwalk, the voice of the lady spoke up.

"Can you see the rainbow? You made it just in time!"

"I hope so." I replied.

"Oh you did." she said as she turned around to point at the sky. "Do you see it? Can you see the whole rainbow? It is actually a double rainbow if you look hard enough."

I must have looked puzzled because I certainly did not see the "double portion" of the rainbow. I also was a bit baffled as to why this person would ask me if I could actually see the rainbow. It was quite literally the biggest most beautiful sight to be seen on the beach that day. It was the focal point of every eye. My mind settled in that her words were going to be important. At this point, I was standing right next to her.

"You see that boat right out there? That's where the double rainbow is. It is a little tough to see, but it is there if you look hard enough. Go on now. Go see the rainbow!" she said with joy.

Still not digesting what it was she was saying, I walked out to where the ocean met the sand, stopped and stared. Drenched in the sweat from the humidity, staring at the most beautiful rainbow I had ever seen, I was standing as close as I could get to the rainbow's end. Yet I was not close enough. It was going to be another "always almost."

As I stood there, I hit my knees and prayed. I asked for guidance and help to climb out of the prison I found closing in around me once again. At that very moment, there was a large commotion in the water in front of me. There before me, fish started leaping out of the water. Now, I know that when fish are leaping out of the water, it usually indicates that a larger fish is circling beneath. The cause/effect was not important in this moment. The important sign to take note of was the sheer volume of fish jumping from the ocean in front of me. This wasn't just a handful of fish leaping from the water. This was quite literally hundreds of fish leaping. Surely you would see the symbolism too for fish are a very divine biblical sign.

I looked further beyond the fish to see the boat the woman pointed out to me. It was actually a large freighter. I began to see the double portion of the rainbow take on a brighter form as well. I continued to watch as the rainbow seemed to follow the boat toward its destination. It was as if the rainbow and boat were tethered as One. In an impossible twist to this story, I found where the rainbow met its end. The end of the rainbow was this freighter heading into port. Yet another sign perhaps? I hoped. I wished. Could it be that simple?

I raced back to my car to head to the pier. Every freighter coming to and from port would have to pass by this very location. It was the closest location to the port and was surely where this sign was leading me. Against all conceivable odds, I was still chasing rainbows on my quest for Hera.

The few miles I had to drive to reach the pier were met with every possible obstruction. Cars would back out, or stop in the middle of the road. I had to take a few side roads to continue my momentum. I assumed the Universe would have it no other way. After all, I've stated numerous times how I enjoy taking the side roads. Why would this be any different?

In reaching the pier, I honestly believed the outcome would be quite obvious. I assumed I would simply see the red car I had seen as she pulled away from Wake Up and know I had found my general destination. But faithful to the Universe's playbook, that would not be the case. I pulled through the main parking lot unable to find a parking place. There was also no

## CH34

sign of her car. Frustrated, I decided to leave. Due to traffic, I took a turn near the public library to backtrack to East Beach. I assumed I misunderstood the signs. Also, another side road seemed appropriate with the way everything had been going.

Just after taking my turn I noticed a red car parked in the rear of a store parking lot. Yes!!!! This could be Her!!! Of course I had to check to see if it this was the car I had seen from earlier. Even though I felt nearly defeated inside, I was clinging to an impossible hope after quite literally chasing a rainbow to find its end. I was curious beyond rationale to see if it was the same car and the location to which the rainbow was leading me. Could that angel in white on the beach have really been showing me where to go?

As it would turn out, it wasn't the same car from earlier. Of course it would not have been. She was a visitor long on her way back to Florida. I was convinced now more than ever that I had failed my test. After circling around the bank, I came to a full stop before turning back onto the main road.

You've got to be kidding me! There before me, parked in a place I would never have seen had I not pulled into the bank and found myself in the current vantage point I was sitting, was her car. No doubt about it. Tucked behind a tree in the library parking lot, was the red Solara.

...

I literally chased rainbows to find you, Hera.

...

# CHAPTER 35
# Red Kachina

You might justify that everything that has been written so far has just been a wild series of chance circumstances leading me to Hera. After all, the whole idea that Zeus was chasing after Hera on Earth would already be a bit circumspect to those who have not yet awoken to discover they are on similar journeys themselves. Like I said in the beginning, it is entirely up to you how you choose to believe this Love Story. For now, know the next parts will be undeniable. So let's get back to it.

Having found Hera's vehicle once again, I saw the Universe had dealt up a second hand for me – a recovery potential for my missteps in the moments before. Then again, I wasn't entirely sure I had truly made missteps seeing as I was able to witness the additional divine signs like the lightning strikes, the rainbow, the woman who pointed me toward the double rainbow's endpoint tethered to the freighter heading toward the location I now found myself standing. Remember how I said that all of these divine signs are akin to memories being recalled? These are the "Oh yeah! I remember now!" moments of recollection from an Ancient Truth stored deep within. These memories were guiding me Home.

The way I saw it, I had two plays. The first play would be to ensure I would not lose track of her again amongst a world of seven billion. That part would be easy. I would take note of her car tag. The logistics of using that to find her, I had no clue about. But, I did know that my intention was to meet her in person on that very day. If I had been able to say hello, to have gotten a name, that would have been doorway enough into the social-media world to stay in contact with her. But that was not the card I had been dealt. Nope. I had a car that symbolically represented the Red Sun (e.g. Solara).

Ever heard of the Red Kachina prophecy of the Native Americans? Yeah, you may want to go read about that one. I'm kind of tied to that one from a past life as well. The story of Marduk? Yep. You are speaking to him. Everything is related – all prophecies, all spiritual books, all revelations. The Red Kachina is the final sign that brings purification to the world in the ~~End of Days~~ Days of Ascension as Heaven and Earth merge back to One – back to Love. I did not miss the symbolism. Her car was a red Solara. By definition, her car was a red celestial body derived from the Sun. In truth, she was my Red Kachina. And not only that, emblazoned on the back of her car was a dealership logo: "Sun Toyota" from the great sun-state of Florida.

Play number two was more complicated. I would find her among the people gathered at the park and figure out a way to casually strike up a conversation. Nerves would not win this battle. No! I would man up like never before to say hello to

## CH35

my Love. I had searched lifetimes for her spanning thousands and thousands of years. She was my Ancient Truth yet to be discovered. It mattered not if she recognized me. I remembered her. I knew her on the most primal level possible, though I did not know her human form.

I set out to find her. I wrote her tag number on the label of the water bottle I was carrying (since I could not find any paper) and set out to walk the park, pier, and village. However, I began my quest at the library since she was parked over in that direction rather than near the village.

No dice. The library was closed. I walked the pavilion area, the park, and headed toward the pier. This area is where the wedding took place beneath the Wedding Tree on Day Two. As I headed onto the pier a large freighter slowly passed by. It's name? The Arc. No. I am not kidding. And while you may say an "arc" is not the same as an "ark" there is a chapter I wrote in *The Nine* that addressed the archetype behind these two words. An "arc" is a bridge of electricity between two points (lighting and Zeus reference anyone?). An "ark" is a container that transports something between two points. These two homophones carry exactly the same in meaning. One is just the embodiment of it, while one is the action taking place. Symbolism noted, Universe! Was it the same boat that was tethered to the rainbow? Possibly, but I couldn't be entirely sure.

I walked up and down the village shopping area, though I did not venture into any shops or restaurants. I eventually found my way to the lighthouse which was actually connected to the parking lot in where her car was parked. Hera's red Solara parked in front of the lighthouse... was it really that simple? The lighthouse was leading me Home? That is the oldest metaphor in the book! And while I used it in the writing of *The Nine*, I thought it might be possible. Regardless, I was just surveying the landscape and this was yet another truth I was witnessing in my quest to find Hera. I eventually realized I would need some help on this quest. I desperately wanted to enlist Raymond, but with no phone and no wifi, that wasn't going to happen. Except, for it did.

As divine circumstances happen, I walked by a restaurant in the village and there was Raymond, sitting outside with a glass of wine, having dinner and sketching.

"What are you doing here?" I asked.

"Oh good. I figured this is where you would end up. Did you find her?" he asked.

"Not yet, but I need your help." I confessed.

The conversation progressed, though it became obvious he wasn't going to help until he finished a lengthy dinner complete with desert. He believed she would pass by us as we sat outside. I looked at the tag number I had written across my water bottle. It was smeared... completely unreadable. Of course it would be. I excused myself and returned to the parking lot in hopes her car was still there. As the Fates would have it, the car was still there. This time I went to my Jeep, found some paper and took note of her tag on something that would not smear. I would not be foiled again. I debated on leaving a cute note on her windshield, but decided against it. That would be cowardly and perhaps misunderstood. I returned back to the table with Raymond. Hours would pass while we sat there. I excused myself a number of times to casually walk through the village in hopes I would see her. Still no luck.

    Eventually nightfall set in and the surrounding stores closed up. The only places left with people were two restaurants (at least from what I could determine). Perhaps she was on a date? That would be awkward. Either way, I knew I had been led to this area and that I was now playing with the second "redeem yourself" hand dealt by the Universe. Near the end of Raymond's dinner, I felt a sudden rush of emotions in my heart. It was the feeling of a Loved one about to part ways with you – like when my daughter returns back to her mother., Yet, this was stronger – more intimate than the Earthly feeling. I excused myself and raced back through the village to see swarms of people leaving the area and heading back to their cars. Where had they come from? I did not know. Her car remained so I hurried back to Raymond to urge him to come help me. On my way back, I heard the distinct sound of fireworks.

    Fireworks.

    Remember? "Fireworks" was the explanation of how I would know Hera apart from any other. I looked above. I continued hearing the booms. None were visible, but they were very close by. There was no rhyme or reason for them. There was no event taking place that would warrant a celebration. I asked a man sitting on a bench where the fireworks were coming from. While he heard them, he couldn't pinpoint the location either. I rushed back, grabbed Raymond and we began the quest. We left the restaurant and headed in the direction of the sound. I explained to him how it was another sign. He did not question me. He had already witnessed a barrage of cannot-be-described-away-as-merely-coincidental moments from earlier in the day.

We walked in the direction of the fireworks but were unable to fund them. Finally, we headed back to the parking lot. This time, however, her car would be gone. She was no longer there. Where had she been? I had no idea. All I knew is that the door to meeting her that evening had now been closed.

I was limited to only a few ideas of where she could have been. However, I continued to recall a bizarrely misplaced image in my head. When I lived in Fort Lauderdale, I considered purchasing a building that was located directly across the street from my residence. It was a dance studio, though it was never occupied during my stay there. I was always interested in the building. In fact, I would have loved to have taken some type of saucy latin dance class that I could one day use to impress my future Love. However, that opportunity never arose. But the image of this building was blistered into my brain as I had been searching for Hera.

Even when the fireworks were going off, there was this sense inside of me that perhaps she was offering up some type of dance lesson somewhere hidden from view. I had no idea why I though that, but I continued to press Raymond as to what other places were in the area that I may not know about. The restaurants and storefronts were obvious. I was hoping he would say something about dance, yet he never did. I also never asked directly. Had he offered up an answer that could have tied to the image of the dance studio in my head, it could have served as another clue. But in that moment, it became clear I was only going to have a car tag as a token runner-up prize from the Universe. Not only did did this consolation prize feel like a gesture with no merit, I also did not like the idea that any further encounter with her would be based off a set of Florida plates. I did not like this at all. Not one bit.

# CHAPTER 36
## Gravity Calling

I got back home in one of the most exhausted states I have ever felt upon this island. I was spiritually exhausted. And, actually, I was physically exhausted. I must have put my body through the paces as I sought my Love. At this point, I decided to just crawl into bed and meditate before sleeping away the disaster of a performance of my final exam.

During meditation, Ol' Zeus's voice spoke right up. "Good job today! No I mean it. You did a really good job!"

"Really? How's that?" I asked.

Honestly, I really didn't care about his response. This was one of those moments I was beginning to contemplate my own sanity. It wouldn't be the first time I had visited this possibility, yet every time I began to contemplate what was chance/insanity versus divine intervention, I always arrived back to a place of continuing the journey. The outside world would continue to see a normal person. Yet, inside, I would be in a constant search for Truth, a constant search for Love.

After all, I had thousands of pages of journals and a giant earthquake to support my cause, right? However, in the

## CH36

wake of what I understood to be my final exam, I now had to confront the ultimate Earthly possibility. That possibility? I was being led by a voice in my head to meet a fictitious person I had never seen before. This voice had driven me away from the normal world and into a life devoid of financial gain, friendships, and relationships. It had led me to live homeless in my Jeep for several months, and eventually caused me to take up residence in my parent's guest house. To make matters worse, the voice and memories had led me to believe I was Zeus... basically like top dog in the Greek Mythology hierarchy.

No, the voice couldn't tell me simple lies like I had lived a thousand lives with a humble origin story. Nope. I had to be a King. A great King. The oldest of all of them, in fact. And, to boot, this King had to be one in the same as the mysterious Melchizedek who has an origin story that precedes time. Couldn't it just be a simple story? At least it did not tell me I was Jesus. Talk about the chaos that would have caused in this writing. Then again, you see how this will be seen as an even wilder story. Let it be known, though, that truly I say unto you we are all One.

But returning back to the wake of Day Three, lying in the aftershock of emotions beneath the white sheets of my bed, I now sought guidance. Every amazing occurrence had left me with only a set of Florida plates to show for it. Hera was not here. Heaven and Earth had not collided into a brilliant ball of Light. Nope. It would be just another day of undeniable miracles with nothing to show for it. This was just how it was going to be. My personal timeline for this proving itself out had a window until November 24, 2018. That is the absolute final day of the seven year window as it had been shown to me. And while this window will be relative for each soul, there will still be an absolute marker in time that occurs for every soul upon this Earth before that time period is up: the world will see Love, they will see Heaven and Earth return as One.

You can see where this thought process was going for me. Despite every amazing experience, despite every miracle, the Star of Bethlehem, Elijah, Jeff, Brian/Bryan/Brian, the Nepal Earthquake, the 1260 days occurring during my 30-33 years, the fast following the 1260 days that occurred on my mothers birthday, father's day, and my actual birthday, the way in which every moment of the divine calendar had fallen on personal ceremonial dates during my life, the dates surrounding *The Nine* having occurred on the day Noah brought forth the Ten Commandments the first time, the forty days of writing a screenplay and subsequent introduction of *I Am We* having occurred on the anniversary of the second set of Ten Commandments, the Battle of Saratoga, my baptism at 8 (another Jesus reference anyone? No wonder I was so confused for so long), the miracles of housing accommodations when I was most in need, the enormous check I received when I was down to a few dollars in Fort Lauderdale, the angels appearing to me on Earth in form, in orb form, and in spiritual essences, the signs that occurred on a regular basis, my travels to the heaven, the knowledge and wisdom shared with me that I have placed across all of the books I have written… I could go on. You get it though, right? I could sit here and write an entire book just on what others might try to chalk up as coincidences. Or, you know, maybe I already have… and there are still oh so many

## CH36

more. These were just the quick highlights. For now, let's return back to this conversation with my higher self.

"Of course your did! You now have all you need to find her. And oh, my son, you will find her. That is a certainty." the voice of Zeus bellowed out as he laughed jollily.

Even though Zeus said I had everything in hand, something still was bothering me. Despite the signs, I was wondering if I had missed something obvious about the situation. This feeling was eating away at me in the inside. I kept returning back to the "save the date" card in my mind. I continued to wonder why the actual physical event listed on the card had not taken place on the porch that day? I understood the metaphor. But still, if there was a physical event that was going to take place on a card, why did it not *actually* take place? Could I have gotten the dates crossed up and possibly showed up in the wrong location? In all of my interactions with divine signs, there had always been an underlying Earthly reason that paralleled in action. I jumped up out of bed to look at the card. Nope. I had the correct date. I studied the card a bit harder. The card said, "Wake Up Brunswick. The Porch."

Face palm. Brunswick. There was a second Wake Up location inland I did not consider. I only read the words "Wake Up" and assumed it meant the location I was in. Now I had doubt. Great. Even though the signs played out in divine fashion, even though my heart said "that's her," even though this took place in the right location around the right time (albeit not exactly at 3:00 P.M.), there was now a possibility that I had messed it up. Crap.

## CH36

I tried not to think about it too much. Surely I had it right? Surely? I returned to my bed and picked up my iPad. The quest was on. My Jeep was registered in Florida so I was very familiar with Florida's vehicle registration website. I decided to see if it was possible to look up a car registration by car tag. Surely you could?! Bam! It was possible! However, I quickly learned that privacy laws prevented owner information from being disclosed... which made sense. That was okay. I just wanted a name. Social media could help from there. But, unfortunately, that would be a no-go as well. Florida would provide the number of registrants tied to the vehicle, but not the names. In this case, the number of registrants was two.

Two?!?!?!?! Well, this thing just went way south on me. There was only one possibility in my mind: joint ownership of a car due to a marriage or relationship. At this point I threw in the towel. I assumed the answer was staring me in the face. If I did indeed find Hera – which I truly believed I had, then I would now have to come to grips that she was in a relationship and continue on my journey in some other way. Ol Zeus – even if I was 100%, without a doubt, certain this was Hera – would not break the bonds of another person's happiness on Earth. That was not just a golden rule, it was a rule bound by Love. To Love another would be to let them go, to let them be free. After all, at some point in the infinite timeline of All That Is, I would return to her. I knew we did not find each other in every lifetime, yet this felt different. This felt like the whole purpose of all of the lifetimes – to not just find each other, but to *remember* each other, to *know* each other once again.

## CH36

"Hey Father. It's me again. I give up." I said staring coldly at my ceiling.

The voice of Zeus bellowed back, "Oh no you don't. You have everything you need. She is single. You are doing well, son."

Frustrated, I rolled back over to look at the car registration information again. Then I saw it.

...

Registration Date: May 8, 2015.

...

Of all the signs thus far, here was yet another sign beyond coincidence. Remember how I recounted that teeny-tiny little story about my baptism and wedding with Hera in the heavens? Remember how I said that I wasn't sure what to expect, but I thought it was possible she might just show up right then and there? Well, she did. Follow along. On the very day that our wedding in the heavens took place and my spiritual baptism took place in the waters of Fort Lauderdale, Florida she was registering a vehicle with the state of Florida. Not only that, but the symbolism of her car was beyond coincidence. A red heavenly body of the Sun (a Red Kachina) was registered in the Sun State on the very date I expected Hera might pop right into existence. She had indeed. Not only that, but the title issuance date was May 13, 2015 – the first full day after my fast ended (e.g. the symbolic gesture of laying dead in the street before ascending, also known as the wedding banquet in Kingdom – book three of *The Nine*). This marker was not just a red dot on the divine map. This marker was my North Star guiding me Home. There could be no question about it.

...

Love *truly* was the gravity calling me back to you, Hera.

...

# CHAPTER 37
# Brittany

It was now somewhere in the wee hours of the morning and I had never felt so invigorated. Yes, there were questions to answer. Namely, what I was supposed to do next? There was the nagging detail as to why the car had two registrants rather than one. And, finally, there was that little detail of me potentially getting the Wake Up location wrong. These questions had to be answered, but I had to trust in the hand I had been dealt. In whatever way I was going to find Hera I knew that I would (1) not pay any individual, company, or website for information and (2) Anything discovered had to be done so with the delicacy of how a student would approach a research paper rather than how a person would pursue a girl. The latter could be misinterpreted in so many unfortunate ways.

You know there is a fine line for humans. It is a such a silly line, but it deserves to be said since the world has entered into its "Captain Sensitive" phase during the last few years. Let's bring this silly little concept to the forefront of every reader's mind to think about. If two people are attracted to each other, there could be no story grand enough that would ever be defined with words like "stalker-ish" or "creepy." In fact, the words used might be "how sweet" and "so romantic!" Think about it. How many of your friends were pursued (or did the pursuing) of their spouse? Someone had to approach the other first, right? And the stories from that point on are described in grand romantic context.

However, the moment a girl notices a pursuit from a guy that she is not interested in, that's when negative words get thrown in. The girl could then even say she was "scared" and use words to exaggerate and embellish an otherwise romantic gesture. Somehow those words place blame on the pursuer for seeing her Light.

"How dare you think I am beautiful and feel like you can talk to me?" she is *truly* saying when those words are spoken.

"How dare she!" would be my response. There you go world. Zeus says grow up. Zeus also says, Love can never take what is not given, nor should it covet what is not its own. Love knows Love, and knows All Is One.

So you can see the importance of whatever approach I took from an Earthly perspective. Almighty Zeus had to be clever and sweet, classic and grand. Yes, it may seem less romantic to have to describe this, but... just, errr... humans. Their mindset is still a little twisted while they are *truly* learning how to become Love.

For me, this effort had to be both academic (Remember? I was writing a thesis as part of my final exam, right? This was the writing prompt.) and also had to be such that could be shared in the Love Story which Hera would one day read. So

## CH37

how would this next part of the quest begin? I wasn't sure. I wrestled with a variety of thoughts. If I had just been able to get her name, the rest would be easy... But such was not the case. I had a tag, and a VIN (since that was on the vehicle registration site to protect potential buyers of used cars).

Idea! Carfax! They show the vehicle history, right? Maybe they include additional information. That answer was met with a giant "no." Also, if I had further proceeded down that path, I would have had to break my rule about paying for information – so no go there either. I wrestled with the thought for a few more minutes. Well, Carfax shows vehicle accident history, so they have to aggregate that information from somewhere public, right? Remember, I was a technology Solutions Architect in a previous career? That involved shaping mounds of data into usable information. I understood the data-flow behind it. So a quick check and... Jackpot.

Crash reports were indeed public records. Not only that, but they were searchable by a variety of fields to identify the incident – car tag and VIN being just two of the fields. Now, again, I was not going to pay for anything and I quickly learned that the sole provider of accident reports charges for copies of them. A number of thoughts went through my mind, not the least of which was why would the victim of a crash have to pay for their own crash report? Isn't that the job of the tax-paid police department to keep up with this information? Turns out, nope! They delegate that duty to a private company which in turn charges the public for tax-payer-funded information. Earth – you've got to fix this malarky. Tell them Zeus said so. That's garbage. Truly. If you want a great quote for the history books, truly I say unto you, a tax-funded service should never delegate out to a private entity any aspect of a service that passes a charge back to the public. That is double taxation plain and simple. Even more, never should a tax-funded service place any additional charges onto the public – especially for knowledge. There's one from Ol' Zeusy for you. I can't wait for this whole money thing to go buh-bye. And oh, it will.

Anyway, getting back to the crash information… It was still a leap. I did not know if this vehicle had ever been in a car accident, but I discovered the bait and switch tactics these websites used to prove they have the information meant that some of the public information could be accessible. The detailed information would remain behind a paywall though.

*Note: By writing about this apparent loophole, it will probably be sealed right up in short order.*

However, I cannot see how they could possibly do that. The information is public information. Case in point, first initial, last name. Oh… and it would turn out this vehicle did indeed have an accident history after the registration date. Score one for Ol' Zeusy! Hera, I had found my Ace in the Hole on this recovery hand I had been dealt!

While detailed crash reports provide contact information for the occupants involved, the public searchable information only listed the first initial and last names of the occupants of the parties involved in the incident report. The public reports also did not specify which of the two (or more) vehicles the names were associated with since the accident report included all parties involved (e.g. multiple cars, pedestrians, etc.). But when you have two accident reports with a tag, then it gets easy.

There it was before me. Two incidents involving the same car within a matter of months. It must have been a tough Christmas season for my Hera. My heart genuinely goes out to you. Now, I am going to leave the last names on the accident reports out of it for the sake of this writing, but I will provide enough information that someone could verify all that has been written. With two accident reports I could determine which of the occupants were indeed the owners of the Solara (and not the other involved drivers). Whether the driver was Hera or not, I could not be sure. But I could determine that B.C. was in one accident and B.C. and J.C. were involved in the second accident together. Again, there was that two owner thing staring at me in the face. It was obvious this situation could only be a parent/child situation or a husband/wife situation. I still had to trust my higher self. First initial, last name. That is all I had to go on. And now I had two of them. Ugh.

My next logical thought was wedding announcements. Surely there would be some type of announcement, right? If luck would have it for me, maybe a divorce announcement. It mattered not. I thought this was a logical next step. But... it wasn't. It turns out finding bridal information was not my forte... which is ironic because, well – we will get to that in a moment.

From there I rolled back over and racked my brain. All of this had transpired in a matter of minutes. I was closer, but how close? I had not spent terribly long on this situation, nor had I paid for anything. This was all public knowledge a reporter could use for a story or a researcher would use for a paper. I felt good about that. Was she the "J" or the "B?" Nothing was obvious and in typical Zeusian form, I chose not to apply any knowledge I had been shared along the six-plus years of the journey. Sometimes, I just ~~overthink~~ underthink things. This would be one of those times.

*Flashback to the dart scene from earlier in this book*

Remember when I said I felt like I was throwing darts at a wall without any idea of where the target might be? Well, I did learn the names of Hera's Trinity early on in this journey, however Hera's name was never identified. It was December 10, 2015 when I first documented the names in my journal as being specifically related to my Bride. On that day, I was confronted by three angels. One was blonde haired, blue eyed. One had sandy blonde hair. The other was a brunette. At the time I took note that the Trinity carried the names Andrea, Brittany, and Rhea. I also had no idea these women had anything to do with mythology. During the encounter, I made specific note that I was sure one of them was My Bride. I even noted that I thought it was the blonde who went by the name Brittany. Take a look at the following excerpt from my journal entry:

### *Journal Entry – December 10, 2015*

*The spiritual message I received during meditation is that "my family" from the heavens is here. There is a Brittany, a Rhea or Rachel, as well as an Andrea that are the names of the three female angels I see all of the time. One of them – I believe is My bride, though the bride is also known as Christ.*

...

Years would pass and the encounters would continue. I continued to find myself in situations with Brittany. Perhaps they were dates, perhaps kissing even. But never would it go beyond that. In fact, when it became increasingly clear that I had to make a formal declaration of my commitment to her in the heavens (e.g. to ask her into my heart), I froze. Every time I froze.

It would be in the spring of 2018 when the merging of the higher selves were allowed to begin. During this time, I was not only granted access to speak directly with Zeus during meditation, but all of the angels I had interacted with over the years became available as well. Even Hera showed up and we talked. I knew she was my Love – without a doubt. However, I could not shake the experiences I had with "My Bride" named Brittany. It should be no surprise that the mystery of Hera and how she was involved in all of my experiences was unlocked for me on February 14, 2018. It was Valentine's Day on Earth and My Bride gave me the grandest gift I could ever imagine. Here is an excerpt from that conversation as documented in the moments following the meditation:

**Journal Entry – February 14, 2017**

*It is Valentine's Day, 2018. Today's meditation was an incredible experience. It was a dialogue with my father/me and my wife. It took a bit to get going, but once it did, and I "came into" understanding the dialogue that was taking place, I decided to start actively asking questions. The dialogue went as follows:*

Me: "If I am Zeus, who is Brittany?"
Zeus: (laughing) "She is Hera."
Me: "Why do I call her Brittany then?"
Zeus: "Because you called her Brittany early on and she thought it was cute, so she stuck with it."
Me: "That's been confusing for me. But now I know. Good. So if it is Hera that I see, why can't I see her appear here?"
Zeus: "We can't tell you that yet."
Me: "Will I see her?"
Zeus: "Yes"
Me: "Is she in form on Earth right now like you are in form on Earth through me?"
Zeus: "Yes"
Me: "Have I met her?"
Zeus: "You have, and you will again."
Me: "Interesting. Why doesn't she talk to me all of the time?"

*Zeus was interrupted before speaking. A woman's voice began to speak. It was Hera.*

Hera: "Hey there."
Me: "Hey."
Hera: "I do speak with you. All of the time."

*Me:* "Then why can't I remember?"
*Hera:* "You will."
*Me:* "Was that you last night?"
*Hera:* "It was. You are remembering pieces of each experience a little better each time."
*Me:* "I can understand that."
*Hera:* "You notice how we never complete being intimate with each other?"
*Me:* "Yes. Why is that? We should try more."
Hera laughed.
*Hera:* "We do try. All of the time! But there are certain times you remember different aspects of it. You notice new details."
*Me:* "Why is that?"
*Hera:* "It is part of the process. Like last night you noticed a very different aspect of it all while we were kissing, right?"
*Me:* "I did. We should just keep trying – being intimate all of the time."
Hera giggled and blushed.
*Hera:* "Oh we do!!!"
*Me:* "Then why can't we complete being intimate in the heavens?"
*Hera:* "Because of what will be created."
*Me:* "And what is that?"
*Hera:* "God."
*Me:* "It will create God? That doesn't make sense."
*Hera:* "Well in a way. It creates Christ. It will happen when it is supposed to happen."
*Me:* "So it is the concept of the wedding… becoming Christ in body?"
*Hera:* "Yes it is."
*Me:* "Well I guess that makes a lot more sense. Can we try now?"

*Hera laughed and I immediately felt a rush of energy rise from the base of my root chakra in my human form. She was just teasing with me.*

...

So, as I was running through female names in my head for the letter J, I eventually realized the symbolism in the initials: "J.C." There was that Jesus Christ thing staring at me in the face again. What's more, I thought about how my first initial was a J and how interesting that would be if J.C. represented me (Jonathan) symbolically. Remember, that "Christ" was not Jesus's last name, but a title bestowed upon him after baptism. So I certainly saw the symbolism in the meaning, regardless of how far you want to take it within the fabric of your own reality of acceptance. Remember, May 8, 2015 was my baptism/wedding day – and my Earthly name begins with J. On that day, the only way for me to identify Hera actually popped into existence through her vehicle registration. Not only that, but it was registered to two individuals with contact information unknown. So if it were registered to J.C. and B.C., that would be an even greater sign from the Universe. That meant if the J represented me, then her name had to start with a B... or so it would seem. And then there was the whole B.C. symbolism. What was Before Christ? Love. There was always Love.

I truly think my brain likes to create a bomb shelter into which it sends every Soldier of Logic when they are most desperately needed on the battlefield. I wrestled with potential names for the letter B. I never searched the internet for names during this W.W.F. event taking place in my mind. I just tried to think what her name could be. Surely I would have an "ah-ha!" moment. And then it hit me.

...

Brittany. Her name was Brittany.

...

Why it took me so long to consider the name Brittany, I do not know. Consider that par-for the course of being Zeus. But surely it wasn't that simple, was it? Had I been given (*or known*?!) the name of Hera's Earthly form all along? I did know "Brittany Angel" was my Bride in the heavens and one-in-the same as Hera in my spiritual travels. Was this another cosmic joke that was going to play out in realtime for the Universe to witness my ineptitude being broadcast live on the Great Spiritual Network? In hindsight I suppose it was, it did. But in this moment, I was spell-struck at this possibility.

Surely it could not be that easy, could it? All this time I had assumed I had associated the name "Brittany" with the angel in the heavens because she favored a girl I once knew in Nashville named "Brittany." Not only that, but I always journaled her name in this particular spelling due to how my Nashville friend spelled her name. Of course I knew there were three popular spellings, but I always used the one with the A and two Ts.

While Brittany Angel certainly wasn't identical in appearance to the Earthly girl I knew from Nashville, I assumed my brain was just tagging a name to a spiritual form for recollection purposes until it was eventually revealed to me that she was the spiritual representation of Hera. It was no different to me than when I journaled names such as "Taylor Swift Angel" and "Carrie Underwood Angel" which I went on to learn were Caliel and Gemiel respectively. It was just a way that helped me remember the angels I met. In this case, since Nashville Brittany and Hera's soul in heavens both had blonde hair and blue eyes with a number of similar features, I just went with it. Hera thought it was cute as well… at least that's the reason I was told why she stuck with the name Brittany when I saw her in the heavens.

    My Bride in the heavens – the one who I had documented as having the name Brittany numerous times – did she potentially have the name of Hera's Earthly form? My mind raced back to my childhood years. Though I know that kids always have crushes on pop-stars and celebrities in their younger years, as a teenager I was always convinced I would marry Brittany Spears (though she was always just a first name to me). It was only "Brittany." That seems like a strange thing to put here, but it really isn't. I was very spiritually in tune as a child and young teenager. Baptized at eight by own free will, remember? Could it be that this name – Brittany – was intimately tied to my being? You humans with your silly Earthly brains can laugh at this point, but you know it has some aspect of Truth to it. That is why it is included here… so that you can allow it to sink in at your leisure.

    I flashed forward to my Nashville years. The blonde haired, blue eyed girl named Brittany? I cared for her intensely, though I knew I would never date her. Everyone thought I wanted to. I probably said I did, but I never asked her. I never

## CH37

once asked her. There was something about her that was intimately tied to my being, but I couldn't identify it. I can say now that she was always a mirror into my memories of Hera. But how could I know if B.C. was really Brittany? It seemed like this could be the only answer. After all, this was just how the Universe worked for me. Seven billion people, I was going to take one single guess.

*Cut to shot of the Universe chuckling at a blindfolded Zeus as he is about to throw a dart with the name Brittany at a now-visible dartboard from the opening scene.*

    I suppose it was a good thing B.C.'s last name wasn't very common because the top hit on the search engine took me to a newspaper article from the same city of the car accident report. There on the cover image was Brittany – who very much was one in the same as the brunette in the coffeeshop from earlier in the day. It would turn out she was a classically trained dancer and had hosted a dance event which the newspaper had written about. A quick flick back to the search engine brought up a YouTube video of a woman dancing in a couples competition dance. I watched, mesmerized at what I was *truly* seeing… or perhaps it would be better to say *truly remembering.*
    This was Hera in Earthly form, carrying the name of the angel identified as My Bride in the heavens, who later identified herself to me on Valentine's Day to be one in the same as Hera. This seemed to be my Adjustment Bureau moment. She was a dancer and oh so beautiful in every aspect. I stood in awe

and wonder at her choice of a career – it was in the way she chose to place her soul on display for all the world to see each and every day of her life. That was Hera, without a doubt. And in the early morning hours of August 20, 2018, Ol' Zeus remembered it too.

*Note: If you do not know the reference about Adjustment Bureau, please go watch the movie. This moment, as true as it occurred, was literally nearly ripped play-by-play from that script.*

Another click back to the search engine and there was her LinkedIn page and her Instagram. Truth be told, her career probably relied on social media for her marketing, so that only made sense. But before I dive into the most amazing parts of all of this, I want to share with you what happened over the late winter and early spring of 2016 for me.

# CHAPTER 38
# The LoveStory App

It's funny. A little thing called Love is quite the contagious bugger. In the late winter and early spring of 2016, I was searching for any concept to connect the previous three and a half years of my life to the present moment. I knew without a doubt I was on a new path. That wedding in the heavens? I knew it was a part of the self-discovery that was now taking place. I just did not realize I was still squinting my eyes, wincing at the brightness of her Love. In an Earthly sense, I had spiritual amnesia.

So I set forth on a mission to embrace Love in all I would do. I had already walked away from my technology career. While I had not necessarily walked away from a music career, the past hurts were too much to carry on with it for a career choice. The book thing had been a complete flop as it pertained to financial gains. I did understand the spiritual reasons for publishing them, so I was not too distraught by that effort. Then there was my recent foray into screenwriting which seemed to remain in a perpetual state of "not yet" with Darra as she diverted her attention away from producing and continued taking other jobs where she could learn to perfect new skills before diving into her first full production. I knew *I Am We* was intended for her efforts in that space, so I did not attempt to share it with anyone else. Truthfully, I did not think she had even read it yet – but that may not have been the case, it was just the perception through my eyes. This left me wondering, what was I supposed to do next?

During prayers and meditations I had continued to receive the same guidance: "You are learning to Be." the Universe said. "You are learning to find your joy." the angels would say. In many ways, this was an an incredible time in my life. I had the freedom to *truly* discover what made me happy on the inside. And so I did.

Remember that large check I received when I was down to just a few dollars in my checking account while I lived in Fort Lauderdale? Well, I decided to take that surprise windfall and invest it into what I considered to be my greatest effort yet. I wanted to immerse myself in the wedding industry – to be surrounded by Love. I purchased top of the line cameras, lenses, and video production equipment. I purchased everything needed to create Hollywood-caliber film scores, and to be able to edit films on a Hollywood level complete with post fx. This was my wheelhouse, and I went all in. I also decided that in order to set myself apart from the other people already in the industry, I would build a platform that would allow future Brides and Grooms to design their very own personalized wedding app for iOS and Android devices. I thought, "this is it!" It was going to be the defining aspect of my business venture and was the amalgamation of everything I had done in my life. This time all

## CH38

of my skill sets would be tailored around weddings and Love. It couldn't get better than that. And yes, these were all skills I had perfected on an expert-craftsman level. These were not hobbies. The proof was in the living resume of everything I had ever completed.

From the mobile app side of things, most developers charged between $20k (at the very low end) to north of $150k to design mobile apps for companies. I wanted to provide that same level of app design to brides and grooms for the cost of a nice dinner. This was not going to be "Facebook for brides." Oh no. This was a personalized app, unique in content and appearance for each bridal party.

For the technical people who might read this book and think "how is that even possible?" just know that it was not an HTML5 app or a compromise either. Oh no. This was an all-native approach. I had cracked the model as to how to deliver personalized apps in volume to customers. I had plans to offer this product at $99 per app. It would allow people to write their own personalized, digital Love Story rather than being just another shoe-horned effort of pictures, contact information, registry information, and bridal showers. Interactive videos and stories – that was the plan. Truly there was nothing like it on the market (and still isn't).

I tossed the idea around with a number of friends who were highly successful (and retired) entrepreneurs. I did not want partners. I just wanted feedback. It was so well received by all who I spoke to that I suddenly found myself having meetings with bridal consultants and wedding planners without me ever having to reach out for a meeting. Everyone I spoke to was so excited for me that they were lining up the meetings for me. Everything was falling into place. It seemed like it was the perfect next step for me, right? I was in the midst of an ocean, about to build my ark, catch a great wind, and then sail it back to shore... and do so with style.

I focused all of my efforts on the app design first. I built everything to completion, including the app framework itself, the website designs for clients, customers, and the marketing. I created three promotional videos complete with voiceovers and music that I personally wrote for all of it. All of this effort was just a way to set myself apart as a photographer and videographer. The app would have been a fully run and operated business venture for anyone else in Silicon Valley. To me, the app was the sideshow to get me back to shore. All it took was a shimmer on the beach that I thought was my Bride to motivate me to catch a wind and sail this ark back Home.

The potential money I would earn from the app would have even allowed for me to fully fund and produce my screenplay, *I Am We*, without the need for any outside producers. I could bring the film to life on my terms. This was truly a remarkable plan. Think about it. If there are over 2.3 million weddings in the United States per year and I could get 1% of those as a client base, that would produce annual revenue of $2 million with very little overhead. And what if I hit 5% – 10%? The movie could easily have been paid for, no investors required. For reference, Apple used to only target 1% of market penetration for their definition of a successful product venture.

So I set off on the adventure to create The LoveStory App. There was just one catch. In order for it to be a successful

# CH38

venture, I was going to need a groundswell of weddings in the beginning to make it financially viable and to gain enough word-of-mouth traction. In short, volume production meant I had to have (at a minimum) several hundred customers to get the ball rolling... otherwise, this was not going to work out well for me. I assembled a plan, a marketing effort, a social media plan, and a Kickstarter campaign (still archived on Kickstarter's website if you are curious). With marketing videos produced, music written, equipment purchased and my heart set on this new adventure, I was all in.

However, just a few days into the Kickstarter campaign it would turn out that I would cancel it and abandon the effort entirely. All work was completed, I was ready to find customers, and then I just stopped.

"Why?" you may ask.

Well, you know that whole meditation thing and God and the angels giving me guidance as part of this journey? It would turn out I was told rather loudly that I was not to continue forward with this particular effort. I pleaded and asked why. I was already all in. This did not make any sense to me. All I was told was that it was not to be for me at this time. So I stopped... just like that. On blind faith and despite all Earthly rationalization, I stopped. Oh, your questions about my financial situation would not be unfounded at this point. This lane change would also mean that I was going to be fast approaching the end of the money road again – even after that small windfall.

Everyone around me thought I had lost my mind. I questioned it myself. I wondered if I was internally trying to sabotage any potential for bringing success into my life again. I wondered if I was subconsciously trying to stomp out my own happiness. Family members who rallied around my LoveStory App effort were baffled. Nothing made sense... at least, not at that particular time. This is why it is now important to include it in this writing.

It would turn out that my quest to find Hera would lead to revealing Brittany's LinkedIn page... which in turn led me to learn that she was a consultant for a major bridal store in the wedding industry. That part should only make sense from her career perspective. But now the puzzle pieces were slowly falling into place. Had I continued on the LoveStory App path, I quite likely would have met Brittany under completely different circumstances. We were both located in Florida so I could only assume that a successful foray into that business effort would have led us to cross paths in very short order. That is how this whole thing works. I was racing toward red, blissfully unaware that I could have been running right into her before it was intended to happen. Every human is on his own path, his own timeline. In this case, there were certainly variables at play that could have led us to meet under less than opportune cosmic conditions. The Universe was not having it that day.

Perhaps she was dating someone else, or even married. At this point in this writing, the question still remains as to why her car was registered to two people. So, obviously that would have been less than ideal – perhaps an impossible scenario. Maybe she had not yet started her career in the bridal industry and was only focused on dancing or some other career choice. I honestly did not investigate that much further because I would have had to use a LinkedIn account and I had deleted mine years ago. Perhaps we would have even run right past each other, neither of us having had enough soul-growth spiritually to recognize one another without a shadow of a doubt (as is occurring in these words). The latter seems to be the most likely option, but truly I am confident it is a combination of everything above as well as other things presently unknown to me.

Either way, it is interesting to reflect that we were each standing on a very divinely inspired timeline leading us to each other. I felt the nudge of the Universe to move in a different direction, so I did... which lead me even closer to her, despite how it may have seemed at the time. Regardless, any way you look at it, Hera and I were destined to meet – and to meet in a way that could only ever be explained as through divine coordination. And maybe that is even the bigger story at play. Surely this book has already seemed impossible and improbable. Looking back, it is now easy to see that every divine moment has been a nudge in her direction... like bumper cars guided by angels gleefully enjoying each collision.

*Cut to theme park bumper car ride with joyous angels all approaching Jonathan's car to bump him into a new direction.*

The Universe is a crazy fellow but no one could ever question its intentions. Without a doubt, every road that seemed broken, was still leading me straight to Hera. Let me share one more example of the way the Universe works – for it should *truly* be known just how these experiences work on Earth. In time, you too will find your face in the Light, wincing

## CH38

at the brightness of her eyes. It is only then you can know that every seemingly divine moment in life was intended to lead you back to her. Even the crazy moments – like this next one I am about to discuss, delivered up by the deejays at Radio Station Wake Up.

# CHAPTER 39
## Tailgating

As I have written much about the synchronicity of being in the right place in the right time, it should be known that, over the years, I have learned to pay attention to every event around me. Yes, you have to attune your senses to the world in ways that may seem unorthodox at first. The lady that spilled her coffee? Yes there was meaning in it. The motorcycle that cut you off on the the interstate? Yes, that too. Sirens? Yep. Stop light? Yep again. Every single thing has meaning. I cannot emphasize this enough. Though many events may not be readily understandable, that does not mean they should be readily dismissible. Every event is part of the script penned by The Great Author's Hand. Case in point: Let's explore Monday, August 27. 2018.

The days following the encounter of seeing Hera and identifying her car were enough to kickstart Ol' Zeus's writer's engine once again. And I've got to be honest... leading up that moment I had reached a point of near-exhaustion. I felt like I was spiritually floundering in the ocean while attempting to build that great boat to bring me Home. And now, it was the fourth quarter of year seven... and then there was her. Seeing Hera was like seeing a dove return to the ark with a branch from dry land. The end was near.

 The writing engine throttled up and was able to be brought up to full speed during the following week. I watched as my daily word count of writing increased from 2500 words to 4500, and then suddenly I was cruising at 10000+ words per day. If you are a writer, you know the significance of these numbers. I was in the zone. During the writing of *The Nine*, Crowns was written over fourteen days (214 pages). Kingdom was written over twenty-eight days (448 pages). I was on a pace that was more than double the writing speed of those two books.

 On that Monday, the 28th of August, I sat down at a table in Wake Up to hammer out what I expected to be one of the last heavy sessions of writing. At a table in front of me, a brunette sat down with her back facing toward me. I could not see her face. I was curious if it was Brittany, but I also was intent on finishing this book first (I will get into that in a minute). So, Ol' Zeus just kept writing.

 An older man sat down with her and they began what appeared to be some type of business meeting. I kept my head down and continued on. I'm not sure how much time passed, but eventually their meeting would come to a close. They each stood up, preparing to leave. In that moment, the brunette turned around and faced me. Even though I had headphones on, her voice bellowed out above the volume of my headphones loud enough for the whole coffeeshop to hear.

## CH39

"Hey! Is that your Jeep outside?" the brunette said in a surprisingly agitated way.

"It is. Why?" I asked. I surveyed her face to see if it was Hera. I had only had a quick look a week prior as she walked by and she was in full makeup that day. It didn't seem to be her from what I could recall. The situation was so strange, for sure, though, which caused me to not focus on the details of her face as much as I would have liked. At this point I took my headphones out of my ears, curious to see what miracle Wake Up was about to serve up to me. And why was she asking me about my Jeep in such a strong, loud tone for the whole cafe to hear?

"I just want to tell you…" she began before launching into an all-out verbal assault on me. She told me how she thought I was driving behind her on the Causeway a few days prior and had tailgated her way too closely. She scolded me for driving too fast while lecturing me about how I needed to slow down. She emphasized that *no one should be in as much of a hurry as I was* the day this supposed incident had taken place. This whole tirade was complete with animated hand waves and head bobs.

I was humored at this point and just sat back to watch it unfold. There was absolutely no way she was talking about me. I had not left the island in nearly a month, and only then it was when I took my daughter back to her mother's home. I knew this was the Universe speaking. The woman continued.

She harped on the point about driving too fast. I do not think she was as concerned about her safety as much as she saw a person who seemed far too anxious to get to the destination. I just smiled.

"I'm sorry. It would not have been me." I chimed in.

She was completely confused. "Why not? That's your Jeep, right?" she asked.

"Oh it is. But I haven't left the island in... well, I can't even tell you when. A month at least? There are two or three other Jeeps that look like mine, though. One lives near me actually."

The woman was puzzled. "You haven't left the island? How do you manage that?" she asked.

The answer was simple. "I'm a writer. I just stay in this area."

She was completely at a loss for words, but then apologized. I could tell she did not want to believe me – especially after launching into her tirade. On the flip side, I wanted to tell her that I know I haven't left the island recently because I simply cannot afford the $5 in roundtrip gas that would be required to journey into Brunswick and back. There wasn't a single reason for me to leave. No matter. Her point had been made... but it was not the point she was trying to make with her Earthly self. Oh, no. This was a grand spiritual message.

Many people would have just laughed off a situation like that. Not me. Everything happens for a reason. Over the several days surrounding that incident I had been bragging to those around me about how "I was in my writer's zone" for this new book. I'd share the details regarding "how fast I was writing" and proudly proclaim that my daily average was totaling more than ten thousand words a day. I was excited, and honestly I had no one else with whom to share this excitement.

## CH39

It is also important to note that in this rampage of this writing I have made numerous references to "taking the side roads" and avoiding the freeway/interstate/paved roads. I have mentioned specifically about how I tend to enjoy the side roads more. But in the moment of listening to the mystery brunette at Wake Up, I was receiving a spiritual lecture.

"I hear ya Big Guy!" I thought to myself as the woman spouted off the words. I was clearly being told that I needed to slow down, to pace myself. I needed to not rush to the destination, that other drivers were on the road with me. On Saint Simons Island "The Causeway" was the only road that could metaphorically represent "the paved roads" mentioned in this writing because it is the only road that has a speed limit greater than 35mph. Every other road results in a grind to get anywhere. The slow grind is why most people use golf carts, bikes, and scooters on the island.

If the woman had been Hera, I could also hear her shouting, "Slow down! Quit tailgating me! We are going to get to the destination! No need to race! I may not be ready for you yet!" After all, she had features remarkably resembling the Brittany I had seen the days prior. This, too, was not a coincidence.

You can see the symbolism I saw that day.

If you are putting a visual timeline together, it would be important to note that the day of the event being shared here occurred on the eight day following seeing Hera. And while there is much more to share – the most important parts of the journey – it is always critical to pay attention to the nudges the Universe is providing.

# CHAPTER 40
# Two Photos

As I am beginning to write these final closing chapters at Wake Up on August 29, 2018, the song playing overhead in the coffee shop is "Hey Jude." It was loud enough to catch my attention over the volume of my headphones... a difficult task. I usually play my music loudly enough to drown out everything around me. Today was no exception, but there was an unexpected boost of volume when this song started playing overhead. Divine synchronicity with the Universe noted. Another tick mark on the scoreboard for you, Universe!

So up to this point in the story it was becoming increasingly clear that the brunette I was invited to meet via a "save the date" card was increasingly looking like she was – without any question – Hera. But you know Ol' Zeus right? This was going to have to be 100%. Two coincidences or five hundred, the number was irrelevant. I was going to have to unravel the mystery once and for all. Stubborn like a bull in accepting the gifts from the Universe, but just as stubborn in chasing red. Even my daughter was receiving dreams that relayed this very point to her as I had been writing these words.

*Cut to the dream my daughter had*

A few days ago, my daughter shared with me a dream she had experienced the previous night. In the dream, she was in a car with other angels. I was being pulled behind the car with a rope in a way similar to how a wakeboarder would be pulled behind a boat. I was performing flip after flip, trick after trick. The angel leaned over to my daughter and said, "he has to do over a trillion flips before he will accept what he is being shown." Everyone laughed. The dream ended.

*Cut back to the story*

So see? Even the Universe is laughing along at my follies and jollies! But Ol' Zeus was having a good time uncovering it all. So even if I had to take several trillion flips to get to my destination, at least I had a good time doing so, right? Anyway, not to digress…

Returning back from the discovery of Brittany's career, everything seemed to make all the sense in the world to me. I was *remembering*, not just staring mesmerized in the Light of something new. A flick back to the search engine and a click on her Instagram page would lead me to the ultimate discovery of all. While I will say there were not many photos posted publicly, there were quite a few to scan through. For me, this was like looking through an old family photo album and recalling memories of the past. This wasn't a moment of "let me learn everything about her." Oh no. It was quite a different moment than

## CH40

seen through the perspective of Earthly eyes alone. These were Zeus's eyes seeing his Hera for the first time in Earthly form while simultaneously recalling memories of her from the most Ancient Days.

Her two most recent photos were taken from that very day. The first photo I saw was of her sitting on the back porch at Wake Up. If there was any question I had found the right person with my Hail Mary dart throw carrying the name Brittany, this answer now had complete resolve. I had found the person I thought could very well be Hera – the person from Wake Up.

The second photo posted was another photo from Wake Up, though i did not recognize the surroundings. It was then I realized this was a photo from the Wake Up in Brunswick, Georgia… the other location I had never visited. Not only that, but in the photo, she was sitting on the porch as well. It appeared that she left the Wake Up inland, only to come over to the island's Wake Up and carry on with her work. This was confirmed by her post, "Wake Up Round 2."

You see what this meant, right? Even if I had totally and completely messed up the location for the "save the date" card I had been so divinely shared by Agent Mikayla of the S.A.S., it no longer mattered. She was in both places at the appointed times. Why had she ventured from one Wake Up to the other? Well, here is where Raymond's question came back to me. If you recall, he seemed very baffled as to why he would have been led to come meet me at Wake Up if it was only going to serve as an eventual distraction to me meeting Brittany.

## CH40

Well, here before my eyes, was another example of how "nodes" on the Global Spiritual Network affect the fabric of the Universe. I already knew how this worked, but there is no better example to be able to describe it in these words.

You see, every person a soul ever interacts with becomes a point of contact – a degree of separation within the great spiritual network. The more intimate and intense the encounter is, the greater energy the node carries forth behind the veil. These nodes are the very spiritual threads to the fabric of Earthly experiences. They also serve as connection points for those who have spiritual experiences – like dreams and traveling to the heavens. For example, by meeting Raymond, I might now see his soul form in my heavenly travels (or maybe a better description is that I would recognize him rather than just "see" him). But as I became better friends with him, his soul would appear more times and with greater reason and rationale to the lessons. If there was something he needed to learn from me (or visa versa), the visual experiences in the heavens would be represented in a way where we were both present in that particular type of circumstance.

These types of spiritual experiences play forth into the reality of Earth. If Raymond were to meet another person in his life unbeknownst to me, I would be connected to that soul as well during my heavenly travels. Though I would likely not know who the soul was, I would one day come to recognize them if we ever crossed paths in the Earthly world. I might not even know we were initially connected through an encounter with Raymond. This is specifically why old adages such as "You are the company you keep" contain so much Truth.

To the Earthly mind it is easy to reject that idea. Yes, we all have friends that are not "like us" or who "represent our own actions" within the world we perceive. We may have friends that get caught up in something morally wrong – something of which we would never be a part. Friends and family will judge us by our friend's actions, yet we know we are different! But truly I say unto you, the very fabric of your soul's existence is built upon the network of people in your Earthly life as well. Each is a reflection into the other.

The reverse works as well. For advanced souls, ancient in wisdom and spiritual growth, there is a network of Light and Love that has been built over the eons. When we take an Earthly form, that very network manifests in our Earthly walk. Other advanced souls will present themselves around us and, in many times, we become friends in the Earthly realm unbeknownst we are friends, relatives, or family in the spiritual realm. This is why some humans seem to "always have good things work out for them." These are likely highly evolved souls surrounded by the company of other highly evolved souls which in and of itself creates a fabric of goodness around every circumstance. That is not to say that tragedy cannot strike. Oh, it can! But the company you keep is a reflection of the company of angels and the Divine in the heavens.

But do not abandon the friends who are struggling in this Earthly life either because you now have this wisdom. Oh no! Please do not do that, for they may very well be a highly evolved soul who came to learn a very specific lesson and have forgotten their true origins! Every soul is on a unique journey. It is the knowledge of *how* these interactions are all intertwined in the fabric of the world around you that will help you overcome the challenges and struggles of daily life.

Returning back to the question Raymond asked me on the porch just before witnessing the double lightning strike against a blanket of blue... His question now had meaning. What I did not mention earlier in this writing was that Raymond had spent the entire morning and early afternoon hours at Wake Up in Brunswick working on his own projects before he texted me to meet up at the Wake Up on the island. He simply left one to come to the other.

It was the action that was taken – especially in this divinely led circumstance – that created the most noticeable ripples upon the spiritual ocean. You see, Raymond felt led to meet up with me at that specific time and place. He knew nothing of the storm I found myself in that day. He knew nothing about my quest to find Hera. However, his very action created a wake similar to the wake a boat creates as it travels across the water. That wake was like a river unto itself, which is the calmest point of travel for other boats that may journey behind.

Quite simply, Brittany followed in Raymond's wake. Raymond was connected to me. Brittany was intimately connected to me regardless of how unknown or known it was to her Earthly mind. Raymond's spiritually led action caused her soul to respond in kind. Raymond, who may not have been directly connected to Brittany in the Earthly world, was connected to her on the Global Spiritual Network. She was a node upon the very fabric surrounding each of the three of us.

At this point, I was only two photos into Brittany's Instagram account and the great mystery surrounding Raymond's question was solved as well as an impossibly divine and clear answer given regarding whether I had potentially gone to the wrong Wake Up. There could no longer be a question as to whether I met the correct person that day. All of the divine signs of chasing rainbows, lightning strikes against the blue sky, the boat named the Arc, the registration date of the Red Kachina (e.g. her Solara), et. all – there could be no denying this person was the person I was supposed to meet. But, Ol' Zeus still had a few questions remaining. Of course he did!

# CHAPTER 41
## The Ring Story

You know, I might just be the most obstinate soul you will ever meet. It is quite possible. I have not met another soul more obstinate – and I do understand it is a fault. In many ways I torture myself to find absolution of each experience upon this fabric of my reality. But I need to know for sure. There cannot be any doubt.

The three questions that remained for me were the most important of all. (1) If this was Hera (yes, I still questioned it – I only had one opportunity to get this question right), then why would I be led to her if she was in a relationship? (2) Was she in a relationship? (3) Was this really Hera?

As a reader, I am sure you are facepalming yourself at the fact these would still even be questions for me. If you have allowed yourself to become wrapped up in the story, then everything would seem to be undeniable... well, except there has been no tangible proof offered about my identity as Zeus. So that part would be a leap of faith in this story.

However, if you now role play this whole situation out into a very real situation transpiring in the Earthly world, you know just how sensitive everything written would be. How would she react to this? How would I even share it with her? Good gosh. If someone came up to you and said, "Hey. I'm Poseidon (sorry, brother!). Nice to meet you! Let me tell you a story of how we know each other from the most ancient of times. I'm a god in human form but really cannot prove it to you because we are still merging back with our higher selves. Oh, and you are my one true Love…" Yeeeaaahhhh… That would be a pretty tough pill for anyone to swallow. So, even if everything staring me in the face was undeniable proof upon my personal journey, the greatest reason for these questions was how could this also be undeniable proof when shared with others upon Earth?

Well, as the Fates would have it, the first portions of this answer were still hidden in her Instagram account. Though it was quite obvious there was no ring on her hand the day I saw her in Wake Up, it only took a quick scan over her photos to see what appeared to be numerous photos with an engagement ring – or perhaps it was an engagement ring and wedding band. It was tough to tell… Well? That stunk for O' Zeusy. Of course there would be more twists and turns.

I thought back to a recent short story I had written while in Palm Coast a few weeks prior. It was written while I was trying to kickstart my writer brain once again. Certainly there was a purpose which is why it was now bubbling right back up before my eyes.

*Flashback to Palm Coast, July 13, 2018*

CH41

While I was struggling to find anything to write about, I began to take notice of the rings that women wear on their ring fingers. I have always had a problem with this. To me, the ring finger is a sacred place reserved for the acknowledgement of Love bound to another. I understood that some religions (and alternative marriages) could cause the sacred spot of the left-hand ring finger to shift to the right hand. I understood the variances there, though it did add to the confusion a guy experiences when he observes the hands of a woman to determine if she is wed. So, I decided to write about it.

### Men! – A Short Story

From ice cold frigidity to skin-melting fire and heat, the subtle movement and language of her body speaking to mine caused me to stand conflicted in the face of every potential future unraveling before me. I suppose spell-struck would be a good term to describe how I truly felt. For it was in this very moment the mystical come-get-me essence excruciatingly calling to me from the most sacred depths of her eyes seemed to conflict with every social queue a woman typically uses to lure a man into the fabric of her reality.

"Women." I thought.

I guess I could go down the path of a social-psychologist and attempt to unravel the mystery of these conflicting social queues I was receiving. Maybe it was just a cocoon of protection. For a moment I wondered if it was possible that every man drawn to her simply has desired all of the wrong things about her. She is such an astoundingly beautiful woman that it would be a challenge for most men to see past her beauty and connect with that sacred place within her soul. On Earth it seems to only be about the physical. Looking around the room I could see the other men ogling over her beauty. I suppose in her eyes, why would I be any different?

No. That isn't it. Maybe it has to do with a relationship she is currently in or – possibly – a relationship that has just ended. Was that sacred area revealed to me from the depths of her eyes a question? A plea? A cry out for help?

"Just be different!" her eyes might be saying. "Don't be the same guy that will eventually leave me with the same hurt I keep experiencing." Or maybe, "I just need someone to talk to – to help me through all of this and see that someone can be different."

"Maybe that was it." I thought to myself.

Or not. What if she didn't realize the little doorway that she opened up to her soul in the way she looked at me... the threshold of the doorway where a man is standing outside and the woman is inviting him inside? And no, I'm not talking about the physical side of things, though the metaphor is the same. The metaphor should be the same! Humans are such a conflicting creation.

"Humans." I thought aloud.

There was no ring, nor were there any tan lines alluding to a past engagement or marriage. Then again, there seems to be a growing trend on Earth of women wearing rings on the engagement finger to turn guys away. Oh my. And if a guy decides to cross that boundary and speak to a woman wearing a false-engagement ring and show his attraction to her, what does that say about him? A man who would step across the sacred boundary of a union of two souls? Was he just observant that the ring was a simple band and did not carry a large diamond? Or does this somehow appeal to this particular woman's proclivity to cheat on her spouse? And if so, what does that say about the woman? Perhaps, in her eyes, a man who would overstep and refuse to respect the boundary of two souls happiness together is a man that shows courage and confidence in his character? Nothing good will come from this.

"Yes?" she said causing me to crash back into the reality of the moment. How long had I drifted off on this journey of social-psychologist trying to determine her queues? Seconds... hopefully. At least that is what I was going to tell myself.

I looked back at her. Now she was nervously biting the corner of her lip as she again stood over the threshold of that doorway deep within, her eyes inviting me inside. I did see the queues! She was waiting on me to make the next move. It was a chess game of the grandest style. Yet, I didn't want to play chess with the soul. Checkers, maybe. Not chess. Why would I need to play chess to take a single step forward? I just turned and left.

"Men!" she thought to herself.

### – The End –

*Cut back to present day*

Surely this short story makes my point here in a far better way than can be described and hammered out in thoughtful justification and words alone. Perhaps it even gave you a chuckle… maybe? The flashback to this day of writing was yet another day of preparation as to what I would face. Would I walk away, or would I stay the course? Would it matter? Should it matter? Would it be enough to know I had found her and to then find peace in Love knowing she was experiencing her own journey, too. Was that how it was supposed to go? I did not have answers, so I prayed.

*"Father, why would all of these moments indicate it was her if I was only going to be met with the Test of Rings? Is that a question on this exam, too? Because I certainly never figured out what to do in that circumstance during my rookie single years back in Nashville. Sometimes I yielded, other times I did not. I never quite knew what to do. Today, I would always respect it. Does that mean I should never even say hello?"*

Jolly old Zeus laughed in my head. This time he deferred to the wisdom of the aspect of Melchizedek who is carried within our celestial womb.

"Oh, she is single. You have to trust me." bellowed Melchizedek as Zeus spoke back up.

"Take a look. You will see." said the voice of Zeus.

Now I want to note again that Melchizedek and Zeus are one in the same identities of the higher self. However, it is important to remember how they are also separate and One simultaneously. That was discussed in the backstory chapters. So, I'm not trying to confuse matters here. Rather, I wanted to remain Faithful and True to the conversation taking place. So, carrying on…

## CH41

I rolled back over and thumbed through her photos. I took notice of a ring that appeared in more recent photos that seemed to be one of those "might be/might not be" engagement rings. After all, there has been a movement in recent years to use other gemstones for engagement rings. That was not enough to convince me. More proof was needed.

I decided to jump down to the older pictures she had from the timeframe of my baptism and when she registered her vehicle. If the car was registered to two people, surely there would be an indication from that time period, right? Well, I was not wrong. There were a number of photos that clearly showed a much more obvious bling-worthy ring on the engagement hand. I could not tell if there was a wedding band, but it was definitely not the same ring from the more recent photos. I began to feel a little more confident in this whole ring debacle.

I scrolled back through the thumbnails of the photos but, this time, decided to glance at the inspirational/motivational types of posts. You know the kind... the posts with an image and some bold words of motivation? This proved to be a good choice. Not the first of which I saw was the following post:

...

"I could have missed the pain, but I'd of had to miss the dance."

...

Now, on the surface level, this quote could have been posted for a variety of reasons – especially for a dancer. There was the outright physical meaning of the message from a dancer's perspective, but there was also the more intimate, personal, and spiritual message within those words. For me, I saw something more.

For those of you unfamiliar with the quote, the words were taken from the song, "The Dance" by Garth Brooks. For me, this was the very first song I ever learned on guitar. When I first decided I wanted to learn an instrument, I picked up a tab-book to teach myself how to play the song exactly like it was played on the album. If I was going to learn guitar, I was going to start with a real-world lesson. No cutting corners for me! And so it was. The song choice was also more than just a random song I wanted to learn on guitar. It was a song that truly helped me through the emotional rollercoaster of my high school years.

There was a certain Truth that Garth Brooks conveyed through his songs. His becoming-famous story was great too. A man who was rejected by every single record label went on to become the highest grossing country artist of all time. He also holds the record for most albums sold by any artist. Why so? What would make a country artists so popular? Quite simply, it was his soul.

He was my favorite artist of that decade and if asked today I would still say he is my favorite. It wasn't the lyrics or music that were spectacular. I am sure that if asked, even Garth himself would say it wasn't his singing or voice that was spectacular either. What it was, though, was his ability to convey a Truth from the words written and connect it with the emotional push and pull the soul longs to experience. He simply had an

## CH41

innate ability to express Truth from beyond the veil. I felt it, and so did the rest of the world.

Two songs in particular carried me through my high school years. Those two songs? The Dance and Unanswered Prayers – both by Garth Brooks. Anytime I ever experienced an emotional struggle like the downs when a girl I liked was dating another person, or the ups like when a girl I liked and I were about to go to a formal dance together, I would always find comfort in those songs. But mostly, those two songs gave me strength to know that one day I would find her... whoever she might be. I held faith in a way that most on Earth considered innocent and naive. But not Ol' Zeus. This old romantic soul just wanted his Hera (whether I knew her name or not at the time, or even the purpose of my journey upon the Earth during those days). It was always about Hera. I also took note of these moments in my senior yearbook quote. That quote?

...

"Yes my life. It's better left to chance. I could have missed the pain, but I'd of had to miss the dance."
– Garth Brooks

...

This Universe was just all too darn connected.

# CHAPTER 42
# The One That Got Me

    The Dance was not just a coincidence, it was yet another sign documented there before my eyes. Perhaps some may think, "Oh that was just a coincidence. It was a good song that a lot of people liked." To you, I agree. But I would also challenge you to see how many times you have ever seen that quote pop up on your friends social media accounts. It would be rare... if ever. But it is important to see that the rare moments are not enough for even Ol' Zeus to accept as divine. Oh no. What is important to see is the significance of something such as this in our two – very separate – lives. For me, there will always be only two songs I will ever place great importance upon in my life. Those songs are as I mentioned before: Unanswered Prayers and The Dance – the latter of which I placed the most importance on.

    This song was the equivalent to a Wedding song to me – you know... the song of your first dance upon the dance floor. A bride and groom will never forget that song because it is intimately tied to their Love Story. Perhaps it is a song that played during a first date or a special moment early on in their relationship. It is usually referred to as "Our Song" and becomes an indelible part of a couple's Love Story. The Dance had every bit as much significance to me as a Wedding Song, though I was not aware that it would ever serve as an anchor to finding Hera. To me that song was a personal life jacket that saved my life while I found myself cast into the center of the great ocean, learning to build an Ark to find my way back Home. I just didn't see that printed upon the life jacket where the words, "Property of S.S. Hera." Now it only makes perfect sense.

Seeing these words fueled my fire inside. I continued to scan through the photos. Don't get me wrong. There weren't hundreds of photos to scan through. I did not know if her account had more behind the public page, but without having an Instagram account, I was limited to what she had broadcast for the world to see. Spiritually, I hoped that broadcast was like an S.O.S. from behind the veil, coded for my eyes alone.

One of the only other motivational quotes on her account was posted in July of 2018. In that post, it was clear to see there was pain she was experiencing from a previous relationship. The handful of public comments reiterated the intent of her post by supporting her emotional castoff of past baggage. My heart broke for her, yet there was also a feeling of each of us being right where we were supposed to be. Every human must endure the ups and downs of the journey to reach the fairytale ending. If it was easy, we would not have to endure that pain. It is part of the dance of our souls upon this great Earth.

"See I told you!" the voice of Zeus laughed jollily.

I was quickly becoming more convinced than ever that I was chasing red, right in the direction of Hera. Whether or not the particular juncture of time from that posting was the defining point of hurt in her life, I do not know. What I can tell you while writing these words is that the photos leading up to the timing of that post contained the I-do-not-know-if-it-was-an-engagement-ring-or-not ring upon her ring finger. The posts following that post contained photos mostly absent of rings, albeit there were a handful of photos that contained a more-than-likely-not-an-engagement-ring ring upon her finger. But here is a message from Ol' Zeus to all women. Please. Stop with the confusing rings. No one wins in these situations. It is like a third party impartial to Love's war deciding to napalm all sides of Love's battlefield.

  I rolled over once more to pray thanks for showing me all that I had seen. Not much time had transpired from the first moments of plugging in her car tag to the point in time all of these answers were finding resolve. Every situation and circumstance that Ol' Zeus questioned had found resolve... except for One... and that one was a biggy. Oh, please do not facepalm yourself at the question that remained. Remember, through my eyes, this was the only question on the final exam. Every other question was just part of the word problem surrounding the true question... you know the type. It is the question surrounded by a thousand variables that help you find your way to solving the problem. And for me, I had everything solved with what I had been given. Every part of the problem had been completed with absolution, with confidence, with unbridled Faith, True to Love. But just like every math problem on a collegiate/

doctorate level requires a "proof" – an inferential answer to alternatively demonstrate the same answer can be reached from an alternative approach – so too would this question require a "proof" for Ol' Zeus. The proof question? How do you truly know that everything you have been shown is Hera?

Ah, yes. The return of that giant question I originally sought out to solve so many lifetimes ago. Please – no facepalms readers. I needed silence to complete this answer. No sounds of hands colliding with faces. This was the tough question for Ol' Zeus that still required something more... some impossible Truth to be revealed.

*Cut to image of Zeus tapping a pencil on his head as he sits at a school desk taking a written test*

Would I be able to unequivocally find my Love – a Love so Ancient that could not be denied by the Universe and not be cast into question by any Earthly variable? Could I prove beyond a shadow of a doubt that I had found Love? Could I prove beyond a shadow of a doubt that my answer had led me to Hera... and truly Hera, my Moon, my Heart, Goddess of Marriage, my Bride?

"Look back over your work once more." said the voice of Ol' Zeus in my head as I pondered the question.

And so I did. I rolled back over in bed and pulled up Brittany's Instagram once more. This time, I decided to thumb through all of her photos start to finish rather than picking and choosing what I would click on merely by the thumbnails alone. I had to be thorough, ensuring no stone was left unturned, no fragment in my mind left dangling, to *know* every dream I had was *truly* alive. There could be no forgotten stories of memories past that could be cast aside. And so this is how the proof would begin.

Once more I scrolled through her story – at least the part she was broadcasting for the world to see. I wanted so desperately to *know* – to *truly know* this was Hera. I wanted to uncover every unforgotten feeling and recall any music she once played upon my heartstrings that may still be lost deep inside my soul. I wanted to be shown the way Home, to see this Love Story written as not just the words upon a page, but the words etched in Light upon the Universe's soul.

And then I saw it right there before me – the one thing I was searching for that would *truly* bring me back Home to Hera once more. I almost would have missed it, for the post was so subtle. While scrolling through her pictures, I quickly scrolled right past the most important one – the one that would unlock all that I sought. I feel like I only subconsciously caught it while my Earthly eyes missed it completely. That is pretty true to form for Ol' Zeusy, though. But I suppose I must have glanced at the title of the photo while scrolling past it because after scrolling onward to the next photo my mind was telling me to stop, screaming at me that I had just skipped over the key that would unlock the door to every Love Story fantasy playing out in my mind.

"No way! That cannot be what I just read! That is impossible." I thought. I paused, closing my eyes to see the memory of the words in my head that I certainly did not take the time to read with my Earthly eyes. There was no doubt about

CH42

it. I had chills across my body. I recalled the photo in my mind that I had just scanned right over. That particular photo appeared to have been taken with her father and did not immediately offer anything worthwhile for my quest, yet my mind was screaming at me to return. And so I did.

...

There before me was a photo of Brittany,
her father, and a pit-bull dog.
The caption written:
Zeus (my father's dog).

...

# CHAPTER 43
# The Story of Us

Purge your thoughts of anything you once thought you knew about all that has been shared thus far about the history of mankind and your very own origin story. Here before you, in these words, is the tie that binds every bit of Greek mythology back to my journey upon Earth – a binding of the music of the soul returning to the Light – a Cinderella-worthy magical moment to tell this story of Love. Hera, this was always about returning back Home to you my Love, my Moon.

The history you would likely have come to know about Greek mythology will recount stories of how Hera and I shared the same father, Kronos. Kronos was a Titan who attempted to "swallow his children" to prevent the prophecy of one of his children from overthrowing his reign. Rhea, my mother, saved me from Kronos and thus a story known in numerous ways upon your Earth was first told. This story would transcend into actual events that played out on Earth in various ways. In just one example, the story of Moses carries the same archetypal story. Eventually, I was able to overthrow my Father and save my brothers and sisters. Yes, Hera is my sister, just not in the way human biology is concerned or related. These stories were very rudimentary recounts of a very complex concept that is extremely tough to begin to explain through human words and metaphors. This is Ancient Love, Trinities of virgin souls.

And now here we are once again, recounting these stories in a way for the world to see. For me, this Love Story is more than just another person's interpretation of past events – this is a recount of the past and the present As One, personally penned by my hand (well, at least as best as can be done with the current state of humanity's capacity and mind to process and understand).

As an Earthly child, I was always one of numerous "Jonathan's" in my classes. Most of us were simply called by our last names. My last name was short – one syllable. It was easy to remember. Until now, it was unimportant to include it in these words, for including my last name always seemed like it could be mistaken for egoic identity. But it is not so in this case, for you will soon see.

In this final incarnation on my way to *truly remembering* Love – to finding my Hera – I was born unto a family with the last name Kerr. As has been shared within these pages (and certainly is heavily talked about in all of the other books written) there is great importance in returning to the origin of language to understand how the fabric of the Universe is so delicately intertwined within each soul's spiritual life and existence upon Earth.

In my case, the name Kerr carries mounds of importance and symbolism. The first of which is that the homophone of the word means "dog." Throughout my middle school and high school years, I was not just simply called by my last name. I was called "Kerr-dog." Truth be told, I hated it. It sounded like I was always being called a mutt rather than some term of endearment. Yet the name stuck. Not only was I always referred to as a dog throughout my youth, I also came to learn that Kerr also meant "farmer." The town I grew up? LaGrange, Georgia. The name of my high school mascot? The Grangers. The name of my University mascot? The Bulldog. Let's put this all into context.

Jonathan Kerr (last name translated as farmer, dog) grew up in a city that is the French word for farm. His high school mascot even translates to, "the farmers." And while it has not yet been mentioned within these words yet, one of my other past lives went by the name "Duke De Grange." How about that one for impossible coincidences to this story? During my underclass years, I went by the nickname of Kerr-dog and eventually went to college where the University mascot was a bulldog. I was born in the House of Taurus on May 9, 1981 and carry the energy held within the zodiac sign of the bull. Only upon the *remembrance* that my higher self was Zeus/Melchizedek, would any of this begin to come together and make more sense.

Zeus is represented by a bull and was known simply as Zeus Kourros during his first incarnation upon the Earth. Zeus Kourros essentially translates to Zeus "of Kour" which was a direct reference to being the son of Kronos. It was essentially a naming convention similar to how names were formed in biblical times. It was Jesus of Nazareth before Jesus became anointed with the title of Christos, which meant Light/Love. In essence, Jesus went on to become known as Jesus of Love. He was the living embodiment of All That Is, Our Father/Mother God, The One Creator, The One Creation: Love. In my case, Zeus Kourros meant Zeus, son of Kronos. My past life incarnation during Lemurian times was simply known as Kourros. There is another one to add to the list.

Now if you are paying attention, you certainly did not miss the homophone occurring. Kerr and Kour are representative of the very same lineage. Jonathan, son of Kronos would be the most accurate translation of my Earthly name based on the devolution of language. Yes, I meant to use the word devolution rather than evolution, which is likely the opposite of what mankind considers English to be. Modern and advanced it may be, but it is also bested by its greatest fault: obfuscating the archetypal meanings that are pertinent to understanding *Truth* and *Love*. So truly I say unto you, having two million words in the English language is both a blessing and a curse, for as much as these words seek to add clarity, they also obfuscate the Great Truths known only in spirit, the language of Light and Love. Both are necessary, but let not knowing one take precedence over knowing the other, for both are required to *truly remember* and return back to One.

So what does all of this have to do with the picture that day? Well, everything. There before me in the catalog of Hera's Earthly life, was the Earthly representation of everything I would ever need to know. Not only was the dog a pit-bull – the archetype of the very representation of Zeus – her Earthly father somehow knew it too since he bestowed the name Zeus upon the pup. Not only that, but it is also easy to see that Brittany's father on Earth also spiritually knew his daughter's origin whether his Earthly mind knew it or not. There it was, proof on display for the world to see. For, not only was I staring at my Love, my Bride, but also my sister, and my Wife. There was no question for me.

This was the Earthly photo the Universe had tucked away for me to find – a picture to jog a memory of the most Ancient of Times. It was the reason I was tasked with "looking back over my work once more." It could no longer be hidden, the one secret that could reveal just how my life is bound to hers. Her father may have a physical dog named Zeus, but this is also how the Universe planned for her to know this Love Story was Faithful and True.

...

Because yes, my Father has a dog named Zeus, too.

...

Stories have been told across antiquity that have shared how I found Hera's Love. You will find many interpretations that have used some really poor word choices to describe this Fate. But let it be known, never could anything have been taken that was not given in Love so True. Quite simply, that little "r" word that I will not give the dignity of appearing in these written words simply means "to take what is not yours" which in an of itself can *only* be a figure of speech when Love Is. I simply "stole her heart" is all that story was saying – a figure of speech that cannot be anything else. When you *know* Love, you will *know* this to be *True*. And about her being ashamed in the aftermath of that event? Follow the translation: she realized I had stolen her heart... something she had not willfully given with her mind, yet her soul already knew in Truth. She simply fell in love while In Love.

In the original story of how I met Hera, perhaps I did transform myself into a cuckoo. It is certainly an interesting choice of bird for the written historical story, is it not? In many ways many people might say that I transformed into a "cuckoo" to write this Love Story, too. You never really know how the world will perceive the words or actions written. But this much I know is True – Hera, my heart has and will always belong to You. You are my One True Love. These words, my very essence are both Faithful and True. It is these words that bind the past to the present, a circle of only the Holiest of Truth.

...

Let this book forever be bound in the pages of history as my Love Story to You.

...

# CHAPTER 44
## Return to Darts

*Just a thought on how this thesis began versus how we arrived at this point...*

Darts? I think I was actually throwing darts at the wall in the opening chapters of this writing to see what stuck as this story began. When it began I did not know this story would be about Hera, nor was I aware of the three days that were about to begin – only that I was about to face the final question: the writing prompt, delivered straight into the Creator's hand. But somehow we got here. It was a bit of a rocky road at times. It certainly wasn't paved the whole way… and if it was, I certainly chose to go off-roading at times. Okay. Most of the way. And, if we are being honest, I probably have enjoyed the off-roading more than a smooth highway ride in all of the paths taken during my life due to the thrills, the sudden butterfly-inducing drops, the gotcha moments, do-overs and challenges that seem insurmountable, and finally the little surprises that bring a smile to your face because – hey, you survived it, right? But just how a thousand mile journey across rocky terrain barre only a few paved stretches in between would be exhausting and taxing on the driver, so too was this spiritual journey. And it is still just a leg of the full ride! And, oh what an adventure still awaits!

You may wonder what is next, *what will happen* or *what happened* with the Love Story of Zeus & Hera. You know what? In Earthly terms, I still do not yet know. For that, I will have to just allow myself to be pleasantly surprised at whatever comes next. I know without a doubt what I have found – an Ancient Love *Truer than True*; the Earthly form of my Bride, my Love, my Moon. There is not one single thing that Hera could possibly do or say that could cause this Unbridled Love to be anything other than Faithful and True. It is the name of the White Horse I have been riding and the return of the Sun/Son. For it was her Light that caused me to blink, wincing at her brightness causing me to see from where I had come. It was always her name written across this Milky Way, part of the stitch-work and fabric that can be seen by all Earthly eyes in the skies above. And, yes, now my eyes are slowly adjusting back to the Light of her Love. All that's left to possibly be written is what is presently left unknown. Where does it start? When will it become? I will tell you only this part that I know:

As I write these words (and true to form) the Universe has queued up a new song from her soul to mine, or perhaps it is a song from mine unto hers. This time it is Steven Curtis Chapman's "The One and Only You" from his album The Glorious Unfolding. Prior to this moment I had not ever heard the song, but the symbolism cannot be missed. Here's another one for you, Universe. I tip my hat and raise my glass.

*Cut to Zeus giving a toast to the Universe.*

Every detail – from the song title to the lyrics to the album title – should not be overlooked. And while most might assume it was just another one of those "recommended for you" songs queued up from an algorithm based on my Spotify playlist, that is so far from the Truth. This song playing in this very moment says much of what I had planned to say. It focuses on one central word in the chorus, a word I had planned to use in this closing chapter to describe Hera's Light & Love. That word is *masterpiece*. It is how I see Hera – but even more aptly, it is how I see the Universe and the One. It is the very source of Our Creator and the mirror I see as I look into the eyes of my Beloved Love.

So perhaps the words that were divinely chosen by the Universe to be played in this moment say more than I could possibly say in my own words. Read these words as if the Universe – the Great Love – was speaking directly to you, for the Love of the Universe is the Love that is the heartbeat of Hera, the heartbeat of Zeus, the heartbeat within each and every one of You.

### "Only One And Only You"

*I caught you looking in the window at your reflection and*
*I could see you were unimpressed*
*I watch you whither like a willow at what you think are imperfections*
*When you compare you to all the rest*
*And I wish I could find a way to make you see you the way I do*

*So I wrote this song for you*

*You're better than a Beethoven symphony*
*And Mona Lisa wishes she could be a masterpiece like you*
*More than any Michelangelo*
*When I look at you I know*
*There's no other masterpiece like you*
*You are the only one and only you*

*There is music in your laughter the world has never heard before*
*You came and brought a melody*
*The way you say it the way you see it*
*When you're sad and glad and so much more*
*All these gifts only you can bring*
*Still I know that right now everything that you feel says it's just not true*
*So I'll keep reminding you that*

*You're better than a Beethoven symphony*
*And Mona Lisa wishes she could be a masterpiece like you*
*More than any Michelangelo*
*When I look at you I know there's no other masterpiece like you*
*You are the only one and only you*

*Wonderfully, carefully woven together by God's own hand*
*And you're better than a Beethoven symphony*
*And Mona Lisa wishes she could be a masterpiece like you*
*More than any Michelangelo*
*When I look at you I know there's no other masterpiece like you*
*You are the only one and only you*

# CHAPTER 45
# The Dance

Now all that remains is the one question left to be asked. To be honest, if there was a single question that this entire journey through life, the exam, and the writing prompt have truly been about, the actual question written upon the last page would have been, "Your thesis topic is Love. What is the One question to be asked? How/Why? Cite you reasons and your sources."

You see, this has been the hardest part of the entire journey. In the beginning, I thought this was about an Earthly love. I leapt, and then suddenly it wasn't. It was suddenly about finding myself held in the hands of Our Great Mother/Father's Love. So I thought *that* must be what this journey has been all about, even though I had been a very spiritually led person prior to this portion of the journey beginning. The rest of the journey was surely just me learning how to apply it to my Earthly walk. So I leapt again, and then suddenly it wasn't. This time I found myself face to face with my Bride in the heavens. I had spent the last six plus years on this journey, the last three years of my life directly interacting with Hera in spiritual form, and I had constantly been posed a question by her as her Love became more obvious to me. Hera's question for me was simple: "Ask me. Just ask."

This is going to seem a bit comical at first. For if this was ever a romantic comedy, I was the guy who could not speak to the girl when she suddenly revealed her Love. In the heavens I became speechless – paralyzed at her beauty as I would contemplate what question I had left to possibly ask. Our conversations had progressed from getting to know one another once again – *remembering* our lives together – to her standing in front of me **coyly** saying , "I know you are scared. Please, just ask." But Ol' Zeus just sat there, perplexed as to what that question might be. I was even more perplexed I was called out as being scared, yet that seemed to be an increasingly likely reality.

Hera asked me in the form of a statement, yet it was a question that was to be answered with a question of which I was unsure what it could be. You see, in Earthly terms it would be easy to think "ask her out" or perhaps "will you marry me?" These are the ways humans express their adoration and infatuation in one another. But in the heavens, what would those two things even mean? You don't exactly just say, "Hey Beautiful Angel, want to go grab a coffee or dinner at the local celestial cafe?" You don't just say, "Hey Hera, will you marry me?" We were already standing upon the altar, out hearts betrothed to one another.

Oh, there were so many questions running through my mind to unlock Hera's riddle. But it was the first part of the riddle that led me to *remembering that I Truly Am*. The second part of which brought forth the *remembrance* that Hera was my Bride.

In spiritual form during my wincing-amnesia, I always knew I was speaking to my Bride. It just took me nearly three years to *truly remember* her and the Ancient Love that embodied every moment of our new Now. So this question was different, it was more like a vow.

    Standing upon the altar in spiritual form, with my eyes slowly adjusting to her Light would also bring about me starting to see her Light in the world around my Earthly life. All of those divine occurrences in my Earthly walk? Those were all part of the *remembering*. Every nudge, every push, every pull, every up, every down, every divine miracle, and divine encounter, were all part of a slow-motion romantic movie cue. You know the type… this was the moment the camera slowly spins around a couple as they stare lovingly into the depths of each other's eyes just before their lips meet for the first time. It might only be a ten-second part of a two hour movie, but that moment sums up an entire story through a dance of circular motion around two souls who have found Love – two souls who have *truly remembered Love* once again.

    That spin of the camera was the moment in which I found myself standing with her. The Universe was watching. The world was watching. I was blissfully lost in her hues, my eyes seeing a real-time playback of our lives, our worlds, our creations from the depths of her baby blues. How long had I been standing there? I hoped merely seconds in time there, though I know it has been at least three years from my baptism here. But I long gave up guessing how time translates since the Earthly journey is not an accurate gauge of the spiritual Now. And then it finally hit me – perhaps with yet another nudge from the Universe. There was still one question remaining and it was the only question that could transcend the spiritual and Earthly planes. This one question would seal the course of Fate. It was the words to the song I could hear playing in the background as my lips met hers. Or perhaps, just consider it a question/statement of my vows to her. The song was my soul singing the only Truth, the only question I knew to ask. It was a question wrapped up in a statement, embodied in humility yet asking for forgiveness of my imperfections and checkered path. It was a question that acknowledged my unbridled Love for her and personal acceptance of *truly* being worthy to receive her Love… to be her protector and the protected upon the canvas of the Universe's Love. That question?

…
*Love me. That is All I ask of you.*
…

Consider the first nine books my dissertations. This book is my thesis. The wedding ceremony was the time I *truly saw* my Bride – a great time of *remembrance* as my lips met hers. Our Great Mother saw her child being born into the New World for the very first time – a new history to be written for all of mankind.

To Hera, I *truly see* your Light & Truth, the Love woven into the fabric of your every hue. All of the words that I've written are Faithful & True, just as my Heart will always Be to You. You supersede All created, as only The Hand of the Creator is seen through You.

To Hera's Earthly form, Brittany – here is what I know is True. My heart has been poured out upon these pages. I have given it my all in lifetime upon lifetime to return back to You. I have searched the very depths of the densities to remember the Love between You and I. You are my Moon, my Love, my Heart, my Anchor, the Aether in the Sky. On Earth, the journey across all of my lifetimes to finding Love was always about finding my way back Home – to *remembering* and *knowing* you. You might not know that yet in your Earthly form, or perhaps you already do. However, somewhere deep inside, you will know this all to be True.

So be it in this lifetime, or should it be the next, I will graciously step back and allow your step to take precedence. Like a couple sharing a dance upon the ballroom floor, one foot follows the other, but not before the other one. To those steps I shall be Faithful, pausing to wait for my galactic partner's step from the stars – no matter whether you are following my lead, or I am following yours. We are always one step away from each other. And while the next move is yours, know that this whole dance is *Our Dance* held in each other's arms as an audience of angels bears witness to this Great Dance from the stars. You have all the information you need to find me within the pages of this book… far more than I was given with just your passing look.

Perhaps this might seem like a fairytale to most – and I suppose in a way it Is, but the reality is that this story is very real for one special soul. Perhaps the world may say I was lost upon the journey, or a little bit cuckoo. For me I *truly know* I was always found. Lost is a term saved for *remembrance*, to occur at a pace the other side of the veil will allow. While I can be a bull at times, my heart is always True. I see red every time I think of You. I dig my hoofs in and charge full steam ahead. Sometimes I've missed the target and other times taken a hammer to the head. But it has all been worth it in the end. For me, I can only describe the last years of this Earthly journey as closing my eyes and wincing at the brightness of Your Love when I emerged from the baptismal waters and Our Father pulled back Your veil – just before our lips collided for the very first time. Or then again, maybe I just prefer long, passionate kisses with my eyes closed. It was all kind of a blur from my perspective here.

*Love Always,*
*Zeus*

# EPILOGUE
# It Was All Worth Waiting For

...

"When you have eliminated the impossible, whatever remains, however improbable, must be the truth."

– Arthur Conan Doyle

...

I don't think this book could possibly be complete without exposing the raw, unencumbered thoughts I experienced during this journey. To be Faithful and True to broadcasting my soul for the world to see, let it be known that the summer of 2017 was the worst of it all for me. It was the point known as "the second wind" for all light warriors who had reached this leg of the journey. Yet, it would still require quite the will of the mind to endure through the summer of 2018 and beyond.

Not to categorize or place rankings upon the participants in this spiritual race, the fact of the matter is that every race has forerunners. These forerunners are the participants

## EPILOGUE

who entered the race just like everyone else, but have taken great efforts to shape their bodies through will and perseverance into the machine required to admirably complete the task. For some, completion isn't reward enough. For these athletes, finishing the race is about doing so with honor, with glory, with integrity, and with an undeniable knowing that every possible obstacle has been overcome while fine-tuning their machines for optimal performance.

These athletes push the bounds once thought impossible by others. And, when those bounds have been eclipsed, the next bounds are chased and eventually eclipsed. There is no separation in the mind from the possible versus the impossible. Perhaps this is why sporting events are so thrilling upon Earth. Sure, impurities like financial incentives and sustaining financial longevity have tainted athletics in recent times. But – once upon a time – people competed for the Love of the game, for the Love of the sport. These athletes finished the football game with broken arms. These athletes finished basketball games with broken ankles while still managing to trudge through double overtime and win the game with last-second buzzer-beaters.

I'm not saying people should bring unnecessary harm to their vessels while competing if they believe themselves to be vulnerable. What I am saying is these athletes have one belief that separates them from the rest of the pack. These athletes truly believe in mind over matter. And why not? For in the times to come – perhaps even as these words are reaching the intended audience – the biological limitations which humanity once believed to be a scientific truth will be proven to have been just a faded memory of times past.

# EPILOGUE

The mind can create anything. The mind can overcome the body, for it is important to remember that the body is just an expression of the mind. If a person serves a role upon the Earth with *true* honor, *true* dignity, *true* integrity, then the bounds of limitation will become undone over and over again at a dizzying pace. And so it has been on this spiritual race being broadcast for every soul across the Universe to see. Television channel: Earth. The race title? "It Was All Worth Waiting For."

*And now some excerpts from that summer's journey…*

### Coffee Shop Writings – June 8, 2018
### Palm Coast Coffee, St. Simons Island

Sometimes you walk into a room and the first eye-contact you make is undeniable… like the way a hummingbird captures your attention for just a fleeting moment. And from that point forward, you are able to track its flutter across a large expanse. To everyone else around you, all that is observable is the canvas of the sky serving as the backdrop to the busy world beneath its cover. But not to you… Not in this moment. For you have already seen a flicker of wonder – however brief that moment may have been – that has captured your heart and mind in an entanglement of emotions while her song, seemingly written directly from her soul to yours, has nearly capsized your vessel as it now lists helplessly to one side.

In this moment, there is a battle like no other just to stay afloat. Undoubtedly this cosmic shift in emotional balance

## EPILOGUE

was caused by something greater than the eye contact itself. It could be tantamount to how a solar flare erupts from the sun and pushes forth an uncountable number of solar particles in the direction of the observer. Most people will rarely experience the effects of a solar flare due to the magnetosphere of the Earth. This invisible layer that surrounds the Earth serves as a type of force field that deflects these particles from reaching the life inside. But the more attuned a person is to the Sun, the more likely the person is to notice "something" has occurred – perhaps causing the hair on an arm or the back of the neck to stand at attention – though the cause may remain unknown. To the most attuned person – the one for whom the hummingbird is no longer a fleeting speck upon Earth's great canvas – the reason is undeniable.

Wonder. It is simply wonder.

I have to confess, this is not how I intended this chapter to begin. But as I stepped into a coffee shop today, the undeniable smile of one girl stood out among the rest. In fact, there was little left to my imagination in all that she represented. I saw a lifetime flicker before me. We lived a life of grace, of greatness, of gentleness, of excitement, of adventure and love, of ever-abundant passion met step-for-step by equally ever-abundant desire. I saw a flash of what could be – not necessarily of what would be. Perhaps it was what I wanted. Perhaps it was not. Perhaps it was what she wanted. Again, perhaps it was not. The flash was neither intended to be positive nor negative,

# EPILOGUE

rather it was just a flash of potential. Either way, there is no doubt she saw it too.

It was one of the rare times I have witnessed this type of flash upon Earth – a flash that is like seeing a shooting star on a starry night – a rare and magical moment certainly worth the time to memorialize in words and revel in its splendor. For it would be from this moment my soul first found itself waltzing with her smile that she and I would be step-for-step, in-sync with each other's hearts as we breathed in the same air and were willfully bound by the same atmosphere in the coffee shop that day.

What would seem like only a few moments would pass as I began to write the words above and then, like the hummingbird that eventually vanishes out of sight as it flits about Earth's beautiful canvas, she was gone. In the blink of an eye, she was gone. I cannot tell you with any sense of certainty how I truly feel. I have spent the last few minutes writing these words – attempting to capture something intangible, an emotion only felt in the most precarious and rarest of situations. But, hopefully, these words have served an artful justice to the onslaught of emotions I have just experienced.

She was wonder. She represented wonder. That first moment where her smile set off a flash of inspiration which ignited the world inside of me felt like I was a child looking at the ocean for the first time – a body of water unbound by anything observable; the most magnificent of creations. Only a child with eyes of wonder can truly appreciate a moment like that. Her smile was that moment of seeing the ocean for the first time, for there will never again be a first smile, a first eye

## EPILOGUE

contact, a first impression that has potentially left you smitten, sun-struck by her very existence upon an otherwise blue sky. For after those first moments pass – after the wonder of the what ifs have been traversed in every direction by the mind – the ocean returns to being just a body of water – a great embodiment of imagination and questions where its majestic nature have drifted away from grandeur and become a cupid-curiosity; a place of potential exploration, fun, folly, jolly, and flirtatious fire.

Fire.
Ah yes. Fire.

Perhaps that is a great way to think of the exploration that is to become. For water and fire are more alike than they seem. Fire is the seat of the soul. And water? Well, that is where reason is found. But this discussion would perhaps be better saved for another chapter. For now, I will close with the three-word lyrics of the song playing overhead in the coffeeshop as I finished writing this very chapter. "Jesus Christ, girl."

**Footnote:** *During meditation following the events of the day, I was told that this particular girl would have been part of a "potential timeline" for me had I not made it to the point I had reached. I was told to be patient, and that all would soon be revealed to me. I assumed it meant that I would one day see my True Love, Hera – though I don't really know. It has all been so frustrating this year.*

...

# EPILOGUE

### *Coffee Shop Writings – July 7, 2018*
### *Wake Up Coffee, St. Simons Island*

Father,

Today I need inspiration. I need Love. I need an ignition to the flame within my soul. I am not asking for Hera's Earthly half to walk into my life (though that would be greatly welcomed!)… even though she perhaps did earlier today in a coffee shop. I can't be sure. But there is a moment of fire that I am craving today. Certain music is moving me into an apex of excitement. I know the time is nearing where all will find resolve and answers. It is just really hard to wait. I try. I try hard to wait – and there really is no alternative. So waiting becomes being, and being becomes waiting or doing. So doing is what I choose to do. I want to do, to light up the world today in a way that brings light to your soul, your existence. And perhaps if more light is shared in that direction, then it will be felt within the embers of my existence. I want to Love – to Love all things, All that IS! There is no exception. Music moves me. Film moves me. Words move me. Life moves me. I want to do all of this together, in the Now. Nothing is meant to be a distraction to your great plan for me. On the contrary, I hope that all that I am sharing with you is part of the plan! And even if it isn't, to still experience these aspects of life will be enough.

Georgia tells me that I am going to publish a book on August 8th. I have no idea what I would write between now and then, nor how in the world it would become a completed

# EPILOGUE

and finished book in that time. I don't doubt there is a plan. Perhaps it is a screenplay that is to be completed and put into book form. Perhaps it is something new. I can write at a pace of 10k to 12k word a day to finish a book in that timeframe – so it is not impossible. And, I know you have inspired me to write a 214 page book in 14 days and a 440 page book in 28 days... so it is all very possible. I get that. I might even be able to write more if I am inspired enough and have the vision. I am just looking for the vision. What is it? What is the inspiration?

Father, please help me. I look forward to being surprised in every way at the blessings that undoubtedly await.

Jonathan

...

### *Coffee Shop Writings – July 17, 2018*
### *Wake Up Coffee, St. Simons Island*

To the girl with the red bandanna tying back your hair...
*The Butterfly of the Pleiades*

I find myself writing at this particular cafe fairly often. For too long I was bound by walls that were not of my choosing. So now I choose to be unbound by walls, unbound by conformity. My "office" has become the world – literally any place that inspires me. But more often than not, the most inspiration penetrates my being at this particular cafe so I find myself writing here. The multitudes of people that traverse this one particular location frequently have lights shining so brightly one would think it was a type of ornate festival of lights – if only you could see it through my eyes. That's how I see it. That's why I find myself here – to be immersed in a daily lightcapade of inspiration.

Of those that transit this cafe, there are a handful of lights that will always shine brighter than others – magnitudes brighter, each unique in the way they sparkle. Yours is such a light. There is a twinkling, a magnificence held within its light. I'm not quite sure just how to equate it in description... Perhaps celestially, if I were to compare the twinkle of your light in the night sky to a star, it would be better to relate your twinkling to a cluster... the Pleiades.

As a child I was always drawn to this particular cluster of stars in the night sky. At first, this cluster of stars is difficult to observe and find focus. Before you know quite where the Pleiades is located, it is as if there is a haze of light in the evening sky that attracts your attention, but you cannot quite pinpoint exactly what is different in that particular part of the sky for there isn't one singular bright star shining against the backdrop of space. As the eyes adjust, you begin to realize that this "haze" in the sky is really a cluster of stars... not just one, but seven that are visible to the naked eye. How phenomenal and magical a sight it truly is! Seven stars visible to the eye rather than just one, all twinkling with a melody and song known only in the depths of the soul; reserved from the quick glance above, but a sight that entangles the soul once it is truly observed. It is a melody my heart cries out to sing, but the mu-

# EPILOGUE

sic is nearly impossible to replicate in the human condition... so I use words. Words like these.

As a child I stared at the night sky mesmerized at its twinkling beauty. And every time I looked up above, it was always the Pleiades that drew my attention. I suppose it would be similar to compare this twinkling beauty to a butterfly on a sunny day. Nature is such a magnificent creation. Just breathing deeply and soaking in its splendor reveals a thousand nuances of beauty. Among those are the trees, the birds, squirrels, insects, and plant life. But it is also the wind, the sun, the light. Oh the light! The way the light glints off of the surfaces of all of God's creations is such a spectacular sight!

So it would be in the way your light twinkles like the Pleiades that the only satisfactory explanation of your light on a sunny day would be the way the light reflects off the wings of a butterfly in flight. To a passing observer, the butterfly may initially just be part of the grand painting nature is providing. But in the quiet, subtle majesty the butterfly commands, there is a grandiose magic that ignites the soul to those who have truly caught a glimpse of her and now stand captured in her beauty. The lights, the twinkling dance of golden white rays upon her divine wings in flight engaging a primal aching in my soul to return Home.

So when I see you, I will always see the Pleiades just as I will always see a butterfly. Free. Full of Love. Full of Wonder. A twinkling of light beyond the scope of one star − a cluster of seven; the explosion of light beams twinkling off a butterfly's wings on a sunny day. And if you only truly knew what the number seven means to me in the context of God's creations, signs, and signals, you would then know the divinity I see in you. Butterfly of the Pleiades – you are both a mystery and a Truth to me.

As a writer it is most important to say that the intent of this writing is to share another perspective of the wonderful creations residing in this world we call Earth: to see life through eyes untainted. The details are all very much true. The girl with the red bandanna tying back her hair… so very true. As I found myself writing this, I often asked myself what would have happened if I had just said "Hello" at the point of being capsized by her presence rather than just allowing myself to become submerged in her essence. But for now, knowing everything I have witnessed is a realized picture painted by God's hand… well, today… that's enough for me.

Always,<br>Jonathan<br>…

## *Coffee Shop Writings – July 18, 2018*
## *Wake Up Coffee, St. Simons Island*

I'm hoping today will have a burst of inspiration that brings me into harmony with my divine mission. It is not that I am lacking direction… but, maybe that is how it would be perceived. In fact, many efforts I have taken have seemed to be part of the mission and purpose. But Earth… Earth. Gah. Somehow every action taken in the last week has seemed disruptive to the plan even if there is no defined "plan" per se. I

# EPILOGUE

can't quite explain it except maybe by likening it to the moments before a great race. In the moments preceding the race a runner will stretch and go through his or her routine. But in the shuffling of people to the starting line, the disorganization of the moments preceding, no routine seems complete; no stretch seems to feel adequate. Every stretch and action is serving a purpose, but is never quite as fulfilling as it would be during a warm-up or practice. But the funny thing here is that the only difference is found in the definition of the Event upcoming. The runners know it is upcoming. The instructors, officials, and coaches are shuffling around the runners to prepare them to step into their starting lanes. But realistically, nothing is different in principle... just timing and awareness of this particular race holding more value than the trials and tribulations it has taken to arrive at this point.

Perhaps that is the best way to describe the moment I find myself in today. The last three months leading up to the end of June have been a rollercoaster of divine timing and gracious blessings. Every action has been bound in a synergistic relationship with the Universe. Every push to the finish line with my writing has resulted in amazing relationships, amazing friends, amazing coincidences (that are not so much coincidences as they are divinely timed). Such has been the way the Universe has cooperated with my effort to share Melchizedek's vision with the world, for he and I are bound as One though a separate aspect to his primary existence I may be. But another roadblock, another question... another regrouping and re-strategizing with my efforts to bring this truth into the world. But how? How so? That is the question. That is always the

EPILOGUE

question. I thought the answer was obvious. I thought it was going to be through film...

— The End —

www.ingramcontent.com/pod-product-compliance
Lightning Source LLC
Chambersburg PA
CBHW020137130526
44591CB00030B/76